FELONY PROBATION

FELONY PROBATION

Problems and Prospects

Dean J. Champion

PRAEGER

New York
Westport, Connecticut
London

For Gerri

Library of Congress Cataloging-in-Publication Data

Champion, Dean J.
Felony probation : problems and prospects / Dean J. Champion.
p.   cm.
Bibliography: p.
Includes indexes.
ISBN 0-275-92993-0 (alk. paper)
1. Probation—United States.   I. Title
HV9304.C46   1988
364.6'3'0973—dc19   88-9744

Library of Congress Catalog Card Number: 88-9744
ISBN: 0-275-92993-0

First published in 1988

Praeger Publishers, One Madison Avenue, New York, NY 10010
A division of Greenwood Press, Inc.

Printed in the United States of America

∞

The paper used in this book complies with the Permanent Paper Standard issued by the National Information Standards Organization (Z39.48-1984).

10 9 8 7 6 5 4 3 2 1

Contents

Preface

In the fall of 1987, the Department of Justice announced that the nation's state and federal prison population grew by almost 5 percent during the first six months of the year. In fact, a new incarceration record was established with 570,519 inmates in U. S. jails and prisons.

At the same time, almost all states were under court order to do something to alleviate their conditions of prison overcrowding. For example, between 1983 and 1984, Tennessee's prisons released so many felons under court-ordered population reduction that an 84 percent increase in the parolee population was observed. During the 1980's, lawsuits filed by inmates alleging cruel and unusual punishment as a result of prison overcrowding skyrocketed, and there is little likelihood that this litigation explosion will abate.

In July 1987, J. Michael Quinlan became the new director of the Federal Bureau of Prisons. The federal prison system is experiencing an overcrowding crisis similar to those occurring in various state institutions. In a December 1987 interview, Quinlan said that the number of incarcerated inmates in federal correctional facilities has grown by 85 percent since 1981. During that same period, bedspace in these facilities has increased by only 20 percent. The prospects for improving the prison overcrowding situation are bleak, inasmuch as new federal sentencing guidelines which will add to the federal prison population went into effect November 1, 1987. Furthermore, parole in the federal system is scheduled for abolition in 1992 as a part of these sentencing reforms.

Maine has abolished parole as an alternative to incarceration, and indications are that other states are moving to sentencing systems that will only add more offenders to already overcrowded correctional facilities. Virtually every state has revised its sentencing guidelines, and a general shift from indeterminate to determinate sentencing is occurring. While more than two-thirds of the states continue to have indeterminate sentencing, the citizenry is discontent with the apparent unfairness and inequity of current judicial and parole board decision making.

All of these events are conspiring to cause corrections officials to re-examine existing policies pertaining to sentencing and granting parole to offenders. Prison construction is costly, and it is unlikely that sufficient numbers of prisons can be built and properly staffed to house the projected doubling of the prison population by the year 1997. Jails in cities and counties are involved as well, inasmuch as many of these locally operated facilities contract with state authorities to house a portion of the prison population overflow annually. Jails are suffering equally from overcrowding.

One solution to the problem of prison and jail overcrowding in the face of rising crime rates is to place offenders on probation. Decisions to impose sentences of probation rest with judges. Together with probation officers who complete pre-sentence investigations on most felons and prosecutors who negotiate plea agreements with offenders, judges attempt to impose a just sentence which will pacify both public and prison officials. Judges are admonished by legislatures to use probation in their sentencing practices as much as possible. And when judges rebel against such suggestions for greater sentencing leniency, the convicted felon sentenced to incarceration probably will not be incarcerated or incarcerated for only a fraction of the originally prescribed incarceration period. The exigencies of our correctional institutions will often result in the release of large numbers of felons short of their projected minimum time to be served.

Increasing numbers of felons are being granted probation. This phenomenon is not new, but it is inconsistent with the sorts of penalties that are prescribed for felonies. Every felony prescribes a minimum of one year *possible* incarceration as well as fines. These possible penalties are infrequently invoked by judges, however, especially for first-offenders and where less serious and nonviolent felonies are involved. But the fact that felonies generally are considered more serious crimes compared with misdemeanors and in view of the possible incarcerative penalties associated with them, more than a few citizens question the practice of placing *any* convicted felon on probation.

This book is about felony probation, the granting of probation to felons as an alternative to incarceration. Felony probation is inexorably linked with prison overcrowding, although it results directly from a judicial decision in sentencing a felony offender. Felony probation is also an enticement used by prosecutors to elicit guilty pleas from alleged felons in exchange for leniency during plea bargaining. But the growing use of felony probation creates enormous burdens for probation personnel, since they must continually devise new and different supervisory strategies to cope with growing numbers of offenders and burgeoning caseloads.

The growing use of felony probation on a national scale greatly increases the importance of behavioral forecasts of criminal behavior. The public is concerned about minimizing the risk to public safety seemingly created by felony probation. Turning out larger numbers of felons as probationers is seen by the public as generating greater risk rather than minimizing it. Thus, officials have undertaken attempts to devise methods and instruments to predict a felon's "dangerousness." Can dangerousness be predicted accurately? Should predictors of dangerousness be used by judges to grant probation to some offenders and deny it to others? Do violent offenders necessarily repeat violent acts if placed on probation? Are property offenders greater or lesser risks than violent offenders?

Recidivism is one of several major issues raised by felony probation. All states are using a variety of probation programs, some in early, untested, and experimental stages, to monitor offender progress or supervise their behavior. Felony probation has increased the importance of community-based correctional programs. Experiments with home incarceration and electronic monitoring systems are underway in several jurisdictions as programmatic and technological innovations suggesting more efficient operation of intensive supervision programs for probationers.

Of course, one option is to incarcerate all convicted felons. This would require considerably more prison space than is currently available. New prisons can be built, but authorities contend prisons are frequently filled as soon as they are constructed. Incarceration expands to fill available prison space. Thus, the jail/prison overcrowding problem will never be eliminated, only minimized. Felony probation is one of the more feasible and economical solutions to this problem. At the same time, the rehabilitative value of probation for probationers cannot be ignored. Many probationers derive some benefit from available programs and services, although not all offenders are "cured." Recidivism is a "given." An important question is, with growing felony probation, what strategies work best to prevent offenders from becoming recidivists? Hopefully, this book will provide some answers to this and related questions.

FELONY PROBATION

Probation in the United States

INTRODUCTION

During 1986, the number of persons on probation increased for the eighth year in a row. One out of every 55 adults was under some form of correctional supervision during the year. By 1987, 2,094,405 persons were on probation in the United States, an increase of 6.4 percent over the previous year (Hester, 1987:1).

Probation is a nonincarcerative sentence imposed by a judicial official, usually accompanied by several conditions and behavioral requirements, and involving variable supervision by a probation officer. Black (1979:1082) defines probation as *the release of a convicted person into the community to avoid imprisonment, under a suspension of sentence, during good behavior, and generally under the supervision of a probation officer.* Essentially, probation is a contract between the court and the offender, where the offender agrees to abide by all probation conditions. Failure to abide by one or more of these conditions may result in probation revocation and subsequent incarceration.

This chapter examines the history of probation in the United States, the functions of probation, and several probation programs. Four major philosophical orientations around which many probation programs have been formulated will be examined. The philosophy of probation will be presented as well as the rationale for felony probation. Finally, some attention will be given to the public risk associated with granting felons probation.

THE HISTORY OF PROBATION IN THE UNITED STATES

Probation was invented in 1841 by John Augustus, a Boston shoemaker. Augustus (1785–1859) had philanthropic interests as well, and he was an early reformer strongly influenced by the Temperance Movement. Considered the "father of probation" in the United States, Augustus was probably the first unofficial probation officer. With cooperation from Boston judges, Augustus assumed responsibility for many offenders who otherwise would have been incarcerated.

Augustus was a guarantor or surety for many criminals, and between 1841 and 1859, judges released almost 2,000 offenders into his custody instead of incarcerating them. Augustus posted bail for these offenders and reappeared with them in court at a later date. If they behaved well in his care, the judge suspended the sentence of incarceration and fined them a nominal amount. According to Augustus, only one offender ever violated his trust and absconded (Bottomley, 1984).

Augustus did not accept everyone for probation. He carefully screened prospective candidates through interviews and checked their backgrounds and social histories. These "pre-sentence investigations" enabled him to select the most successful candidates for probation. For the most part, the offenders he sponsored were low risk, nonviolent criminals. Many had drinking problems. Augustus wanted to reform them. From most accounts, his efforts were successful (Lindner and Savarese, 1984).

As an alternative to incarceration in the 1840's and 1850's, probation was most controversial. It continues to be controversial, and for many of the same reasons citizens cited then for opposing it (Gray, 1986). If criminals somehow avoided imprisonment, they were being "coddled" by judges and others. They deserved to be punished, and probation was not considered "just punishment." Even prison officials opposed probation, but their reasons were often unrelated to probation's rehabilitative potential. Prison guards and other authorities received nominal amounts from the government to cover the cost of food and housing of offenders on a daily basis. Much of this money was appropriated by the prison officials. Diverting prospective prisoners to probation cut deeply into illicit profits.

When Augustus died in 1859, his probation work was continued by other philanthropists including Rufus R. Cook and Benjamin C. Clark. Both of these men worked with the courts during the 1860's and sponsored numerous offenders on probation. Successes were measured by low recidivism rates. In addition, officials were keenly aware of probation's potential as a possible "front-door" solution or safety valve to alleviate *prison overcrowding*.

U. S. jails and prisons have almost always had overcrowding problems. In the early years from 1790 to 1817, incarcerative sentences had to be served completely. Eventually, various states enacted "good time" laws in order to reward well-behaved prisoners (Allen, Eskridge, Latessa, and Vito, 1985:26). New York pioneered this practice in 1817 when the New York State Legislature enacted a "good time" provision leading to the early release of inmates who behaved well and demonstrated industry in their prison work (Allen, Eskridge, Latessa, and Vito, 1985:26; Serrill, 1970:6). Serrill (1970:5) notes that it was common for governors and even prison wardens in certain jurisdictions to pardon prisoners or reduce their sentences in the early 1800's. While the original intent of such "good time" law enactments was to encourage good inmate behavior, the use of early release soon was acknowledged as an alternative means of alleviating prison and jail overcrowding. Today, early release provisions continue to serve these multiple functions. About half the states had "good time" laws by 1869, and by 1944 all states had parole systems.

Besides the early release of prisoners through parole, the alternative of probation to alleviate prison/jail overcrowding was an appealing one, especially to corrections officials in charge of budgetary matters. Despite continuing opposition to Augustus's probation idea among the citizenry, Massachusetts became the first state to formally adopt probation by statute as an alternative to incarceration in 1878. Between 1878 and 1938, 37 states, the District of Columbia, and the federal government passed juvenile and adult probation laws authorizing judges to grant probation at their discretion. And by 1956, Mississippi became the last state to authorize adult probation (Allen, Eskridge, Latessa, and Vito, 1985:44). Table 1.1 shows state and federal progress in adopting probation laws between 1878 and 1938.

Prior to the general governmental regulation of probation, many probation programs were operated among jurisdictions on a private basis. Religiously based programs were common, as various reformist groups established centers or homes to house convicted offenders on probation. Hull House was founded in Chicago by Jane Addams in 1889. And in 1893, James Bronson Reynolds established University Settlement in New York (Lindner and Savarese, 1984). Addams was especially sensitive to the problems of juvenile offenders and sought the implementation of correctional reforms which would benefit them. In fact, many of the early probation programs incorporated by the states were targeted at juveniles. In most states, juvenile probation statutes preceded similar statutes for adults by several years (Johnson, 1928:12–13).

By 1987, 2,094,405 persons were on probation in the United States (Hester, 1987:2). Table 1.2 shows the distribution of probationers for both state and federal jurisdictions.

THE PHILOSOPHY OF PROBATION

The original philosophy of probation may be understood by examining the meaning of the term. It implies "forgiveness" and "trial," or a period during which offenders may prove themselves capable of obeying the law and abiding by society's norms. John Augustus intended probation to be a means of bringing about *personal behavioral change or reform*. Alcoholics would be given an opportunity to learn to live without alcohol, hold jobs, and to support themselves and others. The influence of religious groups and

Table 1.1   Progress in Adoption of Adult Probation Statutes 1878–1938

JURISDICTION	YEAR FIRST STATUTE PASSED	JURISDICTION	YEAR FIRST STATUTE PASSED
Massachusetts	1878	Wisconsin	1909
Missouri	1897	District of Columbia	1910
Vermont	1898	Delaware	1911
Rhode Island	1899	Illinois	1911
New Jersey	1900	Arizona	1913
New York	1901	Georgia	1913
California	1903	Montana	1913
Connecticut	1903	Idaho	1915
Michigan	1903	Virginia	1918
Maine	1905	Washington	1921
Kansas	1907	Utah	1923
Indiana	1907	Federal Government	1925
Ohio	1908	West Virginia	1927
Colorado	1909	Oregon	1931
Iowa	1909	Tennessee	1931
Minnesota	1909	Maryland	1931
Nebraska	1909	Kentucky	1934
North Dakota	1909	Arkansas	1937
Pennsylvania	1909	North Carolina	1937
		New Hampshire	1938

Source: Cahalan, 1986:173.

temperance societies on early probation enterprises is apparent, and religious reform was an early objective of many of these programs.

Rehabilitation

While the original philosophy of probation was *rehabilitation*, this aim was subsequently given much lower priority in relation to other objectives. A gradual disenchantment with probation as a rehabilitative tool occurred as many probationers committed new offenses. In short, rehabilitation among offenders was not occurring, at least not on the scale its promoters had forecasted. Currently, probation serves primarily as a means of controlling a segment of the offender population at varying levels of supervision. Not every offender needs to be incarcerated, despite one or more criminal convictions (National Council on Crime and Delinquency, 1973). Experts continue to disagree whether any type of mass-offender rehabilitation is ever achieved, however, especially when recidivism figures for those on probation are put forth by those opposed to it. However, recent innovations in probation programs have resulted in substantially lower recidivism among probationers, especially while probationers are involved in those programs.

Table 1.2 Adults on Probation, 1986

Regions and Jurisdictions	Probation population 1/1/86	1986[a] Entries	1986[a] Exits	Probation population 12/31/86	Percent change in probation population 1985-86	1986 probationers per 100,000 adult residents
U. S. total	1,968,712	1,265,748	1,140,055	2,094,405	6.4 %	1,178
Federal	55,378	25,797	22,005	59,170	6.8	
State	1,913,334	1,239,951	1,118,050	2,035,235	6.4	1,145
Northeast	366,040	203,996	175,653	394,383	7.7	1,040
Connecticut	36,805	30,237	25,168	41,874	13.8	1,723
Maine	4,451	4,661	4,492	4,620	3.8	530
Massachusetts	86,597	50,925	46,359	91,163	5.3	2,030
New Hampshire	3,096	2,477	1,955	3,618	16.9	472
New Jersey	47,483	28,077	22,530	53,030	11.7	916
New York	99,183	41,168	32,794	107,557	8.4	803
Pennsylvania	75,591	39,183	35,789	78,985	4.5	874
Rhode Island	7,536	4,416	3,778	8,174	8.5	1,093
Vermont	5,298	2,852	2,788	5,362	1.2	1,337
Midwest	408,880	312,341	284,600	436,621	6.8	1,003
Illinois	74,156	46,992	44,945	76,203	2.8	897
Indiana[a]	42,800	45,345	38,880	49,265	15.1	1,224
Iowa	12,063	12,108	11,587	12,584	4.3	598
Kansas	16,204	9,093	9,344	15,953	-1.5	879
Michigan	99,365	77,732	72,235	104,862	5.5	1,571
Minnesota	32,986	28,332	26,091	35,227	6.8	1,135
Missouri[b]	26,081	20,474	15,633	30,922	18.6	823
Nebraska	10,720	12,264	11,719	11,265	5.1	963
North Dakota	1,569	802	827	1,544	-1.6	316
Ohio	66,810	43,975	38,863	71,922	7.7	911
South Dakota	2,249	3,967	3,990	2,226	-1.0	436
Wisconsin	23,877	11,257	10,486	24,648	3.2	701
South	789,702	511,433	464,817	836,318	5.9	1,377
Alabama[c]	16,520	5,400	4,895	17,025	3.1	579
Arkansas	9,268	2,526	1,659	10,135	9.4	587
Delaware	7,139	4,624	3,778	7,985	11.9	1,688
Dist. of Columbia	11,777	10,253	9,723	12,307	4.5	2,522
Florida	130,399	152,522	142,672	140,249	7.6	1,551
Georgia	94,461	57,738	51,636	100,563	6.5	2,290
Kentucky	6,594	4,916	4,669	6,841	3.8	252
Louisiana	26,638	11,767	10,728	27,677	3.9	877
Maryland	67,138	40,648	38,652	69,134	3.0	2,062
Mississippi	6,636	3,018	3,196	6,458	-2.7	354
North Carolina	56,207	32,123	29,686	58,644	4.3	1,245
Oklahoma	21,480	11,237	9,726	22,991	7.0	956
South Carolina	17,979	10,210	9,948	18,241	1.5	748
Tennessee	26,205	16,399	16,313	26,291	.3	740
Texas	269,909	139,033	118,868	290,074	7.5	2,468
Virginia	17,447	6,730	6,448	17,729	1.6	408
West Virginia	3,905	2,289	2,220	3,974	1.8	281
West	348,712	212,181	192,980	367,913	5.5	1,034
Alaska	2,606	1,308	1,029	2,885	10.7	797
Arizona	18,068	9,241	7,026	20,283	12.3	842
California	210,449	126,155	115,862	220,742	4.9	1,111
Colorado	17,612	10,585	10,980	17,217	-2.2	717
Hawaii	7,986	5,102	4,684	8,404	5.2	1,082
Idaho	3,414	2,130	1,774	3,770	10.4	546
Montana	2,637	1,277	971	2,943	11.6	501
Nevada[b]	5,365	2,593	2,440	5,518	2.9	762
New Mexico	4,130	3,831	3,786	4,175	1.1	403
Oregon	23,000	13,589	13,934	22,655	-1.5	1,126
Utah	6,330	3,559	3,511	6,378	.8	610
Washington	45,399	31,630	25,873	51,156	12.7	1,547
Wyoming	1,716	1,181	1,110	1,787	4.1	506

[a] Indiana reported 1985 data for 1986.   [c] Alabama estimated 1986 exit data.
[b] State estimated all data.

Source: Hester, 1987:2.

Of course, when any offender is totally free of any responsibility to report to probation or parole officials, recidivism occurs anyway. One way of approaching the philosophy of probation is to attack the alternatives: jail or prison. It is generally agreed among corrections professionals that prisons and especially jails have little or no rehabilitative value beyond what limited programs are made available to inmates (Huggins, 1986). And experts question whether most of the training an inmate receives is relevant or applicable for acquiring employment "on the outside" (Nelson, 1985).

Some investigators observe that incapacitation through incarceration may have a *criminogenic effect* on inmates (Cohen, 1983:9–10). Thus, imprisonment may lead to longer criminal careers and increasing crime rates. This view is rooted in the belief that associations with other criminals, especially those close associations occurring in prisons and jails, convert such institutions into "schools of higher criminal learning." A first offender learns from career criminals why he/she was caught the first time and what steps to take in the future to prevent detection by police. But the preponderance of evidence suggests that incarceration fails to alter significantly the future behavior of offenders, either favorably or unfavorably (Cohen, 1983:10).

Another view is that the greater the contact with the criminal justice system (e.g., experiencing courtroom procedures, trial, sentencing, and incarceration), the more an offender is labeled as a "criminal" and identifies with that label (Lemert, 1951, 1967, 1974). The logic is that keeping persons away from incarceration through a probationary program of some kind avoids the stigma associated with incapacitation in either jail or prison. Not everyone agrees with this view. However, frequent visits by a parole or probation officer to an offender's place of employment or neighborhood seem to foster similar labeling conditions, as work associates and interested neighbors become aware of such visits and the reason for them.

Selective Incapacitation

One controversial alternative to incarceration is *selective incapacitation, or incarcerating certain offenders and not others, even though similar crimes are committed under similar conditions and the offenders have similar criminal histories* (Forst, 1983; Struckhoff, 1987). Those incarcerated offenders have been "diagnosed" by various prediction devices as high risks to public safety, most dangerous, or likely to commit new crimes if released. Those placed on probation have likewise been predicted by these same measures to be low risk offenders, least dangerous, and unlikely to recidivate by committing new crimes.

Selective incapacitation has been challenged on ethical and legal grounds by several researchers (von Hirsch, 1984; Moriarty, 1987). For example, certain offenders who have drug or alcohol dependencies and/or are unemployed are disadvantaged by selective incapacitation because of these and other "status variables" (Blackmore and Welsh, 1983). Considerable significance is attached to prediction devices forecasting one's future dangerousness. In fact, these types of predictions have been challenged constitutionally.

In the case of *Barefoot v. Estelle* (1983), a convicted murderer, Thomas A. Barefoot, was sentenced to death by a Texas court. Contributing to his sentence was the testimony of a psychiatrist who attested to his probable future criminal conduct. The U. S. Supreme Court held that if there is a probability that a defendant will commit acts of violence in the future or would otherwise constitute a threat to society, then the Texas death penalty statute is valid. Capital punishment for Barefoot was upheld.

In the case of *Jones v. United States* (1983), Jones was committed to a mental hospital for a criminal act. Earlier he had pleaded not guilty by reason of insanity, and he subsequently challenged the hospital commitment as unconstitutional, because it was for a period longer than he would otherwise have been incarcerated if convicted and sentenced to prison. But the U. S. Supreme Court ruled the hospital commitment valid, since Jones's original plea was a presumption of his future dangerousness.

Some persons claim that selective incapacitation results in punishment not for what one has done, but for what it is believed a person may do in the future (von Hirsch, 1984; Moriarty, 1987:3). Proponents claim that selective incapacitation applies only to those offenders who have been convicted of crimes anyway, and thus, selectively applied incarceration is neither unjust nor unfair (Morris and Miller, 1985; Moriarty, 1987:3). Other researchers say that selective incapacitation is discriminatory racially and socioeconomically (Blumstein, 1983). An offender who can afford a good lawyer may be able to escape incarceration through effective plea bargaining (Florida Law Review, 1970) (see Chapter 2, Courts and Judges).

Probation is similarly criticized because it is granted for some offenders and not for others. In spite of the diversity of opinions among professionals about the philosophical bases of probation, rehabilitation and reintegration are dominant themes in virtually *every* probation scheme devised to date.

FUNCTIONS OF PROBATION

The functions of probation include (1) *rehabilitation*, (2) *deterrence*, (3) *crime control*, (4) *reintegration*, (5) *punishment*, (6) *restitution*, and (7) *reduction of prison/jail overcrowding*. The ordering of these functions is unrelated to the priority each has among corrections professionals.

Rehabilitation

Consistent with John Augustus's philosophy, probation is designed, in part, to rehabilitate offenders. This is evident when various probation programs are scrutinized and described. When judges sentence offenders to probation, invariably there are additional conditions beyond *standard probation rules* found in most state and federal codes. Standard probation rules include obeying the law, avoiding injurious habits (e.g., drug and alcohol abuse), reporting regularly to a probation officer, permitting probation officer visits to home or employment, obtaining and maintaining suitable employment, participating in one or more community-based educational or rehabilitative programs, obeying all rules of probation programs assigned, supporting family and children, and paying a percentage of income to crime victims.

Beyond these probation rules are special conditions such as attending Alcoholics Anonymous meetings regularly for a specified period, performing 200 hours of public service, reimbursing victims of crimes for their losses, participation in special educational courses or vocational training, and receiving psychiatric counseling or specific social services. These additional probation conditions are individualized and targeted to meet certain offender needs. In this respect, probation is geared to rehabilitate or treat those who need to be rehabilitated or treated. This is especially evident in cases of drug or alcohol dependencies and withdrawals which often must be accompanied by administrations of medicines in hospital settings.

Deterrence

Probation functions as a deterrent to future criminal conduct. While this statement is debatable and not necessarily applicable to *all* probationers, it does seem to be valid for many offenders who participate in various probation programs. The deterrent effect comes about, in part, as the result of the ever-present possibility of probation revocation and incarceration. No one wants to go to jail or prison. Probationers know that getting caught violating one or more probation conditions may result in having this privilege suspended in favor of confinement in a state or federal correctional facility.

Furthermore, persons who have been on probation previously and commit new offenses, especially serious ones, are less likely to be granted probation again as an indication of trust by the court. Thus, probationers have escaped incarceration, and although while on probation they continue to enjoy fewer liberties than other citizens, these freedoms are immense compared with the restrictiveness of confinement. But some critics are doubtful that probation serves a deterrent function (Harris, 1984). Much depends on how the particular probation program is administered and the level of monitoring offenders receive.

Crime Control

Depending upon the jurisdiction, probationers are monitored more or less intensively. Some investigators say that probation cannot be expected to control crime, because crime is an economic problem extending beyond the scope of criminal justice intervention (Conrad, 1984a). However, in recent years, high technology has gradually insinuated itself into probation practices (Moran and Lindner, 1985; Lilly and Ball, 1987; Lilly, Ball, and Wright, 1987).

The use of house arrest and electronic wristlet and anklet transmitters worn by probationers have greatly modified the nature of probation as we once knew it (McCarthy, 1987; Corbett and Fersch, 1985). At least while offenders are on probation, their behaviors are subject to random checks by probation officers and others. While this does not rule out the possibility that an offender will commit new crimes while on probation, it does impose a series of limiting conditions and operational restrictions that reduce the likelihood of new criminal conduct (Houk, 1984).

Reintegration

Incarceration in jail or prison, especially for longer periods, establishes for inmates certain routines that are alien to life in the community. Confinement to 8' by 12' cells, restricted yard privileges, constant surveillance and searches by guards, and rigid prison rules make adjustment to life on the outside difficult whenever an offender is eventually paroled. One of the most important functions of probation is to reintegrate the offender into his/her community (McCarthy, 1987; Allen, Eskridge, Latessa, and Vito, 1985).

Of course, the offender may not need to be "reintegrated." He/she may *already* be integrated within the community. Thus, probation makes it possible for offenders to remain within the community and work to support themselves, their families, and to offset probation program costs partially by paying monthly maintenance fees from their earnings (Pearson, 1985; Clear and O'Leary, 1983). Many community-based probation programs involving varying degrees of intensive supervision are centered around reintegrating the offender. Some of these programs serve parolees as well as probationers.

Punishment

It is difficult for the general public to see probation as a punishment. Punishment is equated with incarceration of some sort, and anything short of incarceration is simply not punishment. From an administrative/judicial/prosecutorial standpoint, probation is a sentence imposed for a criminal conviction. It involves rules and regulations as well as several other stringent conditions and requirements which must be observed religiously by offenders.

Clearly, experts disagree about the punitive connotation associated (or not associated) with probation (Harris, 1984). For some, justice is the primary consideration, and punishment is the medium through which justice is achieved (Harlow, 1984). Alleged offender rehabilitation runs counter to justice objectives and interests. Others emphasize educating the community to the diverse goals of probation programs and the stringent policies probationers must accept and live by (Steppe, 1986). Yet other experts say more research is needed before meaningful assessments of probation programs can be made and linked with true offender rehabilitation (Smith and Bassin, 1984; Coffey, 1986).

Close and frequent offender monitoring as well as home confinement provisions seem more acceptable to citizens critical of standard probation practices. Also, victim compensation programs and the performance of several hundred hours of community service are interpreted by some persons as punishment devices to achieve justice (Cullen, Clark, and Wozniak, 1985). But the committing of new crimes by probationers does much to undermine program credibility, even though the overall amount of new crimes among probationers is low compared with other criminals and parolees (Travis, 1984).

Indicators of probation as a punishment are the length and severity of the probation period and special conditions imposed by judges (McAnany, 1984). When one or more conditions of one's probation are violated, the courts should assess additive penalties through show-cause hearings. Probation should be a sentence and not just a substitute for a real sentence threatened after future violations (McAnany, 1984).

Restitution

Increasingly incorporated into probation contracts between the court and probationers are provisions for restitution (Wilson, 1983). Restitution to victims by probationers was implemented as law by the Federal Victim/Witness Protection Act of 1982. Federal judges should now order restitution to victims in every case where the victim has suffered any kind of financial loss. Prior to 1982, restitution could only be ordered as a probation condition. After this Act, restitution was permissible as a part of one's sentence in addition to fines and/or incarceration (Herrington, 1986:160). The constitutionality of restitution by probationers was upheld in 1983 in the case of *U. S. v. Lynch,* although the amount to be paid cannot exceed the amount of loss actually caused.

Restitution programs are now in place in most, if not all, states. Massachusetts has an "Earn-It" program where the local courts provide offenders with temporary jobs enabling them to meet their restitution obligations to crime victims (Herrington, 1986:160). Alabama has a Supervised Restitution Program (SIR) which was begun in 1983 (Smith, 1984). The SIR program accommodates and supervises 800 offenders. Excluded from program participation are sex offenders, child molesters, drug dealers, and first-degree burglars. Alabama corrections officials closed three residential work release centers and reopened them as SIR facilities. The successfulness of the SIR program may be measured by the fact that of the 664 program participants served between April 1983 and March 1984, 524 (79 percent) were gainfully employed and had paid over $40,000 in victim restitution. In addition, these offenders performed 164,221 hours of community service and offset program costs by $524,000 through the payment of supervision fees (Smith, 1984).

Reduction of Prison/Jail Overcrowding

The primary functional benefit of probation accruing to the states and federal government is alleviating prison/jail overcrowding (Finn, 1984a). The Texas prison system, for example, is facing a serious overcrowding crisis (Martinez and Fabelo, 1985). Recommendations for alleviating some of the overcrowding in Texas prisons include increased use of probation. Although this has occurred to a degree, the Texas prison population has continued to increase to 38,534, a 2.7 percent increase between 1985 and 1986 (Greenfeld, 1987).

By 1987, 19 states were using local jails on a contractual basis to handle their prisoner overflows (Greenfeld, 1987:4). However, this only served to compound jail overcrowding in those jurisdictions. Probation functions to alleviate *both* prison and jail overcrowding to a degree, although prison and jail populations always seem to expand to their rated capacities in spite of the diversionary efforts of judges and others. Probation re-routes offenders who otherwise would raise prison overcrowding conditions above constitutionally permissible limits and into the "cruel and unusual punishment" range (Dukakis, 1985; Phillips, 1983).

Probation is only one input or strategy for alleviating prison and jail overcrowding, however. Overcrowding generally is a complex phenomenon, with several agencies, organizations, and political bodies responsible for its occurrence. For instance, the relatively recent "get tough" on crime movement has prompted legislatures in various states to adopt harsher penalties for convicted felons. More offenses have mandatory penalties. "Use a gun and go to prison," is a view endorsed by Michigan and other states that have added mandatory incarceration for specified periods (one year, two years, etc.) to the sentences of offenders convicted of crimes involving firearms. This measure alone adds significantly to prison populations.

As a result of such legislative actions and the impact of such actions on sentencing guidelines and judicial sentencing practices, judges are obligated increasingly to operate within narrower sets of sentencing ranges for different offenses. Corrections officials and agencies are often the ones bearing the burden of managing escalating offender populations. The hydraulic analogy is applicable here. As pressures are exerted in one part of the system, these pressures act on other parts of the system and adjustments occur accordingly.

Thus, regardless of whether "front-end" measures are invoked, such as greater use of probation to divert jail- or prison-bound criminals from incarceration, or whether greater use is made of early release or parole, probation and parole personnel must cope with these growing numbers of probationers and parolees. This means devising alternative and more effective strategies for managing these offenders.

One continuing problem with many current probation programs is that they are aimed at persons who probably wouldn't go to jail or prison anyway. Therefore, it is questionable whether probation programs in certain jurisdictions really reduce significantly jail and prison populations. Unlike some of the intensive supervision probation programs in other states, the Colorado Department of Corrections has established a program targeted to affect prison-bound offenders so that their growing prison population problem can be attacked directly (Fogg, 1988:51–52).

Whether probation actually fulfills successfully any one or all of these functions is debatable (Martinson, 1974; Walker, 1985; Orsagh and Marsden, 1987). But most experts would agree that all of these functions are achieved at least partially, depending upon the nature of the probation program and the use of probation by the court.

FOUR PHILOSOPHICAL MODELS OF PROBATION

In recent years, all states and the federal government have modified their existing sentencing guidelines (Shane-DuBow, Brown, and Olsen, 1985). On November 1, 1987, the U. S. Sentencing Commission established new sentencing guidelines for federal district judges to follow when sentencing convicted offenders (U. S. Sentencing Commission, 1987). These federal and state sentencing reforms either directly or indirectly are a part of a nationwide "get tough" policy toward crime and criminals in response to the liberal and often ineffective handling of offenders by agencies of criminal justice in the 1960's and 1970's (Walker, 1985; Cullen, Clark, and Wozniak, 1985).

Articles with alarmist themes are increasingly prevalent in the corrections literature, and each is critical of the administration and implementation of probation in virtually every form (Conrad, 1984b; McAnany, Thomson, and Fogel, 1984). Much of the criticism surrounding probation stems from several competing philosophies which have guided legislative and correctional thinking in recent decades. Four dominant philosophical models have emerged and are identified with specific probation program aims. These include (1) *the rehabilitation model,* (2) *the deterrence model,* (3) *the desert model,* and (4) *the justice model.*

The Rehabilitation Model

As has been seen, rehabilitation always has been a dominant theme influencing adult and juvenile probation programs. It is sometimes referred to as the "medical model" or the "treatment model" because of its emphasis on diagnosing offender problems and devising treatments or cures for them. For example, an offender with a drug dependency is obviously in need of some treatment. As one condition of his/her probation, the judge may order the offender to undergo a withdrawal program at a health center and/or participate in other programs.

The rehabilitation or treatment-oriented model has special features including:

1. Development of individual plans for life in the community (work, study, community service);
2. A requirement of full-time employment or vocational training and community service by each participant;
3. The use of a community sponsor and other support persons who will provide extensive assistance and direction to each participant (Byrne, 1986:8).

A treatment program targeted for a special offender population, drunk drivers, was established by Suffolk County, New York during 1978–1979 (Golbin, 1983). The program for these offenders was called the Probation Alcohol Treatment (PAT) project. Those probationers assigned to the PAT project consisted of 109 offenders who had two or more convictions of driving while intoxicated. Offenders were intensively supervised by probation officers during the next twenty-four months. Only 12 percent of the program participants were rearrested for driving while intoxicated, and program officials regarded this figure as an indication of the successfulness of their efforts (Golbin, 1983).

For another class of probationers, sex offenders, a program of probation involving group psychotherapy was established by the Philadelphia, Pennsylvania Probation Department in 1966–1969 (Romero and Williams, 1983). The sample of program participants included 239 males (consisting for the most part of 48 pedophiles, 39 exhibitionists, and 144 sexual assaulters). During the next ten years, these offenders were followed up by investigators who determined that only 11 percent were rearrested for new sex offenses. Group psychotherapy and close supervision by probation officials were regarded as crucial elements of the successful treatment program.

Proponents of the rehabilitation model are Cullen and Gilbert (1982) who say that:

the ideology of rehabilitation disputes every facet of the conclusion that the constant escalation of punishment will mitigate the spectre of crime. To say that offenders are in need of rehabilitation is to reject the conservatives' notion that individuals, regardless of their position in the social order—whether black or white, rich or poor—exercise equal freedom in deciding whether to commit a crime. Instead, it is to reason that social and personal circumstances often constrain, if not compel, people to violate the law, and unless efforts are made to enable offenders to escape these criminogenic constraints, little relief in the crime rate can be anticipated. Policies that insist on ignoring these realities by assuming a vengeful posture toward offenders promise to succeed only in fostering hardships that will, if anything, deepen the resentment that many inmates find difficult to suppress upon their release back into society (p. 225).

The conventional rehabilitation model of probation is utilitarian in the sense that it specifies treatment or training on an individualized basis for both the good of the community and the offender (Allen, 1985). It is believed by its proponents that the likelihood of future crime is reduced through personalized attention and surveillance, as well as through the provision of training or other assistance offenders might need to survive in their communities (Harris, 1984). Furthermore, blame for criminal conduct is often shifted from the individual to the society, as socioeconomic and racial factors combine to cause personal and social problems for offenders.

Critics see the treatment or rehabilitation model as lacking in several respects. First, there is an "indefiniteness" of sanctions (Harris, 1984). Probation may be revoked for minor noncompliance with probation program rules or for quite serious offenses or new crimes. Second, offenders are often treated as objects. Persons with rights are often treated as "patients" or "cases" with specific illnesses to be cured (Harris, 1984). Third, rehabilitative, interventionist programs are not punishment-centered, and therefore the offender escapes punishments for crimes committed.

The Deterrence Model

The deterrence model is based on the idea that offenders are aware of the criminal penalties that may be imposed if they engage in further criminal activities (Geerken and Gove, 1975). Theoretically, offenders learn about the severity and certainty associated with punishments accompanying specific crimes, and thus they are deterred from committing other offenses. Through the rational acquisition of information about punishment, probationers will consciously calculate the costs and benefits of committing crimes before acting. If the punishment is known, certain, and severe enough, then the rational criminal is effectively deterred (Travis, 1985:76). In this respect, the pleasure-pain principle of Jeremy Bentham comes into play. Offenders are likely to choose actions or behaviors maximizing their pleasure and avoiding pain (1985:76). The threat of imprisonment is painful, and avoiding crime (which may result in imprisonment) seems a natural consequence.

Deterrence is achieved through offender fear of punishment for crimes (Allen, 1985). Certainty of punishment comes about in part as the result of the likelihood of apprehension as well as through the imposition of mandatory sentences for specific crimes committed. However, available evidence suggests that the certainty of punishment is of doubtful value as a general deterrent to crime (Rothman, 1983). For one thing, criminals are increasingly knowledgeable about the law and some of the problems confronting corrections. They know, for instance, that there is little likelihood of incarceration if they are apprehended for certain petty offenses, or if they are incarcerated, it won't be for a long period. This knowledge hardly deters them from committing burglaries, thefts, and other nonviolent acts.

Criminals are also increasingly aware of the advantages of plea bargaining as a means of mitigating their punishment. On one occasion, a person charged with several counts of interstate transportation of stolen property, mail fraud, and conspiracy, and who was also facing many years in prison and stiff fines said, "They offered me eighteen months and three years probation (sic). Hell, I'd plead guilty to murder if I only got eighteen months. The other way, my attorney was going to charge $10,000, plus I could have got ten years or more and fines. This way, I'll do about six or eight months and it won't cost me hardly anything. I can't beat it" (Personal communication, December 1986).

But the effects of probation must be examined in the context of the stigma associated with convictions for crimes (Travis, 1985:76). For many offenders, there is a loss of status, and in some circumstances, offenders are prohibited from holding certain kinds of jobs. Persons convicted of attempted rape or embezzlement will be unlikely candidates for security guards in apartment complexes or accountants for large firms. In addition, there is both specific and general deterrent value arising from probation. The individual offender is deterred conceivably because of the "lesson learned" from being convicted, while others are deterred by the "example" set by the original offender as they see what happens to him/her (Travis, 1985:76).

The Desert Model

The desert or "just deserts" model is rooted in retribution. Retribution is frequently associated with revenge, and society acts through its criminal justice agencies to exact revenge or retribution when criminal offenders are apprehended. The general theme of the just deserts model is that people are entitled to "get what they deserve" for the wrongs they have committed (Allen, 1985:68). In fact, much of the sentencing reform occurring among the states and federal government is geared along just deserts lines.

Proponents of just deserts violently oppose the rehabilitation model because it is inherently unfair. Rehabilitation makes distinctions between persons who commit identical offenses when no such distinctions are warranted (von Hirsch, 1985). Von Hirsch says that persons deserve to be rewarded or punished if they conform to or violate the law, and that one's past conduct justifies subsequent penalties imposed (1985). Some retributionists go so far as to say that electroshocks ought to be administered to offenders, varying in severity according to the severity of the offense (Newman, 1983).

Justification for the just deserts model derives from several assumptions:

1. Persons who violate the rights of others should be punished.
2. While it is not appropriate to add to human suffering, punishment causes criminal offenders to suffer.
3. But suffering through punishment may serve to prevent more suffering than punishment causes (von Hirsch, 1976).

Therefore, probation programs designed around the just deserts model use intensive supervision and surveillance to monitor offender progress. Offenders are likely to be confined to community-based facilities, together with curfews, provisions for restitution, community service, and any number of other punitive conditions. Home confinement and other restrictions are more likely to be applied to probationers within this framework. The level of custody or supervision by probation officers varies according to the severity of the offense for which the criminal was convicted.

The Justice Model

The justice model coincides with the just deserts model to the extent that it also opposes rehabilitation on grounds of socioeconomic and racial discrimination. Disparities in sentencing are often gender-based, or derive from socioeconomic and/or racial or ethnic criteria. The justice model casts doubt on the effectiveness of rehabilitation programs generally, and it is critical of sentencing disparities which violate one's constitutional rights. Thus, sentencing reforms of the late 1970's and 1980's are directed, in part, toward eliminating these disparities.

McAnany (1984:48–49) summarizes several legal principles underlying justice-based sentencing. These principles also serve to illustrate the philosophical underpinnings of the justice model. These are:

1. Criminal law is directed toward the punishment of persons properly convicted of its violation; whatever else the criminal law achieves, it primarily punishes offenders.
2. Because criminal law is punitive in nature, it cannot be used against legally innocent persons however great the social gains for others may be.

3. Criminal punishment is based on the principle of responsibility, i.e., that under ordinary circumstances the individual can make choices of committing crimes or not.

4. While not all conduct prohibited by law is immoral in itself, all crimes are immoral insofar as society through its legislative authority condemns them; choice of crime is choice of social wrongdoing.

5. Blame based on free choice of social wrongdoing is the basis for imposing punishment in criminal law and consists of judgment of condemnation rendered by the court in the community's name, the stigma attached to it, and the sentence to carry out its judgment.

6. Punishment should be distributed in accord with the seriousness of the offense and the culpability of the offender; prior convictions may increase offender culpability.

7. Offenders who commit offenses similar in seriousness should be punished similarly, without distinctions based on fear of future offending or on the needs of society to deter others.

8. Similar sentences need not be exactly alike in nature, but should be alike in the basic quantum of punishment; thus "alternatives" should not be disguised leniency which violates the principle of equality.

9. All dispositional choices, whether by plea, sentence, or parole release decision, should be governed by these principles of distributive justice, which should be incorporated into criteria of selection, whether in the form of guidelines, statutory criteria, or the like.

10. Maximum limits on the most serious sentences should be established, based on community sense of social condemnation but limited by constitutional principles; lesser sentences should be ranged from this upper limit in accord with gradations of seriousness.

11. Other purposes of criminal law, such as incapacitation, protection of the public, deterrence of future offending, and treatment and change of offenders, may be pursued within the limits of these principles, but only insofar as they do not undercut these primary principles.

McAnany derives these principles from a number of authorities including Fogel (1975), von Hirsch (1976), and Singer (1979). The influence of the justice model has been most apparent in both federal and state sentencing reforms in recent years, as states have moved gradually from indeterminate to determinate sentencing systems (see Chapter 2 for a detailed discussion of these sentencing systems).

Like the just deserts model, the justice model applied to probation utilizes close supervisory programs for conducting offender surveillance. Probation officers make frequent visits to offender residences and workplaces. The level of supervision varies according to the severity of the conviction offense, and probationers may be restricted to community-based centers, home incarceration, or some alternative program replete with rules and regulations. Briefly summarizing some of the major features of probation programs with a justice emphasis, the following elements are found:

1. Daily contact between probation officers and offenders for certain crimes;
2. Community service orders;
3. Restitution and/or payment of probation fees and fines.

Some investigators feel that the shift away from the rehabilitative model toward the justice model is primarily symbolic and has a purely cosmetic effect (Cavender, 1984). The justice model is seen as legitimating the government's administration of sanctions. However, other experts see the justice model as the most fair approach to imposing penalties for crimes committed (Fogel, 1981).

Table 1.3 shows a summary of these four philosophical models of probation practice according to the goals of each, assumptions made, theoretical concerns and practical strategies, the role of probation officers associated with each, and ultimate policy implications.

A fifth model has been proposed by O'Leary and Clear (1984). This has been called the limited risk control model which attempts to balance offender risk with a concern for fair punishment (Byrne, 1986:6). The limited risk control model contains the following elements:

1. The seriousness of the offense establishes a range of penalties with the minimum acceptable punishment as well as the most severe punishment.
2. The prediction of future criminal behavior is essential, based upon known risk assessment instruments.
3. Based upon objective risk assessment, judges select one of three control levels for offenders:
    a. Control level I (maximum, medium, or minimum security prisons).
    b. Control level II (local correctional facility, halfway house, home detention).
    c. Control level III (intensive surveillance in community, community supervision in probation or parole, and/or community service and/or restitution).
4. Small caseloads are established with no more than a 10 to 1 client-officer ratio.
5. Weekly contacts and field visits are made to the offender's home and place of employment.
6. Preventive conditions are recognized and high-need areas targeted such as alcohol and/or drug education.
7. Swift and certain administrative review and revocation procedures are undertaken for alleged violation of conditions (O'Leary and Clear, 1984:19).

Table 1.3 Four Models of Probation Practice

	Rehabilitation Model	Deterrence Model	Desert Model	Justice Model
GOAL	Utilitarian: Community Protection via treatment of the offender.	Utilitarian: Crime reduction via threat of punishment.	Non-utilitarian: penal sanction is deserved for deviant behavior.	Non-utilitarian: just and fair penal sanction for deviant behavior.
ASSUMPTION CONCERNING CAUSE OF DEVIANCE	Social pathology. Disorganization. Differential Association. Opportunity. Labeling etc.	Economic model- risk-reward decision by offender.	Multiple social factors. Risk- reward decision by responsible offender.	Rejects "theories" of causation. Offender responsible actor capable of responsible choice.
THEORETICAL CONCERNS	Psychodynamic Treatment-motivated	Punitively Motivated	Punitively Motivated	Punitively Motivated
BASIC CHANGE STRATEGY	Care and control	Threats	Surveillance	Surveillance
SALIENT ROLE OF PROBATION OFFICER	Ego-strengthening via identification and relationship.	Non-treatment role. Surveillance	Enforcement of probation rules	Policing activities Helper as per request. (Advocate for offender)
POLICY IMPLICATION	Decriminalization. Deinstitutionalization. Community re-organization. Psychosocial oriented programs.	Mandated sentences Reduced discretion judges.	Mandated ranges of sentences.	Concept of fairness and egality. Proportional sentencing based on seriousness of offense. Scaling down the levels of punishment. Limiting discretion. Deference to individual's right.

Source: Allen, 1985:68

Using the scheme developed by O'Leary and Clear, the following classification system is derived and presented in Table 1.4. O'Leary and Clear indicate that these preventive conditions are linked directly to the offender's immediate ability to reside safely in the community and are not couched in a rehabilitative context (Byrne, 1986:7). O'Leary and Clear (1984:18) observe that "any assistance rendered an offender must be reasonably related to a crime reduction goal. A supervision agency is not a welfare agency, and an extension of its activities beyond a crime control focus is both inappropriate and dangerous" (quoted from Byrne, 1986:7). Massachusetts and Oregon currently use the limited risk control model in their own intensive supervision probation programs.

Currently, there is no consensus among corrections professionals about which model is best. Each has proponents and opponents, and there are sound arguments favoring and disfavoring each position presented. The im-

Table 1.4 Classification System Using Risk and Nonrisk Control Elements

PROGRAM INDICATED BY LEVEL OF RISK	CLIENT CHARACTERISTICS
LEVEL I: Minimum Community Supervision	Client does not now pose a significant threat to public, no requirements of the court call for close supervision, and client has no important problems that are specifically related to potentially serious violations of the law and that the probation service can reasonably expect to affect substantially.
LEVEL II: Regular Community Supervision	Client does not pose a significant threat to the public, and no close supervision is mandated by the court, but client is currently coping with a significant set of problems related to potential violations of the law. Client has some expectation of overcoming these problems with the assistance of the probation service.
LEVEL III: Intensive Community Supervision	Client has been recently assigned to probation and has a history of violent behavior toward others or is likely to commit a fairly serious violation of the law, or the requirements imposed by the court can be enforced only by close and persistent supervision.

Source: O'Leary and Clear, 1984:79; Byrne, 1986:7.

portance of these philosophies for the present discussion is that probation programs are influenced by them. In order to understand more adequately particular programs, it is important to be familiar with the philosophical models upon which each is based. And similar to these philosophical models, no single probation program has been identified as universally applicable to all probationers. Each program has weaknesses and strengths, and short of incarcerating an offender, all programs have their share of recidivists.

TYPES OF PROBATION

Although probation generally is a sentence in lieu of incarceration in a jail or prison, the meaning of the term as well as its application varies from one jurisdiction to the next (Gray, 1986:26; Barkdull, 1976). This diversification of probation is explained, in part, because of the extensive amount of experimentation occurring during the 1970's and 1980's. Corrections officials and researchers are continually probing, searching for more effective ways of managing growing offender populations. However, there is agreement that probation is a legal sanction. As such, it contains at least three basic elements:

1. Offenders are released into the community.
2. Certain conditions are imposed on the offender as a part of the release agreement.
3. Offenders are under the general supervision of the probation department of a particular jurisdiction (Allen, Carlson, and Parks, 1979; Gray, 1986).

This section describes several types of probation programs currently in place among the states. These include (1) *standard probation supervision*, (2) *intensive supervised probation*, (3) *community-based supervision*, (4) *home confinement or house arrest*, (5) *electronic monitoring*, and (6) *shock probation*.

Standard Probation Supervision

The first thing about "standard probation supervision" is that "standard" changes in meaning among jurisdictions. However, there is a fairly high degree of uniformity among the states concerning standard probation rules. Texas standard probation rules are reasonably typical. These include the following:

1. Commit no offense against the laws of this State or of any other State or of the United States.
2. Avoid injurious or vicious habits.
3. Avoid persons or places of disreputable or harmful character.
4. Report to the probation officer as directed.
5. Permit the probation officer to visit him at his home or elsewhere.
6. Work faithfully at suitable employment as far as possible.
7. Remain within a specified place.

8. Pay his fine, if one be assessed, and all court costs whether a fine be assessed or not, in one or several sums, and make restitution or reparation in any sum that the court shall determine.

9. Support his dependents.

10. Participate in any community-based program.

11. Reimburse the county in which the prosecution was instituted for compensation paid to appointed counsel for defending him in the case, if counsel was appointed.

12. Remain under custodial supervision in a community-based facility, obey all rules and regulations of such facility, and pay a percentage of his income to the facility for room and board.

13. Pay a percentage of his income to his dependents for their support while under custodial suspension in a community-based facility.

14. Pay a percentage of his income to the victim for any property damage or medical expenses sustained by the victim as a direct result of the commission of the offense (Vernon's Annotated Code of Criminal Procedure of the State of Texas, article 42.12).

Caseloads of probation officers are quite large, with officers supervising upwards of fifty or more offenders on a monthly basis. Standard probation supervision may involve weekly or monthly visits by officers to the offender's residence or place of employment. This contact might also be made by telephone. The "standard" contact may even be as informal and anonymous as mailing in a monthly report of offender progress. This report is the offender's self-assessment. It is evident that "control" over offender behavior is minimal if not nonexistent.

Standard probation supervision is responsible for increased public concern for community safety, since unsupervised probationers have virtually unlimited freedom to do what they want when they want to do it. Of course, low-risk offenders are those targeted for minimal supervision anyway, although increasing numbers of more dangerous felons are being granted probation annually in various jurisdictions instead of being incarcerated (Stewart, 1986:98). Perhaps the key word associated with standard probation is *under supervision.*

Intensive Probation Supervision (IPS)

As with standard probation supervision, there is little consensus among corrections professionals about what is meant by "intensive" supervision. This is a relative term, although it refers to "something more than standard probation, but something less than incarceration." Some experts have said that intensive supervision of probationers means to "turn up the heat" through closer monitoring of their activities (Erwin, 1986). An example of intensive probation supervision (IPS) is one established in Illinois in 1984

(Bensinger and Seng, 1986). Prior to 1984, Illinois had no IPS programs and relied exclusively upon standard probation supervision practices in its jurisdictions. The governor appointed a task force in 1983 to study the feasibility of implementing an IPS program on a state-wide basis. The task force recommended that 30 IPS centers should be created, each consisting of two probation officers with caseloads of 25 or fewer offenders. With these units, 750 offenders could be supervised effectively and prison overcrowding would be alleviated (Bensinger and Seng, 1986). The estimated cost of the program was $1.6 million compared with a state prison operating cost of $10 million to service the same 750 offenders.

The "Act Creating a State-Wide System of Probation" was signed into law on December 9, 1983 and mandated the Probation Division of the Administrative Office of Illinois Courts to develop and monitor the IPS programs (Bensinger and Seng, 1986:70). Candidates for inclusion in the IPS program include any offender except those convicted of violent crimes, drug offenses, and repeated offenses. Actually, a screening process is conducted to establish an offender's eligibility for participation in the program. The presentence investigation report is used as well as other relevant background information. Offenders are eligible for the IPS program if they do not pose a danger to the community and if they do not qualify for standard probation (which continues to be used) (Bensinger and Seng, 1986:71).

The Illinois IPS program consists of three phases. Each phase must be completed successfully before the offender moves to the next phase. These phases are as follows:

Phase I Characteristics

1. Three months duration;
2. Face-to-face contact between probationer and the IPS officer at least five times per week;
3. The probationer must submit verification of employment or attend appropriate job training courses;
4. A 7 A.M. to 7 P.M. curfew must be observed, unless employment or community service obligations alter the requirement;
5. Arrest checks are made weekly;
6. The probationer is required to perform a minimum of 60 hours of community service; and
7. Drug testing may be conducted.

Phase II Characteristics

1. Duration is from three to six months;
2. Face-to-face contact between probationer and the IPS officer three times per week;

3. More relaxed curfew regulations;
4. Community service of 40 hours required;
5. Drug testing continued;
6. Arrest checks are made weekly; and
7. Offender must submit verification of employment and continue to attend appropriate job training courses.

Phase III Characteristics

1. Duration is a minimum of six months; and
2. All requirements of previous phases are continued, but at a "less intense level" (Bensinger and Seng, 1986:72).

Between June 1984 and September 1985, 444 offenders were placed in the Illinois IPS program. Over 90 percent had served time in prison. The results revealed that 106 offenders were discharged from the program. These discharges fell into the following categories:

Unconditional discharges	3	(2.8 percent)
Placed on regular probation	21	(19.8 percent)
Returned to prison	60	(56.6 percent)
Absconders	8	(7.5 percent)
"Other"	9	(8.5 percent)

Looking at these figures in view of those who either absconded or were incarcerated, only 15.3 percent could be considered as IPS program "failures" at the time the program was described by Bensinger and Seng. This rate compares favorably with other IPS programs currently operating in Georgia and New Jersey, although these researchers made no attempt to evaluate the successfulness of the Illinois program (Pearson and Bibel, 1986; Erwin, 1986).

Community-Based Supervision Programs

Community-based supervision programs were first established in California in 1965 (Lawrence, 1985:108). While not all states currently have community-based probation programs, many have adopted this concept as an alternative to standard probation supervision. Community-based supervision refers to a variety of therapeutic, support, and supervision programs for probationers, including diversion, pretrial release, halfway houses, restitution, and community service (McCarthy and McCarthy, 1984:5). Their primary goal is to assist offenders in becoming reintegrated into the community. In addition, large numbers of offenders are diverted from prisons, thus alleviating prison overcrowding.

Located within neighborhoods of various communities, community-based supervision programs tend to have similar characteristics which include:

1. Administrative authority to ensure offender conformity to house rules and probation regulations.
2. Job referral and placement services offered by professional staff and/or volunteers.
3. Professional psychiatrists, medical personnel, and social workers available on an "as needed" basis.
4. A large home capable of accommodating from 20 to 30 offenders at a time.
5. Staff counselors available on a 24-hour basis and accessible to offenders at all times to assist with personal problems.
6. A system of staff accountability to the court and responsible for preparations of reports on offender progress.

There is considerable variation among community-based probation programs regarding staff and service quality and delivery systems. Estimates of the cost of operating community-based centers for probationers range from $700 per year per offender to upwards of $2,000 per year. This compares favorably with the cost of incarceration which also varies but averages about $12,000 per year per inmate (McAnany, Thompson, and Fogel, 1984:357). In Texas, for example, it was estimated that in 1983, "per offender" costs were as little as 70 cents per day (about $255 per year) compared with $15 per day per inmate (about $5500 per year) in the Texas Department of Corrections (Lawrence, 1985:109).

Criticisms of community-based supervision programs focus upon the clients that roam freely about the community and general public misconceptions about such programs and the functions they are intended to serve. Also, some persons are concerned that offenders are sometimes abused and their rights infringed upon because of administrative discretionary authority over them and little or no accountability to the court for what happens to the offender (Lawrence, 1985:109). Austin and Krisberg (1982) say that these problems can be overcome, however, if their promoters can present tangible evidence that offender-participants do not necessarily pose serious risks to public safety and if these nonincarcerative sanctions are adequately explained to both public and victims alike.

A common fault of many community-based programs is that their goals are often diffuse and not clearly articulated to the public or the offender (Thomas, 1986). Also, there is sometimes little or no cooperation between various community agencies and community-based programs. Some administrators are simply unprepared to perform their jobs adequately, thus increasing program criticisms rather than minimizing them.

Community-based probation programs are privately operated as well as administered by public agencies. The more effective community-based programs have established boards consisting of both administrative personnel and interested community residents and leaders. These boards have done much to enhance the public image of such facilities and to generate greater acceptance among residents of affected neighborhoods where such programs are located (Lauen, 1984).

The National Institute of Justice has listed ten specific program components of community-based supervision programs as crucial to the successful operation of them. These are:

1. *Facilities*: Each program should have a structured residential component that provides separate housing for pretrial and sentenced offenders; controlled residency increases offender stability.

2. *Programs*: Each center should have at least two or more educational/vocational programs.

3. *Identification of client needs*: Each probationer's needs must be assessed and met; these needs may pertain to food, clothing, emergency financial assistance, and transportation.

4. *Delivery of services*: Each center should provide services by referrals to existing community resources.

5. *Eligibility*: The facility should serve persons in both pre- and post-adjudicatory statuses; federal, state, and local offenders should be eligible for participation so as to avoid unnecessary duplication of services.

6. *Coordination of efforts*: Effective programming requires adequate coordination between criminal justice and community agencies and collaboration between the public and private sectors.

7. *Supervision of individuals*: Offenders need to be supervised outside the center as well as inside it so that community protection can be insured.

8. *Organizational arrangements*: Any organizational associations with other agencies in the criminal justice system or corrections ought to be delineated.

9. *Evaluation and assessment*: Center goals need to be clearly specified and frequently reviewed; both client and program performance should be evaluated frequently by using explicit criteria; such assessments should be used in making any necessary adjustments or changes to existing programs.

10. *Community orientation*: Offender reintegration into the community is paramount, and the center exists as a source of social, psychological, and economic support for offenders (National Institute of Justice, 1973; McCarthy and McCarthy, 1984:414–415).

An example of a privately administered community-based program serving the needs of both parolees and probationers is Talbert House in Cincinnati, Ohio (McCarthy and McCarthy, 1984:415–416). The goals of Talbert House are:

1. To provide a proper climate for the transition of the offender into the community;
2. To provide counsel and assistance to drug abusers;
3. To deal with adolescent drug abusers;
4. To provide an alternative to incarceration;
5. To be of assistance to victims of criminal offenses;
6. To provide crisis intervention on a 24-hour basis through telephone or through a walk-in center; and
7. To provide counsel and secure employment for offenders (McCarthy and McCarthy, 1984:415).

Talbert House operates six residential centers, three for men and three for women. It has an adult therapeutic community as well as a residential youth treatment program for juveniles with drug or mental health problems. Mc-Carthy and McCarthy outline six additional program components. These are:

1. COSOAP (Comprehensive One-Stop Offender Aid Program). Provides a multitude of services under one roof. Includes intake, clinical services, and testing, welfare, legal aid, educational and job placement.
2. Ex-Offender Employment Program. Assisting offenders in vocational and job readiness, counseling for vocational training, testing. Works with 5,000 to 8,000 persons per year.
3. 241-WORK. A temporary day labor program is also a component of this program.
4. 621-CARE. A 24-hour switchboard and crisis center. Averages 4,500 calls per month. Provides backup services for mental health catchment areas and Community Chest Information and Referral.
5. Victim Assistance Program. Provides advocacy services to victims of crime. Counseling by telephone or person-to-person also provided. Over 1,000 victims were served during first two years.
6. Methadone Treatment Program. Program taken over from Cincinnati in 1977. Provides methadone treatment for 150 drug addicts (1984:415–416).

According to Lawrence (1985:112), "community corrections administrators and staff have a major task on their hands. They must clearly define agency goals and objectives. They must assure that these goals are being uniformly implemented, and they must examine program effectiveness from a number of perspectives." It is important that community residents accept these programs, and program support personnel can do much to promote agency-community relations through the creation of boards of community residents and corrections practitioners (Travis and Sheridan, 1983; Gilsinan, 1986).

Home Confinement or House Arrest

Home confinement or house arrest is an intermediate punishment using the offender's residence for mandatory incarceration during evening hours after curfew and on weekends (Ball and Lilly, 1987; Petersilia, 1986a:50–51). Home confinement was pioneered as an alternative to incarceration in prisons or jails in St. Louis, Missouri in 1971. Since then, it has spread to other states including Kentucky, Georgia, Massachusetts, California, Maryland, and Washington, D.C. (Lilly and Ball, 1987).

In 1986, the federal government authorized an experimental program involving home confinement for the Probation Service of the United States Courts. Experts attribute the increasing popularity of home confinement as an alternative to incarceration to two factors: (1) a change in the political climate, and (2) technological developments (Lilly and Ball, 1987:366). The political shift has generally accompanied the philosophical shift in corrections policy from rehabilitative interests to one of crime control. Also, technological innovations such as electronic transmitters and other devices have enabled probation officers and others to monitor offenders more easily and determine their whereabouts at specific times.

In Florida, for example, home confinement was implemented primarily as a means of alleviating prison overcrowding and was authorized under the Correctional Reform Act of 1983 (Flynn, 1986:64). Offenders who participate in this type of probation program are usually low-risk and prison-bound. Home confinement emphasizes continued offender employment, regular surveillance, community service, and victim restitution. Offenders also are assessed for monthly fees ranging from $15 to $200 to offset program costs (Petersilia, 1986a).

The nature of home confinement varies according to the jurisdiction. The probationer may be restricted exclusively to his/her residence or permitted to travel limited distances from it. Or the offender may be obligated to adhere to a specific curfew and be available during curfew periods for contact with probation officials. These contacts may be in person or by telephone.

Home confinement is a punishment-centered community control program (Flynn, 1986:66). It is designed to improve an offender's accountability and responsibility, and thus it has some rehabilitative merit. Community control officers who monitor Florida probationers must maintain a minimum of 28 contacts per month. Also required are regular offender contacts with neighbors, friends, landlords, employers, spouses, police, and creditors (Flynn, 1986:66). Offenders are also required to perform from 150 to 200 hours of public service or provide free labor for various community projects. In 1986, probationers involved in the Florida program performed about 10,000 hours of public service work (Flynn, 1986:66). Program costs average about $3 per day to supervise a probationer under house arrest compared with $28 a day for maintaining incarcerated offenders.

Critics of home confinement as an intermediate punishment have mixed opinions about it. Some investigators say that home confinement is recommended for persons with serious diseases like AIDS or for pregnant women (Petersilia, 1986a). Others argue that home confinement is not punishment. However, Flynn (1986:68) suggests that for some offenders, home confinement might be "unreasonably restrictive." There are issues raised as well concerning an offender's right to privacy under such a home confinment system (del Carmen and Vaughn, 1986:64).

Electronic Monitoring

Electronic monitoring is the use of electronic transmittal devices to verify that an offender is at a specified place during specified times (Schmidt and Curtis, 1987:137). The use of electronic monitoring dates back to 1964 when it was first used in the supervision of mental patients and a few parolees (Gable, 1986). New Mexico Judge Jack Love established an experimental project in 1983 to monitor offenders convicted of driving while intoxicated. Eventually, the New Mexico Supreme Court approved its general use for large numbers of probationers (Houk, 1984).

Electronic devices used to monitor offenders either use telephones at the monitored location or emit signals which may be picked up by receiving devices over great distances. For example, a probation officer only needs to place a call to the offender's residence. The offender answers the telephone and the transmitter emits a signal acknowleding the offender's identity. Or the probation officer merely needs to drive by the offender's residence at certain times and determine from a special receiver that the offender is there. The probation officer does not necessarily have to make calls to the offender. Automatic dialing facilities can be installed so that the offender is called "automatically" by machine at random times when curfew is in effect.

The electronic devices used for monitoring are either anklets or wristlets worn by the offender and not easily removed. While they are not fully tamper-proof, it is apparent from visual inspection whether the offender has attempted to modify their function. In short, it is quite difficult for the offender to physically remove these devices and permit others to wear them in an attempt to fool probation officials. CDS Home Escort, In-House Arrest System, and Contac are just a few of the many monitoring systems available from distributors.

Frequently, these electronic devices are used in tandem with home confinement as a condition of one's probation. Lilly, Ball, and Wright (1987) say that this technology pays for itself in time, especially when compared with the considerably higher costs of incarceration. During an 18-month experimental period, for example, these investigators demonstrated that the initial direct costs associated with the program installation and necessary hardware were high, although the costs of jail and prison incarceration were even higher. In time, electronic monitoring coupled with home confinement would pay for itself through recovering maintenance fees from offenders on a monthly basis.

One concern expressed by at least one investigator related to potential "net widening" as the result of using electronic monitoring (Petersilia, 1986b). Does the availability of this new technology cause judges to impose such probation conditions on offenders who would otherwise qualify for standard (and minimal) probation supervision? In cities where electronic monitoring has been used, net widening has not occurred (Lilly, Ball, and Wright, 1987).

Henry C. Duffie, Chief Probation Officer for the Adult Probation Department of Maricopa County, Arizona, is apprehensive about electronic monitoring as well. He says:

Well, let me say first we're not using such devices. We're experimenting with an electronic surveillance device right now, but we have not gone into it in any big way. There are definite professional differences of opinion among my own staff between those who might be interested in using the new technology and those who are pretty well wed to the old one-to-one relationship or personal relationship. These staff members are not very interested in what they choose to call dog collars on people (Duffie, 1987:124).

But even Duffie admits the electronic system may be considerably cheaper than incarcerating someone in jail or prison.

Shock Probation

Another form of probation is *shock probation. Shock probation or split-sentencing refers to a program where an offender is incarcerated in either a jail or prison for a brief period and then released to some alternative probation program* (Parisi, 1980; Finckenauer, 1982). In a sense, it is not probation at all, since the offender is actually incarcerated (even if only briefly).

Shock probation is designed to:

1. impress offenders with the hardship and psychological problems of isolation and prison life;
2. provide an opportunity to better evaluate the needs of offenders in more detail and help them utilize training and other educational services provided by prisons;
3. provide greater protection to society;
4. "shock" individuals into a realization of the grimness of prison life through the experience of imprisonment; and

5. make offenders aware of the seriousness of their crimes without resorting to a long and potentially damaging prison sentence (Friday, Petersen, and Allen, 1973).

Vito (1984:22) says the major premise of shock probation is that the "shock" of incarceration will cause the offender to avoid future involvement with crime. Thus, shock probation programs encompass two themes: deterrence and reintegration. For example, Ohio established a shock probation program in 1964. Eligible offenders who wanted to participate in the program had to file a petition with the court requesting a suspension of further execution of the sentence. The petition had to be filed no earlier than 30 days and not later than 60 days after the original sentence date (Petersilia, 1987:62).

After the program had been in operation for about ten years, Vito (1978) investigated 1,508 Ohio shock probationers who were placed in that program in 1975. He divided the sample according to the length of sentence they served prior to being placed on probation. Some offenders served from 1 to 30 days, others 31 to 130 days, and others over 130 days. On the basis of subsequent comparisons of reincarceration rates, Vito concluded that probationers who had served from 1 to 30 days had significantly lower rates of reincarceration compared with those offenders serving longer incarceration periods. Thus, Vito concluded that the length of incarceration under the shock probation program can be drastically shortened without affecting reincarceration rates (1984:24).

Subsequently, other states adopted shock probation programs. These included Idaho, Kentucky, Indiana, Tennessee and Texas (Petersilia, 1987:62; Faine and Bohlander, 1976; Waldron and Angelino, 1977). Interestingly, comparisons of shock probationers with probationers under standard probation supervision and incarcerated offenders show little or no differences in reincarceration rates. Therefore, some critics say that shock probation is only minimally effective (Petersilia, 1987:62). However, opponents of shock probation contend that shock probationers often lose their jobs as a result of incarceration, have their community and family relationships disrupted, and are exposed to the labeling and brutalizing experiences of imprisonment. They say that if an offender is a good candidate for a community-based probation program or intensive supervised probation, then shock probation can only serve to harm him/her (Petersilia, 1987:63).

FELONY PROBATION AND PUBLIC RISK

Largely because of prison and jail overcrowding, there is a national trend toward placing larger numbers of felons, even serious ones, on probation (Bensinger and Seng, 1986:69; Vito, 1986:17; Petersilia, 1985a, 1985b; Champion, 1987a, 1987b, 1988c) (see Chapter 4 for an extensive discussion of public risk, offender dangerousness, and recidivism). The basic incongruity associated with felony probation is that persons who commit felonies face prison incarceration of at least one year. Yet, both property and violent offenders, even some murderers, are granted probation annually, and with increasing frequency.

A study by the Rand Corporation of 1,672 men convicted of felonies in Los Angeles and Alameda counties and placed on probation showed that during the 40-month follow-up period, 65 percent were rearrested for new offenses, 51 percent were convicted, and 34 percent were incarcerated in either jail or prison (Petersilia, 1985b). Such high rearrest, conviction, and incarceration rates caused much alarm among the public as well as professionals. The alarm expressed centered largely around the issue of increased risk to the citizenry by loosing large numbers of convicted felons in communities through probation.

But other researchers critical of the Rand report have investigated felony probationers in their own jurisdictions with widely disparate results (Fichter, Hirschburg, and McGaha, 1987; Travis, Latessa, and Vito, 1987). A replication study of 2,083 Missouri felons was conducted between 1980 and 1983 and also involved a 40-month follow-up (Fichter, Hirschburg, and McGaha, 1987). The study disclosed a 22 percent rearrest rate compared with the Rand figures of 65 percent. Furthermore, reconvictions amounted to 12 percent, and even fewer felons were incarcerated.

Similar studies conducted in Ohio and Kentucky showed rearrest rates of about 30 percent and 20 percent respectively, with convictions averaging about 25 percent and 15 percent for these states (Travis, Latessa, and Vito, 1987:11-12). In short, these replications and investigations subjected the Rand report to much criticism, highlighting primarily the extraordinarily high rearrest, reconviction, and incarceration figures presented. Methodological weaknesses and other factors have been cited by critics of the Rand study. But emerging from these criticisms is the prevailing belief among many professionals that felony probation is a plausible and practical alternative to incarceration for certain felons.

The Director of the National Institute of Justice in 1986, James K. Stewart, has said that during the 1980's, more offenders have been sentenced to probation than to prison. Furthermore, by 1984, a record 1.7 million adults were on probation (Stewart, 1986:96). More recent statistics show that that total had risen to 2.1 million adults on probation by the beginning of 1987 (Hester, 1987:1).

Stewart adds that "the public is justifiably concerned about the seven out of ten convicted offenders walking the streets of communities they victimized, creating public fear" (1986:94). Prison overcrowding is largely to blame for increased use of felony probation.

Increased felony probation nationwide has shifted much of the responsibility for offender monitoring and control to probation departments and other officials. Standard probation supervision is woefully inadequate for certain types of offenders granted probation. By the same token, other offenders require little, if any, supervision while fulfilling their probation terms. One continuing question plaguing corrections officials is how to differentiate between those felons who pose serious public risks and those who don't.

The Rand study said in effect that large numbers of felons who were granted probation returned to crime within a relatively short period. But if these offenders had been incarcerated for the duration of their sentences, one implication is their new crimes would not have been committed because they wouldn't be free to commit them.

The Bureau of Justice Statistics has investigated this phenomenon in some detail and has classified offenders into "avertable recidivists" and "non-avertable recidivists" (Greenfeld, 1985). Avertable recidivists are those probationers who would have been in prison at the time their new crimes were committed, provided the sentence of incarceration was imposed and required. Non-avertable recidivists are those probationers who have committed previous offenses and have been punished fully for them. In other words, a non-avertable recidivist is one who is not subject to probation rules or regulations or is free within the community after having served his/her sentence.

Public concern is focused upon avertable recidivists, because they commit new crimes within the time frame of the sentence originally given them by judges. The Bureau of Justice Statistics showed that of all offenders entering state prisons in 1979, about 21 percent were on probation at the time of their new offense. Another 20 percent were on parole or under some form of conditional release when they committed new crimes. This finding prompted legislatures to conclude that had the probationers and parolees been incarcerated for their full terms, the new crimes they subsequently committed would not have occurred. Thus, an argument developed favoring compulsory incarceration for all offenders sentenced to prison terms.

However, the government study failed to take into account the number of crimes involving the participation of others and that would have occurred anyway, despite the incarceration of specific offenders. Little or no research exists, however, showing the amount of crime committed by two or more conspiratorial offenders.

Currently, the emphasis in probation work is developing programs that effectively monitor offenders according to their degree or level of risk. It is extremely difficult, if not impossible, to forecast dangerous behavior accurately. From the judicial point of view, most judges strive for fairness in the sentences they impose. Information provided through presentence investigations of offenders is helpful, and persons with extensive prior records are less likely candidates for probation. At the same time, many offenders with extensive prior records "go straight" after being granted probation, and many firstoffenders go on to commit new and more serious crimes.

The aim of everyone who administers programs for offenders and/or is involved with their ultimate disposition is to impose the proper sentence, whether it be incarceration or probation of some kind. Officials are interested in minimizing the number of "false positives," or those individuals predicted by various measures to be recidivists or repeaters but who do not commit future criminal acts. They are also interested in minimizing the rate of "false negatives," or those offenders predicted not to commit new crimes but who commit them anyway. Unfortunately, the state-of-the-art relating to predictions of dangerousness and public risk is not as advanced as corrections professionals and judges would like it to be.

This is where the proponents of the justice model score their greatest gains. They argue that the sentence ought to be a punishment for past crimes and equivalent to the seriousness of those offenses, independent of whatever forecasts are made about any specific offender's criminal propensities. But the exigencies of prison/jail overcrowding are forcing officials to abandon ideological themes in favor of more practical solutions. In the next chapter, we will examine courts, judges, and sentencing reforms that are an integral part of the felony probation mosaic.

SUMMARY

Probation programs exist in all states. These programs are founded on competing philsophical bases including rehabilitation, deterrence, just deserts, and justice. Each fulfills the overt or covert function of offender rehabilitation. Probation functions to deter criminals, to punish offenders, to make restitution to victims possible, and to alleviate prison/jail overcrowding.

Types of probation include standard probation supervision, intensive supervised probation, community-based supervision, home confinement or house arrest, electronic monitoring, and shock probation. No specific probation program is adopted on a national scale. Each is adapted to fit offender populations which vary among jurisdictions.

Rising jail and prison populations are increasing the numbers of felons granted probation. These increased numbers of both property and violent felons as probationers are causing public concern, and experts are experimenting with numerous programs designed to control and/or monitor offender behavior. Liaisons between the community and corrections officials are imperative if intensive probation supervision programs are to be successful. Intermediate punishments are increasingly popular as strategies for managing increasingly dangerous felony probationers.

2

Courts and Judges

INTRODUCTION

Sentencing felons to probation is the exclusive prerogative of judges. Despite jury decisions, prosecutor recommendations for incarceration, and the information contained in presentence investigations prepared by probation officers, judges may exercise considerable discretion in a majority of criminal cases and invoke some form of probation. They may even set aside "guilty" verdicts by juries. Of course, these decisions are subject to challenge by prosecutors and review by appellate authority. In recent years, such judicial discretion has been challenged in various jurisdictions through a series of sentencing reforms (Shane-DuBow, Brown, and Olsen, 1985). But even with changing sentencing practices and policies, judges emerge as final arbiters of offender dispositions in most cases (Brereton and Casper, 1981; Frazier and Bock, 1982; Farr, 1984; Alschuler, 1976).

This chapter examines some of the more important factors influencing the judicial decision to sentence felons to probation. Crucial to this examination is the prosecutorial role in pretrial plea bargaining. Certain sentencing reforms will also be reviewed as well as their variable impact on judicial discretion. Judicial opinions about felony probation will be examined, together with an inspection of the available alternatives. Finally, virtually all participants influencing the felony probation decision consider the element of offender dangerousness and the extent to which it can be predicted.

FELONY TRENDS IN THE UNITED STATES

Depending upon the statistical source, the rate of serious crime in the United States has both increased and decreased in the most recent decade. First, the UNIFORM CRIME REPORTS (UCR) is the official measure of reported crime in the United States compiled annually by the Federal Bureau of Investigation. The UCR receives its information quarterly from most law enforcement agencies. Among other information, these agencies provide the FBI with statistics showing the number of reported crimes as well as the number of arrests.

Crime in the United States Is Increasing

According to the UCR, between 1985 and 1986, reported murders and non-negligent manslaughters rose by 8.6 percent, reported forcible rapes rose by 3.2 percent, reported aggravated assaults rose by 15.4 percent, reported burglaries rose by 5.5 percent, reported larcenies rose by 4.8 percent, reported motor vehicle thefts rose by 11 percent, reported arsons rose by 6 percent, and reported robberies rose by 9 percent (U. S. Department of Justice, 1987:7–39). "Reported" is used in each case because much crime goes *unreported*. The offenses listed above are known as "Index Offenses," because they function as crude index of national crime trends. They are felonies as well. For the years 1976–1986, index offenses have generally increased, according to the UCR.

The UCR is faulted by experts in several respects. While the following list of criticisms is not exhaustive, it is indicative of at least some UCR inaccuracy. Not all law enforcement agencies report crime. Not all agencies report crime systematically. Crime definitions vary among jurisdictions. Arrests do not mean convictions. If several crimes are committed by a single individual, only the most serious is reported. Crimes are often misclassified. Police often exercise their own discretion and give certain offenders warnings rather than arrest them.

Crime in the United States Is Decreasing

Another popular alternative measure of the amount of crime in the United States is the National Crime Survey (NCS). The NCS is a survey of *crime victims* conducted semi-annually in conjunction with the U. S. Bureau of the Census. It involves interviews with over 136,000 persons in 60,000 households (Bureau of Justice Statistics, 1987a, 1987b).

According to the NCS, criminal victimizations dropped by 22 percent between 1985 and 1986. Reported rapes, robberies, and assaults decreased by 18 percent, reported motor vehicle thefts decreased by 23 percent, and reported burglaries decreased by 32 percent (Bureau of Justice Statistics, 1987b:7). Again, "reported" is used because household members are asked whether any specific crimes have been committed against them. Their reports to interviewers provide the data upon which the NCS is based.

The NCS is also criticized by authorities. Some of the more common criticisms include the fact that victims frequently "overreport" criminal activity because they misinterpret what a particular crime is (e.g., they might get shoved by someone accidentally in a bar and consider that assault), they may be too embarrassed to report crimes (e.g., they may have been involved in gambling or solicited someone for prostitution), they may fear retaliation by offenders if they say anything about the crime, or they may simply forget.

Independent of either the UCR or NCS as an indicator of crime in the United States is *the number of criminal cases* filed and processed by federal and state courts annually. In 1986, 41,490 criminal cases were filed in federal district courts (McGillis, 1987:4). Less than 10 percent of these resulted in trials, but most trials resulted in convictions. Among the nation's 3,235 state felony courts, 1.5 million felony cases were filed in 1986, with fewer than 10 percent resulting in trials. One million felony convictions were obtained (including trial and nontrial dispositions). Since the 27,910 criminal case filings in federal courts in 1980 (the lowest number of filings since 1954), there has been a systematic *increase* annually in the number of criminal cases filed in federal courts (Jamieson and Flanagan, 1987; Meierhoefer and Armen, 1985). State felony courts have experienced comparable increases in caseloads during this same period with proportionately similar trial and nontrial dispositions.

Regardless of whether serious crime nationwide is increasing or decreasing according to official figures and estimates, state and federal courts are deluged with increasing numbers of criminal cases annually. The number of case filings involving felonies is escalating at a rapid rate. In some circles, the 1980's has been labeled as the era of the "litigation explosion" (Meador, 1983) and "assembly-line justice" (Feeley, 1983; Cecil, 1985), although previous decades have been similarly labeled (Blumberg, 1967).

COURT DOCKETS AND JUDICIAL WORKLOADS

In 1986, nearly 300,000 civil and criminal cases were filed in federal district courts (McGillis, 1987). A crude estimate of civil and criminal case filings in state courts is about 23 million (there are about 80 million case filings annually, although a majority are traffic offenses) (Bureau of Justice Statistics, 1987b:35). Approximately 90 percent of all criminal cases result in convictions through "guilty" pleas, and trials are avoided (Stitt and Siegel, 1986; Miller, Cramer, and McDonald, 1978; Meeker, 1984). The point is that despite the relatively low proportion of trials that are actually held, U. S. state and district courts are still incredibly overburdened, with trial court delay as an unpleasant, inconvenient, and inevitable consequence (Mahoney, Sipes, and Ito, 1985; National Institute of Justice, 1986).

Although today's courts are dispatching cases at a more rapid rate than in previous years, court dockets are increasingly crowded, and judges and others are constantly searching for ways to alleviate court workload and pressure (Flango, Roper, and Elsner, 1983). Between 1977 and 1983, for example, civil and criminal case filings increased by over 20 percent, while the number of state and federal trial judges only increased by 7 percent during the same period (National Institute of Justice, 1986). Clearly, these discrepancies suggest somewhat drastic solutions.

Experiments in streamlining case processing have been conducted in several jurisdictions including New Jersey, New York, and selected federal district courts (Conti, et al., 1985; Stienstra, 1985; Aikman, 1986). Some of these experimental programs include appointing temporary lawyers as judges to dispose of less serious cases, particularly those involving civil disputes and traffic violations. These lawyers are called "judicial adjuncts" and carry on their normal law practice while assuming judicial responsibilities on a part-time basis (jurisdictions using judicial adjuncts are careful to avoid conflicts of interest where lawyers might have private interests in cases they eventually judge) (Aikman, 1986). But no procedure is as effective at reducing judicial workloads as *plea bargaining*.

PLEA BARGAINING AND FELONY PROBATION

Plea bargaining is not new, with some evidence of its use dating back to the twelfth century. Today it is so pervasive that many professionals consider it an integral feature of the U. S. criminal justice system (Alschuler, 1979a; Stitt and Siegel, 1986). *Plea bargaining is a preconviction agreement between the state and the offender whereby the offender trades a plea of guilty for a reduction in the charge, a promise of sentencing leniency, or some other concession from full, maximum implementation of the conviction and sentencing authority of the court* (McDonald, 1985:5; Uhlman and Walker, 1979). Over 90 percent of all criminal convictions in U. S. state and federal courts are obtained through plea bargaining (Langbein, 1979; Champion, 1987c). Thus, considerable time is saved and substantial trial expenses are avoided if an agreement can be reached between the prosecution and defense.

Plea bargaining is encouraged to dispose of criminal cases in federal district courts. The U. S. Supreme Court has declared "the disposition of criminal charges by agreement between the prosecutor and the accused, sometimes loosely called 'plea bargaining,' is an essential component of the administration of justice. Properly administered, it is to be encouraged" (*Bordenkircher v. Hayes*, 1978).

Plea bargaining was originally condoned officially in U. S. courts in the case of *Brady v. United States* (1970). Brady was a codefendant in a kidnapping case involving violation of 18 U.S.C. Sec. 1201(a) (1987). Brady faced the maximum penalty of death, provided a jury recommended it. The codefendant pleaded guilty and was therefore available to testify against Brady. Brady voluntarily entered a plea of guilty to the charge, and he was sentenced to 30 years in prison as the result of an earlier plea bargain. He petitioned the U. S. Supreme Court contending his plea was not voluntary, and that he was pressured into doing so because of the impending death penalty. The Court upheld his conviction, despite the fact that he entered into the plea agreement to avoid the possibile imposition of the death penalty.

Individual states are not obligated to adhere to federal sentencing policies or plea bargaining procedures. In fact, Alaska, Michigan, and other jurisdictions in selected states (e.g., New Orleans and El Paso) have abolished plea bargaining outright (Rubenstein and White, 1979; Stitt and Siegel, 1986). However, most states use plea bargaining in some form to obtain criminal convictions (Boland and Forst, 1985; Bell, 1984).

Types of Plea Bargaining

Four types of plea bargaining have been identified. First is *implicit plea bargaining*, where a defendant pleads guilty with an "implicit" expectation of receiving leniency. Second and most common is *charge reduction bargaining* where a prosecutor reduces more serious charges to less serious ones in exchange for a guilty plea from the defendant. Third is *judicial plea bargaining* where the judge offers a specific sentence of leniency in exchange for a plea of guilty. And fourth is *sentence recommendation bargaining* where a particular lenient sentence is offered by the prosecution in exchange for a guilty plea (Padgett, 1985).

Judicial Acceptance of Plea Bargains

Federal district judges are prohibited from participating in plea negotiations between prosecutors and defendants (18 U.S.C. Rule 11, 1988). However, judges supervise plea agreement hearings to determine whether the plea of guilty entered by the defendant was voluntary as well as ensuring that other defendant rights were observed. Judges have the final "say" regarding plea agreements submitted for their approval. Although judges in a majority of jurisdictions at the state and local level also avoid participating in the plea bargaining process because of the potential conflict of interest such participation suggests (i.e., judges who participate in plea bargaining are later in positions to approve or disapprove those agreements they helped to arrange), some jurisdictions such as North Carolina permit optional judicial involvement.

Several U. S. Supreme Court cases have obligated federal judges to monitor these proceedings closely, since a number of important rights are relinquished by defendants through a guilty plea. For example, judges must address the defendant personally and determine if he/she is fully aware of the consequences of the guilty plea (*McCarthy v. United States*, 1969; *United States v. French*, 1983), and the judge must advise the defendant if he/she waives his/her Fifth Amendment rights (*Boykin v. Alabama*, 1969). If the judge fails to address the defendant personally, the guilty plea may be set aside by a higher court (*Kelleher v. Henderson*, 1976; *Shepherd v. United*

States, 1979). In spite of these safeguards, some evidence exists to indicate that in many jurisdictions where plea bargaining occurs, judicial responsibilities are not fulfilled properly (Bell, 1984; Bucknew et al., 1983; Farr, 1984; Champion, 1987c).

In certain state and local jurisdictions, plea bargain agreements are reduced to a one-page summary and submitted several weeks preceding a guilty plea hearing (Kipnis, 1976). In other instances, the essence of a plea agreement is conveyed to a defendant orally by the judge and prosecutor. Sometimes, judges will merely approve the agreement involving a plea of guilt without questioning the defendant at all or through addressing a group of defendants all at once (Miller, Cramer, and McDonald, 1978; Nagel, 1982; Sutton, 1978).

Initiating the Plea Bargain Offer

Prosecutors usually initiate the plea bargain offer, and defense counsel and defendant contemplate its terms and conditions (Miller, Cramer, and McDonald, 1978). If those conditions are not satisfactory, informal discussions between defense counsel and prosecutors are conducted where the parameters of the offer are made explicit and counteroffers are considered. Much depends on the strength and importance of the government's case against the defendant as well as the seriousness of the charges (Meeker, 1984; Mather, 1979).

Prosecutors are also influenced by certain judicial idiosyncracies such as whether particular judges are more or less hostile toward drug offenders or child sexual abusers. In fact, some studies show indirect judicial influence as a significant intervening variable in modifying the contents of plea bargains offered defendants (Champion, 1987b; Brereton and Casper, 1981; Frazier and Bock, 1982). Among their priorities, prosecutors have frequently listed certain idiosyncracies of judges and the kinds of plea bargains they will accept or reject when conducting discussions of guilty pleas with defense counsels (Champion, 1987a; Bell, 1984; Church, 1979; Farr, 1984).

Both the prosecution and defense are sensitive to the advantages of a mutually satisfactory plea bargain. The prosecution is spared the time and expense of a lengthy trial, calling witnesses, and proving beyond a reasonable doubt the elements of the offenses alleged. The defendant is spared greater attorney's fees for trial and the publicity a trial would attract. Also, defendants are aware (or are made aware) that the government's offer is probably going to be less severe compared with the penalties imposed by judges if a conviction is subsequently obtained through trial (Champion, 1988c; Stitt and Siegel, 1986). Evidence shows that sentences tend to be more severe than the penalties contained in the plea bargain if a defendant is offered the plea bargain by the government, rejects it, and is subsequently convicted through trial (Frazier and Bock, 1982; Gertz and Price, 1985; Hagan and Bumiller, 1983; Jaros and Mendelsohn, 1967; McCarthy and Lindquist, 1985b).

An example at the federal level of greater sentencing severity through a trial conviction compared with the sentence imposed for the same offense through plea bargaining is provided in a study of 120 federal judges in six randomly selected circuits for the years 1983–1985 (Champion, 1988a). A total of 13,095 convictions were examined. Of these, 2,365 (22 percent) were obtained through trial verdicts, while the remaining 10,730 (78 percent) were obtained through plea bargaining. Records of convictions in these jurisdictions were subjected to content analysis, and information was yielded concerning type of offense, prior record of offender, age of offender, and other relevant variables. Those records of convictions obtained through plea bargaining were scrutinized to determine whether probation had been used as an incentive to plead guilty.

Additionally, assistant U. S. attorneys were interviewed in each of these jurisdictions on the basis of their prosecutorial connection with the convictions resulting from trials. On the basis of these interviews, it was determined which cases had proceeded to trial where earlier plea bargaining had been attempted. It was also possible to identify those convictions where no plea bargaining had occurred. Table 2.1 shows the initial distribution of convictions by circuit court jurisdiction, the number of plea bargained convictions, and the number of trial convictions involving former plea bargaining.

Table 2.1 shows that 78 percent of all convictions were obtained through plea bargaining. Of those trial convictions, 85 percent had been preceded by plea bargaining attempts. One question generated by this research was whether federal judges impose harsher sentences on defendants who are convicted in federal court through trial compared with those penalties contemplated in plea bargain agreements. Table 2.2 shows the comparative sentencing severity for offenders with and without prior records who entered guilty pleas in plea bargaining, those who engaged in earlier plea bargaining but elected trial instead, and those who did not engage in former plea bargaining. An additional feature of Table 2.2 is a sample of convicted offenders compared on each of the above criteria but where the conviction offense, interstate transportation of stolen property, is the same.

Sentencing severity in this instance is measured by calculating the actual sentence (AS) imposed (in numbers of months) against the maximum possible sentence (MS) a judge could impose under existing statutes and deriving an AS/MS ratio. Thus, if an offender could be sentenced to ten years (120 months) for an offense but receives a sentence of four years (48 months), the AS/MS ratio would be 48/120 = .40. Sentences of probation were counted as "0." Severity is measured in different ways in other studies, but this particular measure permitted direct comparisons for persons with and without prior records and allowed for "relative severity" interpretations. Therefore, two offenders might each receive a year's incarceration, but one offender

Table 2.1 Convictions Through Trial in Six Circuit Courts, the Proportion of Convictions Through Plea Agreements and Proportions of Trial Convictions Where Plea Bargaining Had Been Attempted, 1983–1985

CIRCUIT COURTS	TOTAL CONVICTIONS THROUGH PLEA BARGAINS N	TRIAL CONVICTIONS N	%	TRIAL CONVICTION, PREVIOUS PLEA-BARGAINING ATTEMPTED N	%
Fourth..........1,654	298	18%		261	87%
Sixth..........1,969	375	19%		302	81%
Seventh.........1,466	329	22%		271	82%
Ninth..........2,595	748	29%		686	92%
Tenth..........1,222	259	21%		210	81%
Eleventh........1,824	356	20%		279	78%
TOTALS	10,730 (78%) 2,365	22%		2,009	85%
TOTAL CONVICTIONS, ALL METHODS................13,095					

Source: Compiled by author.

may have faced a two-year maximum sentence, whereas the other offender may have faced a ten-year maximum sentence. The former offender's sentence would be considered proportionately more severe (12/24 = .50) compared with the latter offender's sentence (12/120 = .10). While both offenders serve a year and "a year is a year," there is greater harshness in the sanction imposed on the former offender in view of the maximum sentence he/she *could have received* compared with the latter offender.

Table 2.2 discloses several significant things. First, persons with prior records tend to receive harsher sentences according to the AS/MS ratios calculated for each category identified. Persons with prior records averaged an AS/MS ratio = .15 compared with .07 for first offenders when convictions were obtained through plea bargaining. It is of further interest to note that offenders who were convicted through trials rather than negotiating a plea bargain received consistently more severe sentences. Furthermore, those offenders who did not engage in former plea bargaining but were convicted through trial tended to have more severe sentences than those convicted through plea bargaining, but they also had *less severe sentences* compared with those convicted through trial where earlier plea bargaining had been attempted.

Table 2.2 Sentencing Severity for Plea Bargained and Trial Convictions for Defendants with and without Prior Records, Where Trial Convictions Occurred with and without Former Plea Bargaining, and AS/MS Ratios for Offender Categories According to the Offense, Interstate Transportation of Stolen Property, 1983–1985

ALL CIRCUITS	PLEA BARGAINED CONVICTIONS		TRIAL CONVICTIONS (EARLIER PLEA BARGAINING)		TRIAL CONVICTIONS (NO PLEA BARGAINING)	
	PRIOR RECORD	NO PRIOR RECORD	PRIOR RECORD	NO PRIOR RECORD	PRIOR RECORD	NO PRIOR RECORD
Fourth..	.14	.08	.30	.19	.15	.09
Sixth...	.15	.10	.32	.17	.16	.11
Seventh.	.13	.07	.26	.14	.16	.12
Ninth...	.18	.08	.40	.19	.19	.10
Tenth...	.16	.06	.33	.17	.17	.09
Eleventh	.12	.05	.25	.13	.16	.07
AVERAGES	.15	.07	.31	.16	.16	.09
(INTERSTATE TRANSPORTION OF STOLEN PROPERTY)						
	.11	.06	.21	.10	.13	.08
N =	2,289	1,183	112	40	21	26

AS/MS Ratio = Actual Sentence Imposed/Maximum Possible Sentence Under Existing Statutes (Includes Probation).

Source: Compiled by author.

Finally, Table 2.2 shows sentencing severity for each of these three offender categories (i.e., convicted through plea bargaining, convicted through trial with former plea bargaining attempted, and convicted through trial without former plea bargaining attempted) where the conviction charge was the same for all offenders, interstate transportation of stolen property. This offense accounted for 3,671 convictions. A similar pattern emerges where plea bargaining resulted in less severe sentences compared with those sentences imposed on offenders who were convicted through trial of the same charges. If anything, these data suggest that it pays to plea bargain, and a trial conviction does seem to result in more severe penalties, at least for these federal jurisdictions examined. Similar patterns of sentencing variations have been observed in two other studies of six states including Tennessee, Kentucky, Virginia, Florida, Georgia, and Alabama (Champion, 1988b, 1988c).

The Role of Probation in Plea Bargaining

In view of the changes in sentencing procedures and policies at the federal level and in several states, it is important to examine the role of plea bargaining in relation to some of the functions served by probation. Consonant with the rehabilitative and reintegrative aims served by probation, probation officers have prepared presentence investigation reports (PSI's) for several purposes. These reports provide the sentencing judge with valuable information about the offender's background as well as some indication of the likelihood of his/her success if sentenced to probation. These reports are also used by parole boards when evaluating an inmate's early release potential. With presumptive, determinate, and mandatory sentencing changes in recent years, however, the preparation of a PSI is being given less importance in the sentencing process.

Because judges are expected to sentence offenders within prescribed ranges under a presumptive guideline system or impose mandatory terms of incarceration for certain offenses under mandatory sentencing, the PSI becomes irrelevant as an informative tool, at least in the sentencing stage. However, it must be remembered that judges continue to retain broad discretion in sentencing, even with new, more stringent guidelines in effect. They may stray from presumptive ranges, provided they disclose in writing their reasons or justification for doing so. And it is unlikely that higher courts will curb significantly this discretionary power when it is exercised.

Also frequently overlooked is the power of prosecutors in plea bargaining. These persons have remained virtually unaffected by sentencing reforms. While judges may be increasingly restricted in their sentencing powers, prosecutors decide which charges will be pursued and which ones will be dropped. They are in pivotal positions to influence significantly the course of an offender's punishment. If a Michigan offender is charged with armed robbery, for example, it is within the discretion of the prosecutor to negotiate a guilty plea to a lesser charge, if he/she so desires. Thus, the "use a gun and go to prison" statement and mandatory penalties are rendered impotent, since the prosecutors' powers have not been modified. The prosecutor does not have to charge the defendant with "armed" robbery, but rather, he/she may elect (as an incentive to obtain a guilty plea from the defendant) to reduce the charges to simple robbery. Other aggravating circumstances may be overlooked as well, at the discretion of the prosecutor.

Many states have "habitual offender" statutes which contain mandatory incarcerative penalties. Again, the prosecutor may elect not to pursue an habitual offender charge against a defendant, if the defendant (who is an habitual offender) will plead guilty to some other felony. This tactic was the subject of the landmark case of *Bordenkircher v. Hayes* (1978). Paul Hayes was indicted by a Kentucky grand jury for forgery. It was determined Hayes had been convicted of two previous felonies and was liable under the Kentucky Habitual Criminal Act to prosecution as an habitual offender. Such a conviction would have meant a life sentence in prison for Hayes. He agreed to plead guilty to forgery and accept a five-year sentence (instead of the possibility of a life sentence), and in exchange for this plea, the prosecutor said he would not pursue the habitual offender charges against Hayes. After Hayes was sentenced, he appealed on the grounds that his due process rights under the U. S. Constitution had been violated. Hayes claimed the prosecutor's offer was coercive and amounted to blackmail.

After the case was dealt with in various appellate courts, the U. S. Supreme Court heard it. They upheld the original sentence imposed on Hayes and condoned the prosecutor's tactic of threatening the defendant with more serious charges as valid. Their argument rested on the fact that Hayes was subject to the habitual offender charge anyway, and that the prosecutor was simply indicating what he might do if Hayes elected not to plead guilty to the other charge. Hayes' due process rights were not violated, since he could have elected to plead not guilty to the forgery charges and taken his case to court. Hayes voluntarily consented to plead guilty to the forgery charge in order to avoid more serious charges.

Consistently the Supreme Court of the United States has upheld prosecutorial discretion to make these sorts of offers to defendants and has held such conduct not to be unlawful. However, the Court has cautioned prosecutors about the potential individual and institutional abuses of prosecutorial discretion. This "wrist-slap" has not prevented prosecutors from using such leverage to obtain guilty pleas from defendants in subsequent cases, however. Steinberg (1984) has referred to such prosecutorial power as one form of *nontrial discretionary justice*.

Probation enters the plea bargaining process not only (1) as an alternative to incarceration but (2) as an incentive to elicit a guilty plea from the defendant. As has been seen, judges have the final word in determining the sentence imposed on convicted offenders. Although new sentencing guidelines went into effect November 1, 1987 as a result of U. S. Sentencing Commission provisions, federal judges continue to have considerable latitude in the sentences they impose. But prosecutors hold powerful trump cards in the game of plea bargaining. In fact, prosecutors are in pivotal positions relating to various offender options and dispositions.

A majority of the prosecutor positions in most jurisdictions are political appointments or elected positions. The President of the United States appoints the Attorney General, with the advice and consent of Congress, who oversees all U. S. Attorney offices throughout the nation. The president also appoints U. S. attorneys to head each of these offices. In turn, each U. S. attorney appoints varying numbers of assistant U. S. attorneys as needed to prosecute those cases considered to have prosecutorial merit.

On the state and local levels, district attorney positions in cities and counties are often elected positions. Sometimes these positions are filled through appointments by mayors or other elected officials. Also, state governors may make local district attorney appointments. There is considerable variation among states in this regard.

While each prosecuting attorney at the local, state, or federal level represents his/her government and acts to protect its interests in seeing that citizens comply with the law or are prosecuted for violating it, certain political motives are also evident. Convictions, especially for serious offenses, are eagerly sought, because high conviction rates mean reappointment, reelection, and/or promotion to higher posts within prosecutorial ranks or even judgeships and beyond.

Thus, it is advantageous politically for prosecutors to coax guilty pleas from defendants whenever possible. Besides the savings of time and money, convictions are a source of prosecutorial prestige. Additionally, judges view favorably those prosecutors who can negotiate plea bargains successfully and spare the court the time and effort of conducting a trial. In some jurisdictions, judges rate prosecutors according to various criteria, including their conviction rates, aggressiveness, and general courtroom decorum and demeanor. For instance, judges often remark to prosecutors, "Can't you 'plea' this out?" or "Have you tried to make an offer to the defendant?" The question for the prosecutor invariably is, what does it take to secure a guilty plea from the defendant?

For many defense attorneys skilled in the art of plea bargaining, informal "going rates" for specific offenses are established. These "going rates" are scaled upward or downward depending upon the strength of the government case as well as the strength of the defense. Sometimes, a certain amount of "bluffing" among prosecutors and defense attorneys takes place, eventually leading to a mutually agreeable plea bargain (Maynard, 1984).

It is evident that not all criminal cases are alike. There are some interesting variations that balance the scales of justice favorably for the defendant at times and favorably for the prosecution at other times. An indigent defendant must often rely on a public defender, a court-appointed defense attorney who is paid very little for his/her services. Sometimes, this work is done on a voluntary basis in certain jurisdictions and is rotated among the local attorneys. If the indigent defendant is otherwise innocent but cannot afford witness transportation costs and other relevant fees for a strong defense, the prosecution may be able to offer the nonincarcerative alternative of probation as an incentive for a guilty plea. While the actual number of innocent defendants who plead guilty to felonious charges is not known, at least some defendants enter guilty pleas because they are fearful of being convicted and being punished more harshly.

However, more financially able defendants may be able to construct a reasonably strong defense and persist in a "not guilty" plea. Faced with the prospect of a trial, a prosecutor may opt for a recommendation of probation if the defendant enters a guilty plea to reduced charges. Obviously, many factors are at work which influence the nature of the contents of the plea bargain offered in exchange for the guilty plea.

Another factor considered by both prosecutors and judges alike is prison and jail overcrowding (Finn, 1984b). Several states including Tennessee are under federal court order not to exceed certain rated prison population capacities. While some states contract with local jails to house prison overflow, eventually these local jails reach and exceed their rated capacities as well. Thus, prisons under a "zero population growth" court order cannot admit new prisoners unless an equivalent number of inmates is released.

Prosecutors therefore press for incarceration primarily for chronic recidivists and more serious offenders. But even where serious offenses are involved and convictions obtained, state prison systems may have difficulty finding space to house growing numbers of convicted offenders. Prosecutors and judges sometimes acquire a degree of cynicism toward the system, especially when they see offenders they have sentenced to prison for several years freed within a few months because of the exigencies of prison overcrowding. This cynicism is even detected among police officers who make arrests of suspects initially. Anticipating that certain petty offenders will spend little or no time in jail or prison, some police officers merely give these persons warnings and do not make formal arrests. Again, priorities come into play, and arrests are often reserved only for the most serious crimes.

Until the late 1970's, local, state, and federal judges exercised considerable discretion over the sentencing of offenders. One result of vast judicial sentencing discretion was increased sentencing disparity. Sentencing disparities arise whenever persons who commit the same crimes under similar circumstances are given quite different sentences. One convicted offender may receive probation, while the other may receive ten years in prison for committing essentially the same offense, even by the same judge in the same jurisdiction. Sentencing disparities have often been attributable to race/ethic, gender, and/or socioeconomic differences among offenders (Unnever, Frazier, and Henretta, 1980; Kleck, 1981; Spohn, Gruhl, and Welch, 1986; Kirp, Yudof, and Franks, 1986; Weisheit and Mahan, 1988).

During the 1970's and 1980's, Congress and the legislatures of virtually every state reexamined existing sentencing statutes with the objective of grappling with certain problems associated with sentencing and parole (Smith, Pollack, and Benton, 1987:67). Under the Comprehensive Crime

)l Act of 1984, Congress established the U. S. Sentencing Commission ...... fixed sentence ranges for all federal crimes. The U. S. Parole Commission will be abolished in 1992, and all federal district judges are expected to comply with the new sentencing guidelines. The new laws were designed (1) to reduce, if not eliminate, sentencing disparities, the unjustified lack of uniformity in sentencing due to excessive discretion in sentencing authority in the hands of judges, and (2) to eliminate the unregulated exercise of power of parole boards to release inmates before the expiration of their sentences (Smith, Pollack, and Benton, 1987:67).

The results of widespread sentencing reforms among the states have been overwhelming. Smith, Pollack, and Benton (1987:67) report that between 1975 and 1982, 10 states abolished their parole boards, several established revised guidelines for parole release, 35 states enacted minimum sentence provisions, and 37 states had adopted some form of mandatory sentencing for certain crimes (e.g., using a gun during the commission of a crime). Minnesota, Florida, and Maryland have implemented the most drastic sentencing reforms thus far.

These researchers also indicate that since there is no widely accepted definition of disparity, little is presently known about how much disparity actually exists and whether the sentencing reforms recently introduced by state and federal authorities are doing anything of a tangible nature to reduce these disparities. Both probation and parole are individualized and discretionary. Until the mid-1970's, the rehabilitative function of probation and parole was paramount, and presentence investigations were crucial in assisting judges and parole boards in their decisions about offenders. But drastic changes in sentencing policies in recent years have been more punishment-centered, tending toward the "just deserts" or retributive function. These changes have not eliminated the necessity for PSI's, but they have diminished their importance considerably. And when probation is imposed, the level of supervision prescribed as a probation condition has been made increasingly intense or severe in many jurisdictions. Again, this is consistent with the "get tough" trend in dealing with offenders.

In order to understand how felony probation is or will be affected by recent sentencing reforms, we must examine several alternative sentencing schemes used in different U. S. jurisdictions.

TYPES OF SENTENCING

The range of sentencing systems in the United States involves (1) *indeterminate sentencing*, (2) *determinate sentencing*, (3) *mandatory sentencing*, and (4) *presumptive sentencing* (Bureau of Justice Statistics, 1987a:36).

Indeterminate Sentencing

Indeterminate sentencing is most prevalent among states. Over two-thirds of the states continued to use indeterminate sentencing in addition to other types of sentencing in 1985 (Shane-DuBow, Brown, and Olsen, 1985). Indeterminate sentencing provides the judge with the greatest amount of discretion in sentencing. The judge sets the type of sentence, the upper and lower limits of sentence lengths (within statutory limits), and often designates where the sentence should be served. Parole boards exist to determine an inmate's early release date, however.

Determinate Sentencing

Under determinate sentencing, judges continue to impose the type of sentence as well as its length, for certain kinds of crimes and for particular categories of offenders. Parole boards cannot initiate the early release of any inmate. However, inmates may accumulate "good time" credits which amount to a certain number of days off their original sentence for each month served. Good time credits vary according to the severity of the sentence at the federal level, with more good time credits earned per month for sentences of longer duration than for shorter ones. State authorities permit accumulation of good time credit similarly. Thus, if an inmate obeys prison rules, good time credits are earned and sentences shortened. Good time credits may also be accumulated under indeterminate sentencing as well.

Sentencing reforms in several states have been modified away from indeterminate sentencing toward a determinate sentencing system. One objective of this change has been to limit judicial discretion in sentencing, although judges continue to have considerable sentencing power. Under determinate sentencing, judges continue to grant probation in lieu of incarceration, if they wish to do so, although when they stray from the statutory sentence range (by imposing either longer or shorter sentences), they must usually provide written justification for doing so. These sorts of decisions are subject to appellate review. For extremely serious offenses (homicide, aggravated rape, kidnapping), however, probation is granted much less frequently. Usually there are mitigating circumstances involved such as age or mental retardation (see Figure 2.1).

Another aim of determinate sentencing is to increase the certainty and length of incarceration for various offenses. However, where determinate sentencing has been instituted, increases in incarceration rates have been accompanied by substantially shorter sentences compared with old indeterminate sentencing schemes. In fact, split sentences comparable to shock probation have increased considerably in certain jurisdictions. An investigation of 28 felony courts in 1985 showed that the average prison term imposed under determinate sentencing was from 40 to 50 percent lower compared

Figure 2.1

WOMAN, 70, GETS SIX YEARS IN SEVIERVILLE, TENN.

In September 1986, Mrs. Lee Warner Anderson Fredd, 70, Sevierville, Tennessee, shot and killed her husband, 71-year-old Elmer H. Fredd. On September 3, 1987, Circuit Judge Kenneth Porter sentenced Mrs. Fredd to six years in prison for the slaying. District Attorney Al Schmutzer had originally charged the white-haired woman having heart disease and crippling arthritis with second-degree murder. Evidence showed that the act was premeditated and that Mrs. Fredd's husband had been shot while seated in the bedroom.

The charges were subsequently reduced to involuntary manslaughter through plea bargaining, according to District Attorney Schmutzer, primarily because of her age and infirmity. Judge Porter said to Mrs. Fredd, "I'm sorry you're old and I'm sorry you're in poor health, but we cannot countenance that killing of a man for any of these reasons." Mrs. Fredd alleged earlier that she suspected her husband of infidelity with another woman and that he had asked for a divorce two days before the shooting. Her attorney, Charles Fels, argued that this is a case not requiring incarceration. "She is an elderly, infirm, unwell woman," he said, and recommended that she be allowed to serve her sentence under "house arrest" in Pennsylvania with relatives while undergoing psychological treatment. Fels called the slaying a "tragedy of passion, not a tragedy of premeditation." DA Schmutzer called the killing "vengeful and spiteful." Mrs. Fredd's physician said that if she were incarcerated, it could be fatal.

But because of Tennessee's prison overcrowding, Mrs. Fredd remained free until such time as the women's prison in Nashville developed a vacancy. In the meantime, her attorney continued to press for probation in the form of home confinement and counseling.

Source: *Knoxville News-Sentinel*, September 3, 1987:A20.

---

with comparable offenses under indeterminate sentencing schemes (Cunniff, 1987:v).

In more than a few jurisdictions, the shift from indeterminate to determinate sentencing has backfired. In Washington, for example, the Sentencing Reform Act of 1984 was passed, inaugurating a new "real time" determinate sentencing system (Washington State Sentencing Guidelines Commission, 1985). Washington officials concluded that the sentencing pattern for felony sentences between 1982 and 1985 has changed imperceptibly during the investigatory period when 3,427 felony convictions were examined. And in North Carolina, determinate sentencing went into effect in 1981. While the likelihood of incarceration increased from 55 to 63 percent between 1979 and 1982, the lengths of sentences dropped on the average from 60 months to 36 months (Clarke, et al., 1983). Thus, it is unlikely that the rate of probation will be affected seriously in those jurisdictions where determinate sentencing is practiced.

Mandatory Sentencing

Legislatures in most states have enacted statutes providing mandatory prison terms for certain kinds of offenses (Morelli, 1986). For example, in February 1977, Michigan passed a law requiring a mandatory two-year prison term for any person convicted of possession of a firearm during the commission of a felony. Kentucky has a similar statute. Many states also have "habitual offender" statutes which make incarceration for specified periods mandatory for persons previously convicted of two or more felonies.

It is of interest that many states with habitual offender statutes do not use them because of the potential for aggravating prison/jail overcrowding. This does not rule out the possibility that prosecutors can threaten defendants with an habitual offender prosecution if they don't agree to other terms during plea bargaining. By the same token, charges involving possession of a firearm during the commission of a felony do not have to be pursued by the prosecutor, and this can be a part of the plea bargain subsequently formulated. In fact, Shane-DuBow, Brown, and Olsen (1985) contend that the largest amount of discretionary abuse occurs among police and prosecutors, and that little or nothing can be done at a sentencing hearing later to balance the scales of justice (Eskridge, 1986:72).

The landmark case of *Bordenkircher v. Hayes* (1978) not only condoned plea bargaining, but lent approval to the prosecutorial strategy of threatening prosecution of more serious crimes if defendants don't plead guilty to lesser ones. In the case of mandatory penalties, an issue arises concerning the mandatory minimum penalty provided by statute, given the offense(s) for which the guilty plea is entered. The judge must advise the defendant of the mandatory minimum penalty provided by law which must be imposed. However, if the judge chooses to stray from the mandatory minimum penalty by imposing a sentence of probation where a period of confinement is prescribed, it is his/her obligation to provide written justification or the reasons for that departure from the statutory penalties. The defendant must also be advised of the outer limits of these penalties (*U. S. v. Garcia*, 1980) .

It will be recalled that the U. S. Supreme Court held that Hayes' rights to due process had not been violated, in spite of the threatening nature of the prosecutor's remarks. There were no elements of coercion or retaliation, since Hayes faced those additional charges rightfully. But it is quite apparent that if a prosecutor offers NOT to prosecute on certain charges, this tactic can be quite persuasive in eliciting pleas of guilty to lesser charges. Mandatory sentencing leading to mandatory prison terms of specified lengths affects prison and jail populations only when the prosecutor decides to place charges involving mandatory sentencing against defendants. But because of prison overcrowding problems and the exacerbation of such problems resulting in part from prosecutors filing charges against defendants which carry mandatory incarceration, such charges are often deliberately avoided. But since the potential exists for prosecutors to exercise this option, many defendants feel pressured to enter guilty pleas to reduced charges. Again, this underscores the pivotal role of the prosecutor in virtually all criminal cases. Thus, despite the fact that most states have mandatory sentencing for certain offenses, large-scale increases in prison populations have not occurred as the direct result of these mandatory sentencing provisions.

A controversial tactic sometimes used by prosecutors is "overcharging" defendants with assorted crimes, although this is not necessarily prevalent in all jurisdictions (Nardulli, Flemming, and Eisenstein, 1985). In a 1986 cocaine case involving two university football players, prosecutors entered 26 charges against these defendants as the result of three or four transactions involving illicit drug sales. These charges included possession of cocaine for resale, possession of cocaine, selling a controlled substance (cocaine), conspiracy to sell a controlled substance, manufacturing "crack," use of cocaine, etc. Each charge was intertwined with the others, with fines and mandatory incarceration upon conviction totaling over $500,000 and 300 years. The compounding of charges had escalated the case into "Class X" felonies involving possible life imprisonment. Through plea bargaining, however, all charges were dropped except possession of cocaine to which guilty pleas were entered, and the football players were given 90-day sentences with work release, three years' probation, and no fine. One player was offered a professional football contract and the sentencing judge permitted him time away from jail to practice regularly. The prosecutor got his felony conviction, the judge was spared a lengthy trial, one football player got his professional contract, and some community residents were outraged. Therefore, much depends upon decisions made by the prosecutor whether mandatory sentencing will be invoked by the judge. Of course, if such charges are pursued, the judge must adhere to the law and impose the mandatory sentence.

Presumptive Sentencing

Legislatures establish various sentence lengths for all criminal offenses. Actually, three sentencing ranges are created. The middle, or presumptive, sentence is the recommended one, while the higher or lower penalties may be substituted if warranted (Goodstein and Hepburn, 1985:27). Presumptive sentencing requires that judges adhere to the presumptive sentence lengths prescribed by law, unless there are aggravating or mitigating circumstances. Aggravating circumstances might include use of a weapon during the commission of the crime, serious injury to the victim, or especially brutal treatment of the victim by the offender. Mitigating circumstances might include one's age (very young or very old), whether an offender is mentally ill, whether the offender may not have participated directly in the crime (he/she might have driven the getaway car in a holdup), or whether the offender gave information to police leading to the arrest and conviction of others.

Again, if judges stray beyond the ranges permitted under presumptive sentencing, they are usually required to submit in writing their rationale or justification for the decision. If probation is granted but incarceration is prescribed, this decision usually may be challenged by prosecutors and others. However, the judge's argument for moderating the sentence is frequently upheld on appellate review. In short, attempting to "force" judges to conform to specific presumptive sentencing standards is futile, since judges can always find ways of getting around any types of sentencing standards (Eskridge, 1986:73).

Also under presumptive sentencing, parole board authority is either abolished or drastically limited (Smith, Pollack, and Benton, 1987:71). Under the traditional parole system, parole boards were authorized to revoke one's parole for parole violations and return the parolee to prison. Currently in some jurisdictions, if early releasees violate the terms of their parole or early release as prescribed by a judge, they may be subject to the additional charge of contempt of court and a new trial where another prison term may be imposed.

Eskridge (1986:70) summarizes presumptive sentencing guideline models as including four elements:

1. A standard sentencing range established by law.
2. A statutory presumption that sentences, as established by sentencing judges, will fall within the legally defined range.
3. A legal proviso allowing sentencing judges to move sentences outside the guidelines in light of aggravating or mitigating circumstances unique to each individual case.
4. A requirement that sentencing judges make formal written justification in the event a sentence falls outside the guidelines.

SENTENCING REFORMS AND FELONY PROBATION

Prior to the massive sentencing reforms at state and federal levels occurring in the 1970's and 1980's, most jurisdictions adhered to the indeterminate sentencing scheme. Indeterminate sentencing is based on the treatment or rehabilitation model, where individual needs of offenders have been emphasized. Probation, parole, and rehabilitation are stressed, and fair sentencing is theoretically achieved through individualized punishments according to each offender and his/her needs and the circumstances of the offense committed. Parole boards determine early release dates based on predictions of an inmate's dangerousness to society (Goodstein and Hepburn, 1985:12–13).

However, indeterminate sentencing has been criticized on at least three different counts. First, it has generated considerable sentencing disparity. Two different offenders can commit identical crimes under similar circumstances, yet one receives probation and the other five years in prison. Much discretion lies in the hands of the judge and parole boards regarding an offender's final disposition. Second, it is questionable whether rehabilitative programs actually rehabilitate. Prisons offer inmates vocational and educational training, and those on probation are similarly exposed to such "rehabilitation." However, there is much uncertainty about the successfulness of these programs and whether offenders are actually rehabilitated. The fact that offenders are obligated to participate in them introduces the element of coercion (e.g., sometimes inmates are threatened with parole denial for not participating in certain prison rehabilitative programs), and persons coerced into doing something are less likely to benefit from the activity compared with those who participate voluntarily.

Finally, judges and parole boards rely on predictive devices designed to forecast an offender's future behavior. No instrument yet devised is capable of predicting one's future behavior in any absolute sense. Factors such as one's age and prior record are important, but these are insufficient criteria upon which to forecast one's future and determine one's parole eligibility or probationary status. Therefore, errors of prediction enter the picture and affect adversely or positively one's early release or probation chances. Already discussed have been "false positives" and "false negatives," respectively those persons predicted to be dangerous and who turn out not to be, and those persons predicted not to pose risks but turn out to be dangerous.

The Shift from Indeterminate to Determinate Sentencing

Dissatisfaction with indeterminate sentencing and the apparent disparities it creates has caused federal and state authorities to reexamine their existing sentencing schemes. In 1972, sentencing "guidelines" were established by the U. S. Parole Commission through a pilot project. So-called "empirical" guidelines based on several predictive criteria were established in several federal district courts in Vermont, Colorado, Illinois, New Jersey, and Arizona (Block and Rhodes, 1987:5). Several states, most notably Minnesota, created new sentencing guidelines as well in the late 1970's which centered around a presumptive sentencing scheme.

By the early 1980's, all states had revised their sentencing provisions to include some form of determinate, presumptive, mandatory, and/or guidelines-based sentencing. It is beyond the scope of this book to examine in detail the precise changes in sentencing schemes occurring in each state. However, it should be noted that a majority of states continued modified indeterminate sentencing of one sort or another together with these other sentencing schemes.

Targets for change included judges and parole boards. The intent of most, if not all, sentencing reforms was to curb the discretionary powers of these decision-making authorities, presumably to reduce general sentencing disparities and increase offender release predictability. Other aims were to increase the certainty of incarceration for criminal behaviors as well as sentence lengths.

The Real Results of Sentencing Reforms

Did the sentencing reforms have their intended effects? Yes and no. Between 1975 and 1982, 10 states beginning with Maine abolished their parole boards, and 37 states had adopted some form of mandatory sentencing for specific offense categories (Smith, Pollack, and Benton, 1987:67). The abolition of parole boards is certainly a "final solution" to the problem of unchecked parole board early release discretion. Incarcerated offenders may still earn early release from prison as they accumulate sufficient "good time" credits. In some jurisdictions, good time credits amount to one day off for each day served. In other jurisdictions, different formulas are used to calculate good time. In any case, even mandatory sentences are not served in their entirety because of the good time credit an inmate may earn. Therefore, legislators interested in seeing that offenders are incarcerated for the full term of the sentence imposed by the judge have been thwarted in their legislative efforts and intent by prison good time provisions.

Judicial discretion is an entirely different matter. States such as California have found the shift to determinate sentencing largely "cosmetic and reactive" (Hammrock and Santangelo, 1985). Did judges at the state and federal levels experience serious reductions in their sentencing discretion? Generally, no. With the exception of offenses such as murder and habitual offender statutes, judges continue to wield considerable power in determining whether to incarcerate offenders, placing them on probation, and determining the length of their incarceration if incarceration is imposed (Goodstein and Hepburn, 1985:30).

Colorado is a good illustration of how determinate sentencing has been ineffective in modifying judicial sentencing behaviors. A first offender convicted of burglary may be placed on probation or incarcerated for a minimum of three years. If the judge elects incarceration, he/she is bound to observe the minimum sentence under Colorado's presumptive sentencing scheme. Therefore, there is a tremendous gap between probation and a three-year sentence, creating for the judge a difficult sentencing decision (Goodstein and Hepburn, 1985:30). At the federal level, judges may depart from existing sentencing guidelines and impose probation, provided they issue a rationale in writing stating the reasons for this departure (Block and Rhodes, 1987:7). However, some experts cite factual inaccuracies about inmates and their offenses which have been known to interfere with judicial objectivity when using sentencing guidelines or departing from them (Pope, 1986).

At the federal level, although sentencing guidelines were established for federal district judges to follow, it is uncertain whether most judges will adhere to these guidelines. Departures from these guidelines are permitted, but as is the case in states using guidelines and sentencing grids, judges must explain in writing their reasons for departing from those guidelines (Block and Rhodes, 1987:7). Among federal judges, "while the U. S. Sentencing Commission does not expect departures from the guidelines to occur with great frequency, it is not known how often they will occur, which direction they will take, and how large they will be" (1987:7).

Another intended consequence of many of these sentencing reforms was to increase the certainty of incarceration as well as lengths of sentences imposed. Again, there are mixed results among the various states where substantial reforms have been implemented. A 1983 study of sentencing outcomes was conducted involving 15,000 felony offenders in 18 predominantly urban jurisdictions in the United States for offenses of homicide, rape, robbery, aggravated assault, burglary, larceny, and drug trafficking (Cunniff, 1985:1). Interestingly, the average prison term in determinate sentencing jurisdictions was 40 to 50 percent lower than in those jurisdictions using indeterminate sentencing.

In a later study of 23,389 felony convictions in 28 jurisdictions throughout the United States, two significant findings emerged which are relevant here (Cunniff, 1987). First, in those eight jurisdictions where determinate sentencing was used (encompassing Florida, Colorado, California, North Carolina and four other states), 87 percent of the offenders were sentenced either to jail or prison. In those indeterminate sentencing jurisdictions (including Washington, Oklahoma, Missouri, New York, Ohio, Tennessee, Texas and 13 other states), 65 percent of the convicted offenders were sentenced to either jail or prison. Table 2.3 shows the percentage distributions of incarceration for each jurisdiction and whether the incarceration was in jail, prison, or either jail or prison.

Therefore, at least for those jurisdictions covered by the Cunniff study, determinate sentencing resulted in greater incarceration rates, despite the fact that many of these incarcerations were in jails rather than prisons. This

Table 2.3 Percent of Sentences to Incarceration for Each Jurisdiction, by Place of Incarceration, 1985

Jurisdiction	Percent of all sentences to:		
	Incarceration (jail and prison)	Prison	Jail
Overall average	75%	45%	30%
Determinate	87%	42%	45%
Dade County	89	58	31
Denver	44	43	1
Hennepin County	76	26	50
Kane County	82	40	43
King County	81	24	57
Los Angeles County	90	41	49
Mecklenburg County	60	55	5
San Diego County	93	41	52
Indeterminate	65%	48%	17%
Baltimore City	59	56	3
Baltimore County	57	36	21
Dallas County	65	63	1
Davidson County	84	41	43
Erie County	69	40	30
Essex County	63	41	22
Franklin County	*	58	*
Harris County	61	59	1
Jefferson County	65	56	9
Jefferson Parish	59	27	31
Lucas County	79	51	28
Manhattan	78	53	25
Maricopa County	60	36	24
Milwaukee County	61	34	27
Multnomah County	63	39	25
Oklahoma County	38	32	6
Orleans Parish	53	39	14
Philadelphia	71	33	38
St. Louis	57	42	15
Suffolk County	77	39	38

Note: Percents may not add to total due to rounding.
*Data on persons sentenced to work release were not collected. Consequently, the information on the use of jail in Franklin County is incomplete and no entry is provided for total incarceration.

Source: Cunniff, 1987: 9.

is significant because determinate sentencing is *supposed to result in higher incarceration rates*. This is precisely what occurred. However, jails are short-term incarceration facilities and not intended to house offenders for more than a year. Sentences of more than a year are most often served in state prisons or penitentiaries. Table 2.4 is even more enlightening. It shows the percent of offenders sentenced to probation under both the determinate and indeterminate sentencing schemes.

With the exception of the burglary category, offenders were granted probation more frequently under determinate sentencing compared with indeterminate sentencing. It should be noted that these figures reflect either

Table 2.4 Percent of Sentences to Probation for Each Conviction Offense, by Jurisdiction, 1985

Jurisdiction	Homicide	Rape	Robbery	Aggravated assault	Burglary	Larceny	Drug trafficking	All cases
				Percent sentenced to probation for conviction offense of:				
Overall average	14%	33%	26%	50%	44%	57%	66%	47%
Determinate	16%	37%	29%	54%	44%	60%	75%	52%
Dade County	11	13	5	19	15	20	27	16
Denver	18	5	25	51	59	66	81	56
Hennepin County	17	62	50	79	77	86	98	73
Kane County	18	19	38	51	62	69	71	59
King County	15	44	3	74	72	93	84	73
Los Angeles County	16	37	32	54	45	64	79	56
Mecklenburg County	21	14	17	56	43	53	72	45
San Diego County	22	34	38	73	49	82	69	58
Indeterminate	13%	30%	25%	47%	44%	56%	57%	44%
Baltimore City	10	39	36	20	41	70	57	42
Baltimore County	0	0	20	23	51	63	76	54
Dallas County	20	25	17	31	33	50	59	35
Davidson County	14	13	12	25	21	25	25	21
Erie County	12	9	31	52	35	48	66	41
Essex County	11	20	8	54	63	74	67	51
Franklin County	18	9	25	32	36	41	48	36
Harris County	10	30	11	38	37	45	53	39
Jefferson County	19	4	25	43	33	36	50	36
Jefferson Parish	33	6	17	52	38	61	63	49
Lucas County	15	0	17	33	24	64	63	47
Manhattan	2	12	21	43	19	40	33	27
Maricopa County	21	42	37	61	57	74	74	63
Milwaukee County	25	44	47	78	69	77	82	64
Multnomah County	27	57	42	72	55	80	79	61
Oklahoma County	6	23	13	69	78	82	79	68
Orleans Parish	17	7	23	54	47	68	64	50
Philadelphia	7	31	33	48	53	54	55	42
St. Louis	32	13	22	44	47	54	58	45
Suffolk County	6	31	37	55	54	64	58	52

Note: The data in this table reflect all probation sentences, that is, probation only and probation with jail

Source: Cunniff, 1987:12.

straight probation or a split sentence (shock probation) with a short jail term followed by probation (Cunniff, 1987:12). And again, as in the earlier 1983 study conducted by the same researcher, the average length of prison terms was from 40 to 50 percent *shorter* under the determinate sentencing scheme compared with the indeterminate sentencing system (Cunniff, 1987:v). This is precisely the opposite of what was predicted and intended as the result of shifting from indeterminate to determinate sentencing.

One plausible explanation for this perplexing state of affairs has been provided by Goodstein and Hepburn (1985:38). They say that "discretion operates on a hydraulic model: if it is eliminated in one part of the system, it will increase at another." The "increase" in discretion occurs among police and prosecutors.

The Discretion Shift

The police, of course, always exercise discretion regarding who to arrest and what charges will be filed. While they may later be called as witnesses if the case comes to trial, generally their discretion ends here. However, changing the method of sentencing offenders is likely to cause priority shifts among prosecutors about which cases to pursue and which ones to drop. These prosecutorial priority shifts, in turn, will be perceived by police as either encouraging or discouraging when they are contemplating the arrest of a criminal suspect. At present, little is known of the relation between police discretion and the sentencing of provisions in various jurisdictions. What *is* known, however, is that the rationality associated with police discretion is influenced by a multiplicity of factors including how the prosecutors will eventually dispose of the case (Gottfredson and Gottfredson, 1988:70).

The major discretionary shift occurs among state and federal prosecutors. Casper, Brereton, and Neal (1981) says that "little evidence of increased plea bargaining [occurs] as a result of the determinate sentencing law" (Goodstein and Hepburn, 1985:38). This is hardly surprising. There is no logical reason for determinate sentencing to increase the *amount* of plea bargaining per se. Rather, the *nature* of plea bargaining might be expected to change as prosecutors have new cards with which to play the plea bargaining game. As a matter of fact, determinate sentencing, mandatory sentencing, presumptive sentencing, and/or the use of sentencing guidelines will probably equip most prosecutors in affected jurisdictions with more powerful bargaining tools.

Judges must hear cases brought before them by prosecutors. Prosecutors decide which charges to file against which alleged offenders. Thus, as offenders are faced with greater (sometimes absolute) *certainty* of incarceration *if convicted*, especially of serious charges, a logical implication of these sentencing reforms might be an even higher incidence of guilty pleas to less serious felony charges. It is still too early to tell if this sort of trend is occurring in those jurisdictions using determinate sentencing. But as has been seen, in selected determinate sentencing jurisdictions already investigated compared with indeterminate sentencing jurisdictions, split sentences and probation appear to be increasing, while sentence lengths are shorter. Undoubtedly this is a partial reflection of the kinds of charges brought against offenders in plea bargain agreements and in criminal trials.

Goodstein and Hepburn observe that "plea bargaining, which has been left unregulated in virtually every determinate sentencing model, permits unregulated discretion to be exercised and may increase the power of the prosecutor with respect to other actors in the criminal justice system" (1985:38). Shane-DuBow, Brown, and Olsen (1985) agree and argue that the greatest measure of discretionary abuse lies with prosecutors. However, certain kinds of prosecutorial vindictiveness have been challenged successfully in recent years when defendants have attempted to exercise their constitutional rights (Erlinder and Thomas, 1985).

JUDICIAL VIEWS ON SENTENCING FELONS

Although judges are supposed to be impartial arbiters in their sentencing of felons and others, it is evident from research of judicial attitudes that they differ significantly regarding their individual rationales and beliefs which tend to influence the sentences imposed (Lurigio, 1987; Brantingham, 1985; Wald, 1986). However, among judges, prosecutors, and many criminal justice practitioners, there is widespread consensus on the goals to be achieved through recently enacted state and federal sentencing reforms. This agreement suggests that:

1. The old style indeterminate sentence (1 year to life) is unacceptable largely because the old assumptions regarding the success of rehabilitative programs are no longer considered valid.
2. Incapacitation and deterrence have now become the primary goals of sentencing.
3. Personal crime is more important than property crime.
4. Violent crime is more important than non-violent crime.
5. Sentences should be proportional to the offense.
6. Mandatory sentences are probably unworkable.
7. The characteristics of the offender as well as the offense should be considered.
8. Some kind of appellate review of sentencing is desirable (Smith, Pollack, and Benton, 1987:67–68; Judicature, 1984).

The manifest goals of the police, prosecutors, and courts are to control crime and protect society from dangerous criminals. The means of achieving these objectives have shifted in the last several decades from rehabilitating offenders through treatment to deterring and punishing them through just deserts and justice. Especially for judges who sentence offenders, the two primary ways in which a sentence imposed can safeguard the public against future crimes are (1) through example, where the offender's sentence may deter others from wrongdoing, and (2) where the treatment prescribed for the offender may cause him/her to correct his/her way of life (Chandler, 1987:11). As we have seen, neither of these alternatives may function as a deterrent for any particular offender or potential offender.

In any event, judges must decide the appropriate punishment. At the federal level and in many state and local jurisdictions, probation is encouraged as a nonincarcerative alternative, when it is reasonable to impose such a sentence. "Reasonable" is an elusive term and varies in meaning among judges in all jurisdictions. Probation program innovations establishing a higher degree of probationer monitoring and control have greater credibility among judges and prosecutors compared with programs typified by standard probation supervision (which usually means little or no supervision). Some professionals contend that "one of the greatest changes in the administration of criminal justice in the . . . courts in the last generation has been the adoption of probation" (Chandler, 1987:14).

Glaser (1984) has outlined six principles for judges to consider when sentencing felons. These principles are:

1. Maximize fines and minimize incarceration.
2. Minimize criminalization.
3. Interrupt crime sprees.
4. Lock up tightly those who, if released, are likely to inflict public damages at a rate that can reasonably be assessed at much more than the cost of their confinement.
5. Minimize the unsupervised involvement of offenders with each other, and maximize their bonds with nonoffenders.
6. Provide intensive vocational education and realistic work experience, with incentives for good performance, at occupations that both appeal to them and have good postrelease job possibilities (1984:22–28).

These principles reflect the cost-effectiveness of probation over incarceration (fines and nonincarcerative alternatives), the isolation of criminals from other criminals as a means of interrupting their networks (shock probation or split sentencing can sometimes disrupt drug connections or other criminal social networks), the selective incapacitation of the most serious offenders, the increased interaction of offenders with noncriminals through work release and community-based probation programs, and the rehabilitative influence of relevant job training. Therefore, sentencing judges must consider each sentence as a multifaceted decision which is likely to influence greatly an offender's future conduct.

One of the more difficult decisions judges must make is whether to sentence felons to probation or incarceration. They are faced not only with competing correctional philosophies but also with an aggregate of constituents who carefully scrutinize the sentences they impose. In many jurisdictions, "court-watchers" sit in courtrooms for hours on end, observing judges and the decisions they make in each and every criminal case. These court-watchers may be concerned citizens or newspaper reporters, but their impact is sometimes overwhelming. On any given day, a judge may impose a harsh sentence on a petty offender for cosmetic value, if court-watchers are present. On other days when court-watchers are not present, the judge may dismiss a similar case or impose probation.

Another important factor influencing judicial sentencing practices is prison/jail overcrowding. There is only so much room in state prisons and local jails. Most actors involved in the sentencing process are aware of this fact. Therefore, a judge's decision is based, in part, on what the statute prescribes as punishment, the aggravating and/or mitigating circumstances, the record of the defendant, and the practical concern for aggravating the overcrowding problem.

In 1986, a survey was conducted of 296 judges, prosecutors, parole commissioners, and wardens in New York State and the federal government. The survey centered on sentencing, its purposes, and its implications for offenders and society (Smith, Pollack, and Benton, 1987:68). These respondents were asked (1) whether sentencing a defendant to prison acts as a deterrent to crime by others in the community, (2) whether the main purpose of sentencing a criminal is to punish and/or incapacitate him, and (3) whether prison sentences should be changed to "flat" sentences without parole, i.e., without supervision backed by the threat of reincarceration after release.

Most respondents including judges tended to agree the main purpose of sentencing criminals is for punishment and/or incapacitation. Also, most judges and prosecutors agreed that imprisonment of offenders acts as a deterrent. Parole/probation officials were in general disagreement with the idea that imprisonment functions as a deterrent to crime. Almost all respondents rejected the idea that flat sentences without parole ought to be established.

In another 1985 study of a relatively small sample of judges in Illinois, judges were asked questions concerning their feelings about the value of probation for felons. In this study, probation was defined as "intensive supervised probation" with a rather high degree of monitoring by probation officers. Most judges said that from their own experiences, such probation programs were quite useful, even for those cases involving "high-risk" offender groups (Lurigio, 1987). In the same study, prosecutors interviewed disagreed and felt that most probation programs would not be particularly effective in monitoring serious offenders. These differences of opinion are understandable, since prosecutors are primarily concerned with obtaining convictions and seeing most of those convicted also incapacitated.

FELONY PROBATION TRENDS IN SELECTED JURISDICTIONS

Petersilia (1985d) has said that felony probation is increasing nationwide, especially in California where prison overcrowding is forcing judges to opt for this nonincarcerative alternative. Is the use of felony probation increasing in other jurisdictions as well? And if so, to what degree?

Two studies are of interest here. First, a survey was conducted in 1985 of 166 city and county prosecutors in several randomly selected jurisdictions of Virginia, Kentucky, and Tennessee (Champion, 1987b). This represented a response rate of 64 percent from an initial questionnaire mailing of 260. Subsequently, random samples of prosecutors from the selected jurisdictions were interviewed. Content analyses of felony convictions in these selected jurisdictions were also conducted for the years 1970 through 1985, identifying offense information, age and gender of offender, whether the conviction was obtained through plea bargaining or trial, and several other salient factors.

Disregarding whether offenders had prior records or were first offenders as well as the specific offenses involved, the incidence of felony probation was tracked for the sixteen-year period, 1970–1985. Table 2.5 shows the distribution of felony convictions, the proportion of convictions obtained through plea bargaining, and those convictions where probation was granted. No attempt was made to determine the type of probation sentence imposed, and split sentencing with short jail terms was counted as probation as well.

Table 2.5 shows a systematic increase in the use of felony probation for all jurisdictions combined. Further investigation revealed that when first offenders were compared with recidivists, the probation rate for first offenders across all offense categories rose from .71 in 1970 to .82 in 1985. However, the use of probation for recidivists systematically declined during the same period from .38 in 1970 to .22 in 1985. Also, when convictions were divided according to violent and property crimes for all years combined, probation was used 16 percent of the time for violent offenders, whereas it was used 65 percent of the time for property offenders. Probation also increased systematically for offenders in advancing age categories. In effect, the older the offender, the more likely probation was imposed. This finding held for those with prior records, first offenders, and for different types of crimes (violent and property offenders) as well. A subsequent investigation of judicial sen-

Table 2.5 Kentucky, Tennessee, and Virginia Area Jurisdictions, Numbers of Felony Convictions, Plea Bargained Convictions, and Proportion of Convictions Involving Probation, 1970–1985

YEAR	TOTAL FELONY CONVICTIONS N	CONVICTIONS THROUGH PLEA BARGAINING		CONVICTIONS INVOLVING USE OF PROBATION	
		N	Prop.	N	Prop.
1970	2,980	1,427	.48	845	.59
1971	3,174	1,925	.61	1,078	.56
1972	2,999	1,846	.62	1,071	.58
1973	4,221	3,429	.81	2,023	.59
1974	3,485	2,599	.74	1,559	.60
1975	4,003	3,103	.77	1,830	.59
1976	3,715	2,906	.78	1,743	.60
1977	3,217	2,423	.75	1,478	.61
1978	3,983	2,915	.73	1,807	.62
1979	4,121	3,334	.81	2,067	.62
1980	5,113	4,220	.82	2,658	.63
1981	4,326	3,563	.82	2,244	.63
1982	4,780	3,989	.83	2,619	.69
1983	4,355	3,612	.83	2,383	.66
1984	5,032	4,378	.87	2,977	.67
1985	4,868	4,321	.89	2,981	.69

Source: Compiled by author.

tencing patterns in Alabama, Georgia, and Florida disclosed similar trends (Champion, 1988c).

In a study of 120 federal district judges in six randomly selected circuit jurisdictions reported earlier in this chapter, the incidence of the use of felony probation was examined for the years 1983–1985 across all jurisdictions (Champion, 1988a). During the investigative period for the circuits examined, 13,095 felony convictions were obtained either through plea bargaining or trial. Of the 13,095 convicted offenders, 4,714 (36 percent) were granted some form of probation. Table 2.6 shows the distribution of these 4,714 felony probationers across all jurisdictions according to first-offender/prior record status as well as type of crime (i.e., property or violent offense).

Table 2.6 shows that at least for these federal jurisdictions, felony probation was granted to an increasing degree for the three-year investigative period. Of course, this may or may not be representative of all federal circuits, but it does include nearly a fourth of all federal district judges in six different circuits as well as a substantial number of felony convictions.

It is uncertain currently as to how the new federal sentencing guidelines will affect these trends. As of November 1, 1987 new guidelines went into effect influencing sentencing decisions of nearly 575 federal district judges.

Table 2.6 Felony Probation Across All Years and by First-Offender/Prior Record Status, Property/Violent Offenses, 1983–1985, for Six Circuit Jurisdictions, N = 4,714 *

YEAR	ALL CONVICTIONS	RECORD FO**	PRIOR	TYPE OF CRIME PROPERTY	VIOLENT
1983.......	.32	.62	.21	.55	.27
1984.......	.34	.66	.23	.58	.28
1985.......	.39	.67	.26	.61	.31
AVERAGES...	.36	.65	.24	.58	.29

*Number of felony probations out of 13,095 convictions.
**First Offenders.

Source: Compiled by author.

These judges continue to have broad discretionary powers unchecked by the new guidelines, and some form of probation remains an alternative sentence they may impose.

Block and Rhodes (1987:2–3) say that as a result of these new federal sentencing guidelines, a number of significant changes in sentencing patterns is likely to occur. First, straight probation without any conditions or confinement (standard probation supervision) will probably be reduced substantially. Currently, some confinement includes split sentencing or shock probation, mixed sentences, and probation with some jail included. Offenders with sentences of no more than six months may receive a probation term that includes community-based supervision (Block and Rhodes, 1987:2). Sentences of more than six months are likely to be split between some jail and some community supervision.

Any sort of probation for particularly violent offenses will decline appreciably. About 41 percent of the violent offenders in the federal system received some form of probation prior to November 1, 1987. It is estimated that this figure will drop to about 25 percent because of the new sentencing guidelines. For robbery, probation and split sentences will decline from 25 percent to 5 percent, according to Block's and Rhodes' projections. Probation for drug offenses will also decline from about 34 percent to 13 percent. Theoretically, the amount of time served by incarcerated offenders will increase on the average from 16 months to 29 months, although this increase is only for selected serious offense categories.

Because of the Comprehensive Crime Control Act of 1984 and the Anti-Drug Abuse Act of 1986, the minimum and maximum sentences for career criminals and drug offenders will increase significantly. Income tax evasion penalties have doubled from previous sanctions, and tax evaders are more likely to be incarcerated and less likely to receive probation of any kind (Block and Rhodes, 1987:3-4).

But uncertainty remains about how federal judges will respond to the new guidelines. Even more uncertain is the reaction of U. S. attorneys and their assistants who prosecute cases and plea-bargain with defendants. This "hydraulic" factor may offset any additional prison/jail overcrowding projected to occur as one result of these new sentencing reforms. Block and Rhodes (1987:3-4) also note that substantial sentence increases have been established for certain crimes that are rarely prosecuted. Thus, it is unlikely that prison populations will be affected, at least as far as prosecutions for these rare offenses are concerned. However, these researchers do anticipate significant prison population increases due to new drug laws in comparison with how drug offenders were formerly treated.

Each state has established or is in the process of establishing sentencing reforms designed to "get tough" on crime and criminals. There is no universally acceptable sentencing system adopted by all states at present, and therefore, uneven effects of sentencing reforms among the states are expected. In some instances, the reforms implemented in certain states have caused those states to re-think their reforms. Maine abolished parole boards in 1975, for example, but now Maine is faced with rapidly escalating prison populations. As one result, Maine is now seeking new alternatives (more reforms?) to remedy the unanticipated effects of old reforms.

SUMMARY

General concern is expressed over the amount of crime in the United States and the apparent ineffectiveness of various offender programs for controlling or reducing it. One result is every state as well as the federal government has implemented sentencing reforms which affect probation in various ways. Indeterminate sentencing is gradually being replaced by presumptive, determinate, and mandatory sentencing schemes thereby reflecting a general shift from the traditional treatment or rehabilitative philosophy to one of just deserts and justice.

Plea bargaining is useful in securing over 90 percent of all criminal convictions at local, state, and federal levels. Prosecutors play pivotal roles in the plea bargaining process, and it is anticipated that they will play an even more crucial role in view of changing sentencing patterns. New sentencing schemes are giving prosecutors greater and unchecked negotiating power in their attempts to elicit guilty pleas from criminal defendants.

Although efforts have been made by legislatures to limit the discretionary powers of judges and parole boards, judges continue to remain relatively unaffected by sentencing changes implemented thus far. The main impact of sentencing reforms to date has been to shift some discretionary power from judges to prosecutors.

The use of felony probation in selected state and federal jurisdictions has increased significantly in recent years, although for those states and jurisdictions adopting new sentencing guidelines, it is presently unknown what changes will occur regarding the incidence of felony probation. Continued prison/jail overcrowding will influence arrest decisions by police, prosecution and charging decisions by district attorneys, and sentencing decisions of the judiciary at all levels.

Projections by experts suggest a general decline in the use of standard probation supervision, particularly for specific offense categories such as robbery and drugs. Although sentencing reforms are designed to increase generally the amount of time served in prison as well as the certainty of incarceration, it is too early to tell whether these changes will eventually develop. Some jurisdictions report greater use of split sentences with significantly shorter periods of incarceration under determinate and presumptive sentencing compared with indeterminate sentencing. Although prison population increases are anticipated, judges, prosecutors, and others may employ a variety of strategies within their discretionary authority to curb such increases.

3

Prison/Jail Overcrowding and Felony Probation

INTRODUCTION

A sentence of probation in general is dependent upon discretion exercised by several criminal justice agencies and their actors as well as the offender and type of crime committed. Initially, police exercise discretion in their arrests of alleged offenders, and on the basis of evidence and other considerations, district attorneys decide which cases should be prosecuted or dropped. As has been seen, prosecutors play pivotal roles and act at more case-handling decision points than any other officials (Hall, 1987:3). And although judges in recent years have had to adhere rather closely to stricter sentencing guidelines in most jurisdictions, they also make crucial decisions about whether to grant probation or withhold it. Despite the reactions of their constituents toward the political or idiosyncratic nature of their sentencing decisions, judges are moved to consider as well various factors external to the courtroom, the offender, and the nature and severity of the offense (Wald, 1986; Finn, 1984b; Price et al., 1983).

Probably the most significant and visible problem currently confronting the criminal justice system in general and corrections specifically is *prison and jail overcrowding* (Gottfredson and Taylor, 1983). This is because prison/jail overcrowding not only affects and influences all criminal justice organizations and agencies but is reciprocally affected and influenced by all of them as well. Petersilia (1985d:36) strongly alludes to this interrelatedness, although the primary focus of her Rand research was to learn whether increased felony probation, one consequence of prison/jail overcrowding, presents unacceptable risks for public safety.

This chapter examines prison and jail overcrowding and its influence on the incidence of felony probation. As police officers, prosecutors, judges, corrections officials and legislators act in their different capacities to alleviate the overcrowding problem or aggravate it, probation and parole departments and their staffs are invariably affected by virtually every solution proposed. Thus, the changing roles and caseloads of probation officers in response to prison and jail population reduction programs will be addressed. Finally, the delicate balance between citizen interests and public policy and the nonincarcerative sentences meted out as felony probation will be explored.

PRISON AND JAIL OVERCROWDING

Every state prison system has an overcrowding problem (Sapp, 1984). The federal prison system is similarly overcrowded (Greenfeld, 1987). An indication of the severity of prison and jail overcrowding is provided by Bureau of Justice Statistics figures showing that between 1978 and 1983, new prison construction provided 122,317 new prison beds, although prison population growth during the same period exceeded that figure by 33,255 (Allen, Latessa, and Vito, 1987:92). Also, between 1978 and 1983, new bed space for jails increased substantially, but again, jail population increases exceeded new bed space by 37,121 (Allen, Latessa, and Vito, 1987:92).

Table 3.1 shows federal and state prison population capacities at the end of 1986. Between 1985 and 1986, state and federal prison capacities were increased by 24,000–32,000 beds. But during this same period, the prison population grew by over 41,000 inmates.

In Table 3.1, *rated capacity* refers to the number of beds or inmates assigned by a rating official to institutions within the state. *Operational capacity* is the number of inmates that can be accommodated by the prison staff, existing programs, and services. *Design capacity* (which is often the same as "rated capacity") is the number of inmates originally intended to be served by the facility according to planners and architects (Greenfeld, 1987:4). On the average, state prisons were operating in 1987 at about 106 percent of their highest rated capacity, while the federal system was operating at 27 percent above its highest rated capacity.

Seventeen states reported a total of 13,770 prisoners held in local jails by the end of 1986 as well, directly attributable to overcrowding in their own state prison facilities. Table 3.2 shows the number of state prisoners held in local jails between 1985 and 1986. Tennessee's prisoner population held in local jails virtually doubled during the 1985–1986 period, for example. Substantial prison population increases in local jails were also observed for Virginia, New Jersey, Louisiana, and California (Greenfeld, 1987:4). These additional prisoners in local jails add to jail revenues through state-jail contractual agreements, although jail overcrowding problems are frequently exacerbated as a result.

Measures of Prison/Jail Overcrowding

Determining whether a prison or jail is overcrowded is more complicated than merely counting beds and prisoners and seeing if prisoners equal or outnumber the beds. Using the prison's or jail's rated or design capacities as

Table 3.1 Reported Federal and State Prison Capacities at Yearend 1986

Jurisdiction	Rated capacity	Operational capacity	Design capacity	Population as a percent of:[a]	
				Highest capacity	Lowest capacity
Federal	27,938	34,890	27,938	127%	159%
Northeast					
Connecticut	6,072	4,968	3,781	114%	183%
Maine	1,033	1,033	1,033	124	124
Massachusetts	3,265	...	...	174	174
New Hampshire [b]	689	689	539	110	141
New Jersey	10,401	11,394	9,777	105	123
New York	37,743	39,502	35,891	97	107
Pennsylvania	...	...	11,048	138	138
Rhode Island	1,456	1,440	1,359	94	100
Vermont	597	597	547	113	124
Midwest					
Illinois	19,705	19,705	15,943	98%	122%
Indiana	8,710	...	...	113	117
Iowa	...	2,702	2,918	95	103
Kansas	3,502	5,015	...	108	155
Michigan	...	16,784	...	124	124
Minnesota	2,495	2,495	2,633	94	99
Missouri	...	11,588	...	91	91
Nebraska	1,562	1,513	1,542	125	129
North Dakota	...	471	471	89	89
Ohio	...	...	13,282	169	169
South Dakota	1,189	1,090	1,189	88	96
Wisconsin	...	4,591	...	124	124
South					
Alabama	10,374	10,374	10,374	108%	108%
Arkansas	...	4,620	...	102	102
Delaware	...	2,563	2,404	110	118
District of Columbia	6,769	6,577	...	100	103
Florida	35,982	32,290	25,561	90	126
Georgia	...	16,323	...	106	106
Kentucky	4,921	5,327	...	101	107
Louisiana	11,080	11,080	11,080	100	100
Maryland	...	13,646	9,544	98	140
Mississippi	5,878	...	...	95	95
North Carolina	...	...	16,575	107	107
Oklahoma	7,642	7,260	...	126	132
South Carolina	9,212	9,212	8,163	122	138
Tennessee	7,801	...	...	92	92
Texas	40,392	38,373	40,392	95	100
Virginia	10,159	10,159	9,753	115	120
West Virginia [b]	1,547	1,640	1,547	86	91
West					
Alaska	2,336	...	...	105%	105%
Arizona	...	9,911	...	95	95
California	32,853	53,887	32,853	107	176
Colorado	3,760	3,760	...	98	98
Hawaii	1,252	...	1,252	174	174
Idaho	1,149	1,470	1,149	99	126
Montana	936	1,190	936	93	119
Nevada	...	...	3,911	115	115
New Mexico	2,363	2,593	2,363	104	114
Oregon	...	4,057	2,815	117	168
Utah	1,805	1,805	1,537	98	115
Washington	5,324	6,040	5,324	108	123
Wyoming	...	950	...	91	91

... Data not available.
[a] Excludes State-sentenced inmates held in local jails due to crowding where they have been included in the total prisoner count.
[b] Capacity figures for males only.

Source: Greenfeld, 1987:5.

Table 3.2 Number of State Prisoners Held in Local Jails Because of Prison Crowding, by State, Yearend 1985 and 1986

States housing prisoners in local jails	Prisoners held in local jails			
	Number		As percent of all prisoners	
	1985	1986	1985	1986
Total	10,143	13,770	2.2%	2.7%
Alabama	398	514	3.6	4.4
Arkansas[a]	115	458	2.5	8.9
California	1,122	1,566	2.2	2.6
Colorado[a]	245	343	6.8	8.5
Idaho	9	0	.6	0
Illinois				
Kentucky	43	48	.2	.2
Louisiana	791	886	13.7	14.0
Maine	2,923	3,449	21.0	23.7
Massachusetts	51	36	4.2	2.7
	2	1	—	—
Mississippi				
New Jersey[a]	933	1,169	14.6	17.3
South Carolina	1,486	2,244	11.6	13.2
Tennessee[a]	429	451	4.1	3.9
Utah	628	1,201	8.3	14.3
	33	77	2.1	4.2
Vermont[b]	11	8	1.7	1.2
Virginia	786	1,257	6.5	9.7
Washington	49	62	.7	.9
Wisconsin	89	0	1.6	0

—Less than 0.05%.
[a]For States not including jail backups in their jurisdiction counts, the percentage of jurisdiction population was calculated on the combined total of jail and prison.
[b]Vermont reported 8 inmates in local lockups.

Source: Greenfeld, 1987:4

measures is unreliable as well, since many prisons/jails are old and some are continually undergoing modernization or renovation with some cells or blocks uninhabited for lengthy periods.

Two principal measurement levels of prison/jail crowding have been identified: (1) individual-level crowding and (2) aggregate-level crowding (Gaes, 1985:107).

Individual-Level Crowding. Gaes (1985:107–108) has said that individual-level prison/jail crowding can be measured by individual data including *spatial density, social density, personal space, privacy,* and *perceived crowding. Spatial density is the amount of floor space per occupant.* An 8' by 8' room has 64 square feet of space. Table 3.3 shows the spatial density of all state prisons as of June 30, 1984. A proposal by the U. S. Department of Justice in 1980 proposed that a standard of at least 60 square feet be provided for inmates spending no more than 10 hours a day in that space, and at least 80 square feet for those inmates spending more than 10 hours a day in that space (Innes, 1986:4). But in 1984, 62 percent of all state prison inmates were housed in cell units of *less than 60 square feet* regardless of time spent in them (Innes, 1986:4).

Gaes (1985:107) says that *social density is the number of people in a given area.* The social density of a two-person cell is two. Social density is considered more important than spatial density regarding influencing inmate violence, however (Paulus, McCain, and Cox, 1985). *Personal space is the amount of space that does not have to be shared with others,* such as individual cells or rooms. *Privacy is the proportion of time the prisoner can be alone.* Inmates may have single cells during the night, but they must spend most of their daytime hours with other prisoners. Finally, *perceived crowding is self-reports of inmates of how crowded their surroundings happen to be.* These are admittedly unreliable and nonstandardized, and thus it is impossible to make meaningful comparisons among jails or prisons according to perceived crowding.

Aggregate-Level Crowding. Gaes (1985:109–110) says that aggregate data are based upon individually compiled data. Three aggregate-level crowding measures are used. These include the *crowding density ratio, aggregate measures of prison housing,* and *crowding in common areas.* The crowding density ratio is understood only in relation to some commonly used standard of space allocated to each inmate. Thus, *the crowding density ratio is the number of single-inmate cells (or two-inmate cells) that can be put into a dormitory meeting a specific square footage capacity.* Aggregate measures of prison housing consist of the percentages of a prison's population housed in different types of bunking arrangements, such as single cell, double cell, small dormitories, or large open bay dormitories (Gaes, 1985:110). *Crowding in common areas refers to crowding in dayrooms, recreation yards, prison libraries, or dining halls.* Therefore, a library designed to accommodate 30 prisoners per hour is considered overcrowded if 60 prisoners per hour use these library facilities. Gaes says that few, if any, studies have used crowding in common areas as the index of prison/jail overcrowding thus far.

Table 3.3, compiled by the U. S. Department of Justice Bureau of Justice Statistics, uses spatial density to reflect variations among state prisons. Southern prisons tend to have the highest spatial density, while prisons in the Northeast have the lowest density (Innes, 1987:5). Gaes (1985:109) contends that the most typical aggregate-level unit of analysis among prison crowding researchers is the prison, while the most common measure is a density ratio based on the number of inmates housed in a prison relative to its capacity. Table 3.1 uses this measure to reflect prison overcrowding, whereas Table 3.3 relies upon the average amount of square footage (an individually-based measure, spatial density) available to inmates for overcrowding estimates.

Prison Overcrowding Compared with Jail Overcrowding

Prison Overcrowding. Prisons differ from jails in several important respects. First, they are designed to house more serious felons for periods of one or more years. Therefore, facilities for long-term confinement, recreation, vocational/educational training, counseling, and other services and activities must be provided. Second, prisons differ according to the level of custody associated with specific offender categories. These custody levels include minimum security, medium security, and maximum security (Wright, 1986). A third important difference is state prisons are state-operated and are therefore subject to a high degree of control by state legislatures.

State prison systems are operated almost entirely from legislative appropriations, although the federal government allocates monies for special projects, innovative constructions, and other assistance. Finally, corrections officers in prisons compared with those who operate jails generally tend to be better-qualified and trained, because of selection and recruitment standards established by various states. While guard positions do not pay as well as comparable jobs in the private sector, sufficiently large numbers of persons are attracted to such positions because of job security, fringe benefits, and less risk (Lombardo, 1981).

Prisons are also breeding grounds for inmate gangs and long-term coalitions that often have greater control over prisoners and their lives than prison officials (Suall, 1987:23; Webb, 1984). In 1985, for example, state and federal prisons reported 114 gangs, usually based on race or ethnic characteristics (U. S. Department of Justice, 1985). Gang membership in Illinois state prisons alone was as high as 5,300 inmates, about a fourth of the entire Illinois inmate population.

The Oklahoma prison system is illustrative of the overcrowding problems of other state prisons. Between 1974 and 1983, the Oklahoma prison inmate population more than doubled from 3,230 to 7,480 inmates (Oklahoma State Board of Corrections, 1984). In view of the fact that the operational capacity of Oklahoma prisons in 1987 was only 7,260 inmates, the problem facing Oklahoma prison officials was more than a little apparent in 1983. At the end of 1986, Oklahoma's prison population had grown to 9,596, although its rated and operational capacities remained at 7,642 and 7,260 respectively (Greenfeld, 1987). And by 1987, Oklahoma prison overcrowding was barely in the top ten states with substantial overcrowding problems.

Jail Overcrowding. Jails compared with prisons are designed to accommodate short-term offenders or persons charged with various offenses. However, jails in some jurisdictions may release certain inmates within hours after their arrest while some accused felons and sentenced prisoners may remain incarcerated in these "short-term facilities" for several years (Kizziah, 1984).

Persons arrested by police, including juveniles, are typically brought to jail initially, where they await their disposition. These may include serious felons, persons arrested for driving while intoxicated, vandals, misdemeanants, persons illegally hitchhiking along interstate highways, persons arrested for public drunkenness, loiterers, vagrants, shoplifters,

Table 3.3 Number of State Prisons, Number of Inmates, Average Square Feet Per Inmate, and Percent in Multiple Housing, by Use of Unit and State, June 30, 1984

	Number of prisons	General housing			Special housing			Other housing		
		Number of inmates	Average square feet per inmate	Percent of inmates in multiple occupancy	Number of inmates	Average square feet per inmate	Percent of inmates in multiple occupancy	Number of inmates	Average square feet per inmate	Percent of inmates in multiple occupancy
U.S. total	694	335,282	57.3	70.1	32,671	57.1	30.0	13,930	93.3	65.8
Alabama	12	7,068	59.6	83.8	464	57.7	.9	139	77.5	77.0
Alaska	12	1,428	71.4	76.7	119	66.0	52.1	43	49.6	72.1
Arizona	12	6,337	77.0	76.4	654	61.5	89.3	63	230.1	19.0
Arkansas	7	3,263	76.2	76.6	304	70.0	91.8	98	126.5	69.4
California	36	32,607	48.0	89.2	3,479	47.8	19.9	3,064	44.8	78.1
Colorado	9	2,047	76.1	27.9	522	96.1	33.9	17	128.5	94.1
Connecticut	13	4,337	49.8	44.1	278	55.8	53.2	440	59.0	37.0
Delaware	6	1,754	87.9	43.3	5	60.0	0	78	72.3	75.6
District of Columbia	5	1,951	90.1	83.4	414	57.3	12.6	232	89.3	100.0
Florida	40	21,180	54.4	85.0	2,202	64.3	32.6	414	64.9	96.9
Georgia	23	11,250	82.5	79.2	943	62.5	21.2	470	680.4	47.7
Hawaii	7	1,127	37.8	93.4	161	35.6	82.0	421	20.4	99.8
Idaho	3	962	45.7	91.5	83	52.4	50.6	46	45.2	100.0
Illinois	25	13,951	57.3	62.8	1,449	56.6	17.5	367	71.9	33.8
Indiana *	11	8,138	52.4	70.5	421	51.4	24.9	82	90.3	62.2
Iowa	10	2,250	63.0	47.6	353	49.7	4.8	83	99.5	61.4
Kansas	7	3,255	38.9	73.4	447	52.2	9.4	37	69.5	78.4
Kentucky	10	4,392	71.8	64.3	136	61.3	7.4	8	371.4	37.5
Louisiana	11	9,207	71.7	89.0	869	80.6	61.7	333	77.7	83.2
Maine	4	935	49.6	60.0	65	54.0	0	11	56.0	0
Maryland	14	10,621	49.7	55.8	1,433	41.3	50.1	299	135.3	69.2
Massachusetts	13	3,914	60.4	50.2	425	50.5	29.2	186	65.5	36.0
Michigan	29	11,798	66.8	34.0	881	56.9	0	471	90.0	56.9
Minnesota	7	1,875	65.9	3.3	149	74.3	1.3	224	83.7	4.0
Mississippi	6	3,887	49.9	99.0	442	50.2	41.2	229	49.3	100.0

74

State										
Missouri	11	6,812	47.9	70.2	898	54.4	18.2	153	52.6	94.8
Montana	3	790	55.9	58.1	41	64.4	0	5	740.0	0
Nebraska	5	1,460	61.8	55.4	75	59.9	29.3	78	103.7	89.7
Nevada	8	2,426	54.3	71.4	479	54.9	37.6	164	34.5	90.6
New Hampshire	1	276	42.2	12.7	81	41.9	13.6	156	88.1	21.8
New Jersey	11	9,040	64.0	48.2	704	73.1	0	299	83.1	72.9
New Mexico	4	1,247	77.5	37.8	275	66.1	0	22	66.4	0
New York	41	28,056	66.8	36.1	2,268	59.4	7.0	942	93.0	21.5
North Carolina	79	13,518	54.7	84.5	1,139	61.8	17.9	1,230	80.4	68.6
North Dakota	2	427	69.2	29.3	4	52.0	0	5	72.0	0
Ohio	13	13,756	53.2	85.2	2,237	57.2	51.3	314	103.3	69.1
Oklahoma	14	5,591	65.2	71.3	325	91.5	1.2	687	52.9	77.6
Oregon	7	3,195	46.4	72.5	213	47.8	2.8	13	203.8	92.3
Pennsylvania	9	10,785	51.2	55.0	994	55.6	25.9	503	81.2	69.0
Rhode Island	6	919	63.4	66.7	150	69.6	77.3	32	111.1	65.6
South Carolina	19	6,690	44.8	88.3	539	63.7	39.7	304	56.4	73.0
South Dakota	2	721	49.8	53.1	72	48.3	38.9	3	60.0	0
Tennessee	13	6,443	56.2	91.4	973	54.0	57.9	231	154.9	91.8
Texas	27	31,274	39.8	90.5	2,933	41.2	48.2	554	87.6	34.7
Utah	2	1,178	67.8	50.9	235	50.0	0	44	118.0	77.3
Vermont	6	412	59.3	64.8	36	68.0	44.4	58	50.5	98.3
Virginia	41	8,650	66.7	62.1	614	70.1	5.9	63	115.8	60.3
Washington	15	6,090	47.2	80.3	298	55.8	28.9	95	60.0	49.5
West Virginia	3	1,293	71.0	56.7	130	94.5	70.8	47	287.6	100.0
Wisconsin	17	4,053	69.7	26.0	224	82.2	4.5	70	98.5	52.9
Wyoming	3	646	89.7	22.9	36	79.0	0	3	79.0	0

• Seventy-two units in Indiana, housing 72 inmates, could not be classified and are excluded.

Source: Innes, 1986:3.

probation and parole violators, disorderly conduct, and fleeing prisoners from other state jurisdictions (Wood, Verber, and Reddin, 1985). Persons awaiting trial are housed in jails, as are federal and state witnesses, some state and federal prisoners from prison and penitentiary overflows, work releasees, and persons serving weekend sentences (Corliss, 1983).

Jails also differ from prisons in that they are funded by local sources. Jails are most often city- or county-supported, and jail guards are often recruited by police chiefs or county sheriffs. Jail guards are among the most poorly trained, educated, and paid employees in corrections work (Kerle and Force, 1982; Allinson, 1982). Sometimes this work is performed by community volunteers with little or no corrections training. Guards are often hired after informal interviews with casual background checks for previous records. Many jail guards receive no correctional training whatsoever. In comparison, prison corrections workers must complete a specified number of preservice and inservice hours of training and meet other selection criteria before being hired to work in state correctional facilities (Camp and Camp, 1985). For example, Florida established the Correctional Training Institute in 1973 at Raiford, Florida to conduct courses and training programs for prospective corrections recruits (Wainwright, 1985). Most other states have similar programs.

Compared with state prisoner turnover, jail inmate turnover is fairly brisk. Because of the intended short-term nature of jail confinement, many jails spend little or no money on vocational/technical or educational programs, group and individual counseling or therapy, and other activities normally found in most prison systems. Many jails have no recreational areas for inmates other than large, dormitory-like rooms where they eat and sleep. Medical assistance is provided on an "as needed" basis, inasmuch as most jails cannot afford to hire and maintain full-time medical personnel.

Jail overcrowding is comparatively more difficult to control than prison overcrowding. Aggressive policing leading to numerous arrests creates spasmodic jail overcrowding in certain jurisdictions (Kizziah, 1984). The courts aggravate the situation as well by prescribing unusually high bail for low-risk offenders. Backlogs of court cases and the sluggishness of the trial process add to overcrowding as well. Poor offender classification is often blamed as a primary contributing factor to escalating jail populations in many jurisdictions (Brennan, 1985; Price et al., 1983).

A measure of the seriousness of jail overcrowding is provided by Kline (1987). By mid-1986, jail occupancy was at 96 percent of the rated capacity for all U. S. jails. Between June 1985 and June 1986, there were 16.6 million jail admissions and releases. Only 47 percent of the population of jail inmates were convicted offenders serving jail terms. Also by June 1986, jail occupancy exceeded rated capacity by 8 percent. Of the nation's 612 jails in jurisdictions with large jail populations, 23 percent (139) were under court order in 1986 to reduce their inmate populations (Kline, 1987:4). Table 3.4

shows the rated capacity and percent of capacity occupied for jails in jurisdictions with large jail populations. Incredibly, in 1986 there were 207,007
jail inmates in 612 jails with a cumulative rated capacity of 191,069.

Among the reasons cited by the courts for mandatory jail population
reductions were inadequate recreational and medical facilities, poor visita-
tion practices or policies, poor food service, inadequate segregation procedures and policies (i.e., placing juveniles in the same cells with adult
offenders), the lack of educational, counseling, or training programs, fire
hazards, and poor disciplinary procedures. *The chief reason for court-ordered jail population reductions, however, was overcrowding.* Despite these
court-ordered changes and improvements in both prisons and jails, however,
compliance among jurisdictions has been uneven and slow (Call, 1987).

Why Prison/Jail Overcrowding Is a Problem

Prison/jail overcrowding occurs as the result of many factors. Aggressive
policing leads to more arrests. Prosecutors pursue greater numbers of serious
cases. Judges sentence increasing numbers of offenders to incarceration.
Prison overflows swell the jail populations of various states. Pretrial
detainees, witnesses, suspects, probation and parole violators, DUI arrests,
and unconvicted persons unable to make bail add to already high jail population figures. Detainer warrants result in temporary jail admissions where inmates are held for crimes committed in other states or because they have
allegedly violated federal laws such as immigration or interstate transportation of stolen goods (McShane, 1985). Eliminating parole boards and curtail-
ing the early release of prisoners, the movement toward mandatory and
determinate sentencing, and misclassifications of offenders also increase
prisoner numbers. Table 3.5 shows 1976–1986 trends in jail and prison incarcerations as well as arrest, probation, and parole/early conditional release
figures against comparable U. S. adult resident population growth for the
same period.

The U. S. adult resident population has grown by 17.5 percent between
1976–1986, but jail and prison incarcerations have increased by 85 percent
and 100 percent respectively. At the same time, probation and parole/condi-
tional release have respectively increased by 121 percent and 98 percent.
Despite extraordinarily high levels of probation and parole by 1986, jail and
prison populations systematically rose as well.

Whatever the reasons for prison/jail overcrowding, no one today disputes
that overcrowding exists. And most persons agree that overcrowding is a
serious problem (although there are those who contend overcrowding is
"deserved punishment" for wrongdoing and shouldn't be alleviated; it is a
part of one's punishment and thus should be expected as well as deserved).

Below are seven problems directly or indirectly attributable to prison/jail
overcrowding:

Table 3.4 Jails in Jurisdictions with Large Jail Populations: Rated Capacity and Percent of Capacity Occupied, 1985 and 1986

Jails in jurisdictions with large jail populations	Number of jails		Rated capacity		Number of jail inmates		Percent of capacity occupied	
	1985	1986	1985	1986	1985	1986	1985	1986
Total	614	612	179,729	191,069	190,221	207,007	106%	108%
Jails not under court order to reduce population	477	473	126,965	130,926	134,967	144,252	106	110
Jails under court order to reduce population*	137	139	52,764	60,143	55,254	62,755	105	104

Note: Data are for June 30 of each year and cover all jails in jurisdictions with an average daily inmate population of 100 or more in the 1983 jail census.
*The court-ordered capacity for these jails in 1985 was 54,375 (1,611 inmates higher than the rated capacity). In 1986 it was 60,801 (658 inmates higher than the rated capacity).

Source: Kline, 1987:4.

Table 3.5 Trends in Adult Resident Population, Adult Arrests, and the Number of Adults Under the Care, Custody, or Supervision of State or Local Correctional Authorities, 1976–86

| Year | Adult resident population of the U.S.[a] | Total adult arrests | Number of adults | | | |
			Jail	Probation	Prison[b]	Parole and conditional release[c]
1976	151,313	7,212,244	147,470*	923,064	235,853	156,194
1977	154,299	7,740,766	152,127*	974,296*	247,507	168,052*
1978	157,322	7,875,997	156,783	1,025,528*	260,176	179,909*
1979	160,463	7,904,727	169,550*	1,076,759*	271,295	191,767
1980	162,791	8,261,253	182,317*	1,127,991*	285,667	196,786
1981	166,354	8,696,185	195,084*	1,179,223	322,972	203,418
1982	169,045	9,959,728	207,853	1,450,799	363,713	203,331
1983	171,504	9,737,684	221,815	1,532,721	381,665	230,115
1984	173,705	9,570,903	233,018	1,688,597	404,245	250,138
1985	175,749	9,899,070	254,986	1,913,389	435,589	283,139
1986	175,807	10,387,449	272,736	2,035,593*	470,659	309,477*
% change						
1976–86	17.5%	44.0%	84.9%	120.5%	99.6%	98.1%

*Indicates that a number was estimated or is preliminary.
[a]Population estimates in thousands.
[b]Prisoners with sentences greater than 1 year.
[c]Includes both mandatory release and parole.

Source: U.S. Dept. of Justice, no date.

1. *The legal problem*: Under 42 U.S.C. Sec. 1983, numerous lawsuits have been filed by prison and jail inmates in recent years alleging civil rights violations. Other suits have involved constitutional rights violations, arguing that overcrowding is "cruel and unusual punishment." "Double-bunking" or placing more than one inmate per cell has been challenged, although the U. S. Supreme Court has condoned double-bunking in previous rulings (*Bell v. Wolfish*, 1979; *Rhodes v. Chapman*, 1981). However, the overcrowding issue was successfully pursued against the Texas Department of Corrections in the case of *Ruiz v. Estelle* (1982) (Call, 1987; Contact Center, Inc., 1986). The Fifth Circuit Court of Appeals said, in effect, that it found that the Texas Department of Corrections (TDC) imposed cruel and unusual punishment on inmates in its custody as a result of the totality of conditions in its prisons. The TDC was slow in complying with court-ordered improvements, however. In October, 1987, the court acknowledged TDC compliance and suspended hefty fines for contempt imposed a year earlier (Martin and Ekland-Olson, 1987:246).

2. *The inmate violence problem*: Overcrowding in prisons/jails has been linked with inmate violence and aggression toward other inmates (Lane, 1986; Ekland-Olson, Barrick, and Cohen, 1983). Therefore, inmate safety has

emerged as problematic. Stronger inmates often prey on weaker ones. In jails, unconvicted and innocent inmates are frequently victimized by other inmates.

3. *The problem of more disciplinary infractions*: Institutional rule-breaking has been associated with increases in prison/jail populations (Ruback and Carr, 1984). Rule-breaking, in turn, affects a prisoner's chances for early release. Some researchers recommend that conclusions should not be drawn too quickly about the relation of overcrowding and inmate violence and assaults. Ekland-Olson, Barrick, and Cohen (1983) say that the age structure of a prison population is a better predictor of inmate violence than simple overcrowding, where greater proportions of younger inmates seem more susceptible to committing more infractions and assaults. Prisons containing larger proportions of older offenders seem less likely to exhibit large amounts of rule-breaking behaviors.

4. *The problem of more suicides and natural deaths*: Suicides in jails and prisons are not uncommon (Anson, 1986; Library Information Specialists, Inc., 1983; Burks and DeHeer, 1986). In jails, for instance, there were 277 deaths in 1986 (Kline, 1987:4). Of these, 52 percent (145) were from natural causes, while 39 percent (107) were from inmate suicides. The other deaths arose primarily from inmate violence. Some persons speculate that inmate suicides are largely the result of a crisis reaction to the depression and anxiety often accompanying arrest and initial incarceration (Kennedy, 1984). However, other investigators say that suicides and many natural deaths are concomitants of prison/jail overcrowding (Paulus, McCain, and Cox, 1985).

5. *The problem of psychiatric commitments and stress*: It is well-known that a portion of prison and jail populations consists of mentally ill offenders who should be hospitalized rather than incarcerated (Paulus, McCain, and Cox, 1985). Overcrowding seems to exacerbate psychological problems, however, as increasing numbers of offenders in prisons and jails with high population density seek or are recommended for some type of psychological counseling or psychiatric assistance (Paulus, McCain, and Cox, 1985; San Francisco Jail Overcrowding Committee, 1985; Maryland Criminal Justice Coordinating Council, 1984; Cox, McCain, and Paulus, 1985:12).

6. *The problem of unworkable prison programs*: Even in prisons well-equipped with vocational/technical training programs, counseling services, and other educational facilities, overcrowding makes it difficult to individualize such services the way these services were originally designed to be applied (Phillips, 1983; New Jersey Governor's Management Improvement Plan, 1983; Hawkes, 1985).

7. *The problem of recidivism*: Overcrowding and recidivism are interrelated, but experts are unsure about the precise connection (Paulus, McCain, and Cox, 1985; Austin, 1986). In a study of 21,000 prisoners who were granted early release from Illinois prisons between 1980 and 1983, Austin (1986) found that such early releases did not affect the Illinois crime rate ap-

preciably. There was a general rise in reported crime to police of less than 1 percent associated directly with the early release of these prisoners. Other researchers say that overcrowding leads to greater rates of reconviction among released offenders, however (Paulus, McCain, and Cox, 1985). One explanation for this increased recidivism may be in-prison vocational/educational program inadequacies stemming from overcrowding. Although these programs are rehabilitative in nature, overcrowding interferes with their proper functioning, and the prisoner-beneficiaries of such programs and services eventually emerge from prison unrehabilitated or unassisted by these programs.

This list of problems is certainly not exhaustive. But it is representative of the sorts of conditions directly or indirectly resulting from prison/jail overcrowding. Some of these problems cannot be remedied easily. Suicidal inmates cannot be readily profiled and treated. Natural deaths will occur, even in optimum incarceration conditions. And where inmates are permitted to congregate socially, inmate violence cannot be completely prevented. Also, some prisoners are completely unresponsive to *any* program aimed at rehabilitating them or improving their employment or social potential when released. However, various criminal justice agencies can act to lessen the likelihood of the occurrence of these problems. A key correctional priority, regardless of the motive or obvious vested interests of certain agencies or officials, is to alleviate prison/jail overcrowding.

Methods of Alleviating Prison/Jail Overcrowding

Although the story may be apocryphal, Prime Minister Winston Churchill consulted with his Cabinet Ministers during World War II at the height of the Battle of Britain. Germany was about to bring Britain to its knees through great shipping losses due to the German submarine activity. "How can we solve the U-boat menace?" Churchill shouted. One of his ministers replied, "Well, we can heat the Atlantic Ocean to 212 degrees, and when the U-boats surface to cool off, we can sink them with our surface ships!" "How can we heat the Atlantic Ocean to that temperature?" Churchill queried. "I think up solutions. YOU work out the details!" retorted the cabinet offical.

Canvassing the criminal justice literature for solutions to prison/jail overcrowding discloses numerous proposals being implemented in various jurisdictions. Many are tangible and potentially workable. Other proposals, although valid, are less tangible and near-impossible to implement. Perhaps the most abstract proposals call for systemwide cooperation and coordination to rectify the overcrowding problem (Hall, 1987; Kastenmeier, 1986; Kapsch and Luther, 1985).

Kapsch and Luther (1985) say that "to reduce prison overcrowding, Oregon's criminal justice system requires *agreement on the purpose of criminal sanction* as well as overall *coordination* of the entire system, not just corrections. A *clear, consistent philosophy* should focus on the system's total sanctioning capacity and be managed through systematic considerations of both punishment and risk." [Italics mine]

Kastenmeier (1986:38–41) says:

While numerous factors have contributed to the increase in prison populations, criminal justice policy changes may be the most obvious and most controllable factor. . . . the crisis [crowding] can be lessened if the various elements of the criminal justice sector—police, prosecutors, defenders, judges, community and correctional personnel—*share in policymaking* with legislators and other government officials and *work together cooperatively and creatively to fashion an integrated criminal justice policy.* [Italics mine]

And Hall (1987:5) says "while many communities have taken great steps, experience has also confirmed the complexity of the jail crowding problem and the futility of seeking a panacea through one or two changes. *Long-term success requires a variety of solutions and, most important, the time, patience, and attention of the entire criminal justice community.*" [Italics mine]

These passages have been selected deliberately, not to belittle their significance or demean their authors, but rather to highlight the complexity of the prison/jail overcrowding problem and the interrelatedness of this problem with virtually every component of the criminal justice system. These solutions are noble ones, but it is unlikely that they will ever be attainable. The mere fact that experts cannot agree on the philosophical bases of criminal sanctions, the most appropriate sentencing systems, and the efficacy of parole boards and probation programs suggests that criminal justice systemwide cooperation to solve the overcrowding problem is likewise elusive. Churchill's cabinet member knew how to solve the U-boat menace, but implementing the solution was an entirely different matter.

Various states have enacted emergency measures to be exercised by governors in the event prison populations become intolerably high. But these emergency solutions usually result in a correctional game of musical chairs between state and local officials (Kastenmeier, 1986:38). The state orders prison population reductions by either granting prisoners early release or confining them to local jails for temporary housing. This increases caseloads for parole officers and skyrockets jail populations which are already high. Less control of offenders through increased parole officer caseloads often leads to rearrests, reconvictions, and reincarceration, with the whole process of prison overcrowding starting all over again. Among the states with emergency prison overcrowding acts are Louisiana (Westerfield,

1984), Texas (Martinez and Fabelo, 1985), and Washington (Sims and O'Connell, 1985; Washington Governor's Emergency Commission on Prison Overcrowding, 1983).

At least eighteen solutions for alleviating prison/jail overcrowding have been proposed. Generally, these may be categorized according to whether they are "front door" solutions or "back door" ones (Garry, 1984; Kastenmeier, 1986). Front door solutions are those proposals operating to limit prison and jail intake such as pretrial diversion, probation, fines, dispute resolution, community service, decriminalization, and house arrest. Back door solutions are proposals which affect immediate prison and jail populations such as early release through parole, furloughs, parole authority to reset sentences to shorter lengths, increasing good time credits, and new prison/jail construction.

Front door solutions include the following:

1. *Diversion*: Maryland, California, Connecticut, and Oklahoma are four of several states establishing diversion programs for short-term or low-risk offenders (Austin, Krisberg, and Melnicoe, 1985). Many defendants housed in jails are pre-trial detainees or persons arrested for DUI or public drunkenness. Maryland courts have attempted to alleviate prison overcrowding by diverting short-term prisoners to jails instead of prisons (Maryland Criminal Justice Coordinating Council, 1984). For jail inmate population reductions, Maryland proposals include eliminating confinement for specific non-violent offenses and an elimination of bail for others. Connecticut jails and prisons, which average 1,500 more prisoners annually than their rated jail and prison capacities, have caused officials to adopt pretrial release programs for certain offenders and eliminate bail for others (Connecticut Prison and Jail Overcrowding Commission, 1985).

2. *Probation*: The increased use of probation for both felons and misdemeanants alleviates some of the pressure from jails and prisons. But again, the correctional "musical chairs" game shifts the problem of supervising offenders to understaffed and inadequately funded probation departments (Finn, 1984a; California Joint Committee for Revision of the Penal Code, 1984; Martinez and Fabelo, 1985; Sumner, 1985:86).

3. *Shock probation*: Split-sentencing or shock probation temporarily raises jail populations for 30-day, 60-day, or 90-day periods, but the long-range impact is to reduce overcrowding (Westerfield, 1984; Oklahoma State Board of Corrections, 1984; Maryland Criminal Justice Coordinating Council, 1984).

4. *Restitution/victim compensation/community service*: Restitution, victim compensation, and community service often are additional conditions associated with one's probation or pretrial diversion. The intent of these alternatives is to avoid incarceration by providing services to the community as a punishment and restitution to victims for losses suffered (California Joint

Committee for Revision of the Penal Code, 1984; Illinois Governor's Task Force on Prison Crowding, 1983).

5. *Limiting prison size and allocating space to judges*: A Connecticut proposal is that a certain number of prison cells be allocated to each trial judge in order that they may be responsible for keeping prison populations within constitutionally permissible capacities (Blumstein and Kadane, 1983). Theoretically, this would obligate judges to seek nonincarcerative alternatives for less serious offenders at the time of sentencing, thus conserving valuable prison space only for the most serious offenders.

6. *Build more prisons*: An obvious solution to prison overcrowding is to build more prisons. However, the cost of new prison construction is prohibitive for many jurisdictions. Also, new prisons seem to fill quickly to capacity, thus creating the need for more new prisons (Dukakis, 1985; Rhode Island Governor's Commission, 1984; Allied Engineering, 1985). One alternative is to renovate buildings previously used for other purposes. This is being done in various states and appears to be economically feasible compared with new prison construction (Miller and Cansfield, 1987:22).

7. *Changing bail provisions*: Especially for jail populations, one major factor contributing to escalating numbers of inmates is that defendants cannot afford bail or bail is denied. Rhode Island, for instance, has standardized bail guidelines. One recommendation has been to change these guidelines and eliminate the requirement of bail for certain non-violent, low-risk offenders (Rhode Island Governor's Commission, 1984).

8. *Decriminalization of certain offenses*: Proposals to decriminalize certain minor offenses would alleviate a certain amount of jail and prison overcrowding. Legalizing marijuana possession or prostitution would decrease substantially the number of drug and soliciting offenders arrested and prosecuted annually. Maryland has undertaken a reexamination of its existing criminal statutes to see whether different sanctions can be imposed that will reduce or eliminate state terms of confinement for certain non-violent crimes and whether other crimes should be decriminalized (Maryland Criminal Justice Coordinating Council, 1984). Massachusetts is also contemplating such reviews of its statutes (Phillips, 1983).

9. *Diverting pending misdemeanors from jails*: Many jail inmates are incarcerated for various periods awaiting trial for minor misdemeanor offenses. Serving these offenders with special notices or other citations commanding their appearance in court at a later date is recommended as a nonincarcerative alternative (Westerfield, 1984).

10. *Selective incapacitation/better classification*: Selective incapacitation is a hotly debated proposal for alleviating prison overcrowding. Proponents suggest that dangerous offenders can be identified and confined, while those less dangerous offenders should be granted probation or some other nonincarcerative alternative. However, opponents of selective incapacitation

argue that it is racist and discriminatory at best, as well as raising moral, ethical, and legal issues.

Some experts have promoted the notion of "selective deinstitutionalization" which combines effective classificatory devices with estimates of offender risk to public safety in determining who should be incarcerated and who shouldn't (Gottfredson, 1984; Garry, 1984). Brennan (1985) raises the usual issue of false positives and false negatives associated with risk prediction measures. He says that a common weakness of existing measures is the overprediction of violent or recidivist behaviors. Once these measurement problems have been resolved, however, jail overcrowding can be reduced significantly through effective classification of low- and high-risk offender groups.

11. *Home confinement/house arrest*: The use of house arrest or home confinement is a reality in some jurisdictions and in the experimental stage in others (Lilly and Ball, 1987). In California, the Joint Committee for Revision of the Penal Code has sought measures to alleviate prison/jail overcrowding by examining practices for monitoring offenders in other states. While the California State Legislature passed the largest prison construction program in the state's history in 1983, it is anticipated that this accomplishment alone will only temporarily alleviate the crisis of overcrowding. One viable alternative to incarceration is home incarceration, because it requires minimal probation officer monitoring of offenders and it is considerably less costly compared with incarceration (California Joint Committee for Revision of the Penal Code, 1984).

12. *Private sector contracting*: Since the federal government and many state correctional agencies have failed to deal adequately with the prison/jail overcrowding issue, proposals have been advanced advocating the privatization of prisons and jails (Robbins, 1986; Logan, 1986; Immarigeon, 1987; Lindquist, 1984). The privatization or private operation of prisons and jails by commercial interests on a profit-making basis is certainly not new. In the 1800's, many early probation programs were privately operated, especially those catering to juvenile offenders. By 1984, 1,877 privately operated juvenile programs were operating in the U. S. holding 31,390 juveniles, while 28 states reported privately operated prerelease, work-release, or halfway house facilities. Among the largest privately operated facility states were California, Massachusetts, New York, and Ohio (Mullen, 1985:4).

Today, the private operation of prisons and jails for profit by organizational professionals is rapidly becoming a feasible alternative for resolving persistent overcrowding problems. Private interests claim that correctional institutions can be operated efficiently and profitably. At the same time, administrative credibility can be established and low recidivism rates will be observed (Hackett, et al., 1987). Private interests argue that they can save taxpayers money by building prison facilities more quickly and cheaply, and operating them more efficiently. Furthermore, with little or no governmental bureaucratic intervention, new ideas and correctional philosophies can be implemented with little or no resistance from vested interest groups, staff hiring can be rendered routine, and overcrowding can be reduced significantly (Robbins, 1986:24). Blumstein (1968) and Kline (1987) suggest that as an additional incentive, private corporations can receive bonus payments from the government for each client's lack of recidivism during a fixed time period. Regarding prison contracting on a private basis, Hackett et al. (1987:3) have summarized some of the principal issues as shown in Figure 3.1.

Therefore, the question is not whether private interests will be permitted to take over corrections facilities from the various state and local jurisdictions, but rather, how much control will private interests exercise in their operation? It is still too early to tell whether private enterprise in corrections will achieve the successes it forecasts.

13. *Probation Subsidization.* The quality of intensive supervised probation programs and the ability of administrators of such programs to manage larger numbers of offenders can be improved through greater subsidization of such programs. For example, in the Department of Justice's 1986 appropriations bill signed by President Ronald Reagan, $614 million was allocated for 11,988 positions for the Federal Bureau of Prisons. This is an increase of 485 new positions over the 1985 figures. Also, $556 million was allocated for 10,876 positions, an increase of 435 positions and nearly $34 million over the previous year. The majority of remaining funds served to activate a federal detention center in Oakdale, Louisiana, and new housing units at ten other existing federal institutions. By comparison, $1 million was added for 50 additional correctional officer positions and $2 million for community treatment center programs (American Correctional Association, 1986:42).

State appropriations for probation programs reflect priorities similar to the federal system. California's Probation Subsidy Program was first tried in 1965, and Minnesota, Colorado, and Oregon subsidized community-based programs in 1975, 1976, and 1978 respectively (Lawrence, 1985:108). Today, most if not all states have some community-based programs for probationers. Community-based probation programs are much less expensive to operate compared with the costs of incarcerating offenders. But as Lawrence (1985:109) so aptly points out, "the expectation that community alternatives are always less expensive than institutional programs means they are given a smaller budget in state funding, thus offering only minimal services to a larger number of clients." More money allocated for community-based programs won't automatically improve program quality, but it won't hurt program quality either. One reason community-based programs in some jurisdictions fail to have the necessary public support and confidence is their restricted budgets do not permit their personnel to operate effectively in the

Figure 3.1

PRISON CONTRACTING: THE ISSUES

Legal issues

1. What are the legal issues in prison contracting?
2. What liability protection will a government agency and contract need?
3. How should the responsibility and authority for security be divided between the contracting agency and private operator?
4. What provision is there for protecting inmates' rights to appeal decisions affecting them?

Policy and program issues before deciding to contract

5. What specific preanalysis should a state undertake prior to the contract decision (e. g., cost analysis, legal issues analysis)?
6. What are the reasons for considering or not considering contracting prison operation with private enterprise, particularly with for-profit firms?
7. How should publicity regarding change in private operations be handled (e.g., agency, media, public)?
8. Should contracting be for (a) existing facilities; (b) a new institution replacing an existing facility; or (c) a new institution not replacing an existing facility?
9. What level of offender should be assigned to the contracted facility? What are the differences in attempting to contract minimum versus medium versus maximum security facilities?
10. How many inmates should the contractor be expected to house? What provisions should be made for fluctuations in that number? What control does the contractor actually have over the number of inmates? Should minimums, maximums, or both be established in the contract?
11. How will inmates be selected? Will the private organization be able to refuse certain inmates (e.g., AIDS victims, psychologically disturbed offenders)?
12. What authority and responsibility should a private contractor have for discipline and for effecting the release date of inmates? What will be the relationship of these decisions to the State Board of Parole?

RFP and contract issues

13. Should contracting be competitive or noncompetitive? Are there enough prospective contractors to provide real competition? What are the relative merits of for-profit and nonprofit organizations as prison operators?
14. What criteria should be used to evaluate private proposals (e.g., percentage values for cost and quality of service)?

Figure 3.1 *(Continued)*

---

15. On what basis should the contract price be established (e.g., firm fixed price, fixed price per unit, cost plus fee)?

16. What provisions should be made to reduce service interruption (e.g., problems with transition periods, defaults by contractors, work stoppages, fallback provisions)? Should there be provisions to protect the private contractor (e.g., government obligations)?

17. What performance standards should requests for proposals and contracts establish?

18. What should be the duration of the contract and what provisions made for renewal?

19. What provisions for monitoring performance are needed in the RFP and proposal?

20. What provisions should be made for present correctional employees (e.g., rehiring rights, job benefits)?

Monitoring and evaluation

21. How and to what extent should contractor performance be monitored?

22. How should government evaluate the results of contracting?

23. What results can be expected from contracting (e.g., cost, service effectiveness and quality, alleviation of crowding, effects on other prisons in system)?

Source: Hackett, et al., 1987:3.

management of offender-clients. If you can't afford to hire competent counselors and ancillary help, then those persons served do not get the needed assistance risk/needs assessment inventories say they need. The domino principle is apparent here. But it can be reversed in part through greater state appropriations for community-based probation services.

So-called "back door" measures to alleviate overcrowding in prisons and jails include the following:

14. *Parole*: The present shift from indeterminate to determinate, presumptive, and some mandatory sentencing is taking its toll by removing paroling authority from parole boards or abolishing these boards entirely. Although a majority of states continue to use parole boards for early release decisions, it is difficult to project if this will continue to be the case within the next ten years. Under the emergency prison overcrowding provisions enacted by various state legislatures, governors are granted temporary authority to

reduce prison overcrowding by effecting early releases for inmates, regard-less of the risk they may pose to society (Sims and O'Connell, 1985).

Rapid and substantial prison reductions by means other than administra-tive powers of the governor can also be achieved by parole boards em-powered to shorten prisoner sentences (Eisenberg, 1985c). Oklahoma was among several states forced by the courts to take drastic measures to reduce prison overcrowding in the early 1980's. Besides increased use of fines, suspended sentences or split sentences, Oklahoma officials were able to ef-fect great reductions in prisoner sentences through parole board action (Ok-lahoma State Board of Corrections, 1984).

15. *Removal of mentally ill prisoners to hospitals*: Maryland is among several states mandating the removal of as many mentally ill prisoners as possible from prisons and placing them more appropriately in hospital set-tings (Maryland Criminal Justice Coordinating Council, 1984). While there are no precise figures about the number of mentally ill offenders currently incarcerated, some experts suggest that as many as 40 percent of all local, state, and federal inmates may have mental illness problems of one type or another which require hospitalization rather than incarceration (Rockowitz, 1986a). For example, in 1985 the Oklahoma Department of Corrections ad-mitted 60 percent of 796 mentally handicapped persons who scored 75 or less on the Beta intelligence test to its minimum or higher security prisons (Davis, 1985). In some jurisdictions, mentally retarded persons have been placed in prisons and jails to "protect them from the rigors of the street" through "mercy bookings." Rather than help them, evidence suggests that jail and prison stress may exacerbate latent convulsive, psychotic and be-havioral disorders (French, 1986).

Johnson, McKeown and James (1984) say that of the 3,493 jails in the U. S. in 1984, there were 600,000 mentally ill persons confined there at dif-ferent times. Many of these persons were confined because of their inability to function in their communities. Many were chronically ill and posed no threat to public safety. Yet they were incarcerated rather than hospitalized. The identification and removal of such persons from prisons to hospitals would permit more efficient use of space for more serious offenders (San-tamour, 1986; Cohen, 1986; Rockowitz, 1986b). The Georgia State Prison has adopted a system to identify and deal appropriately with mentally retarded offenders. The three-stage approach includes studying each inmate's file with an IQ of 70 or below, interviews with persons who have had contact with the inmate over time, and a direct interview with the inmate. Inmates classified as mentally retarded are provided with special educational/voca-tional programs (Hall, 1985).

The Texas Department of Corrections also has a screening mechanism for identifying mentally ill offenders. The Mentally Retarded Offender Program was created in response to federal court intervention, and all mentally retarded inmates are identified as they enter the system. After they are thus classified, they are transferred to sheltered units where they receive special services apart from the general prison population (Pugh and Kunkel, 1986).

16. *Reduction of sentence duration by adjusting the proportion of time served*: Singer (1984) suggests that the just deserts philosophy does not require incarceration for every offender. There are degrees of deserts accompanying any crime. He notes that a fair approach to reducing prison overcrowding does not adhere in a system of sentencing guidelines, but rather it requires an adjustment in the percentage of the original sentence actually served.

17. *Increasing good time credits*: Closely related to reducing sentences according to Singer's scheme above is the increase of good time credits earned per week or month. In 1985, Pennsylvania authorities conducted a study showing that their state prisons had more than 5,500 prisoners double-celled and were 33 percent over their rated capacity (Pennsylvania Commission on Crime and Delinquency, 1985). It was recommended that one effective means of alleviating prison overcrowding would be to increase earned time or good time credits for state prisoners which would ultimately lead to their early release. California authorities endorsed a similar program whereby inmates could earn increased numbers of good time credits effecting their early release apart from parole board discretion (California Joint Committee for Revision of the Penal Code, 1984).

18. *The use of furloughs*: In a review of U. S. state correctional institutions, prison officials were queried concerning how their prison systems adapted to overcrowding (Sapp, 1984). Among the alternatives used by at least nine states were furlough programs, where offenders who were about to be released anyway were granted temporary leaves from prison custody to visit families, friends, or others. The most frequently mentioned solution was the use of community-based parole facilities, however.

19. *Changing the nature of prison/jail housing*: In 1983, a study was conducted in California of the cost-effectiveness of four alternative jail housing arrangements according to five criteria: construction costs, staffing, safety, legal liability, and manageability (Farbstein and Goldman, 1983). The targets of the study were pretrial inmates housed in single-bed cells, double-bed cells, 8-bed cells, and 16-bed dormitories. Jail administrators preferred single-cell arrangements because they were safer, reduced inmate stress, and were less likely to generate personal injuries and lawsuits against local authorities and the government. Although 8-bed cells offered less space than single or double cells without providing more privacy than found in the 16-bed dormitory, the dormitory-style housing was preferred ultimately because of lower maintenance costs and greater space utilization.

It is apparent from these front door and back door solutions for alleviating prison/jail overcrowding that most are directed at the former where prosecutors and judges play crucial roles. Most relevant here are those proposals encouraging greater use of diversion and probation supervision rather than incarceration. These proposals result in a significant shift in the responsibility of supervising and monitoring offenders. The shift is from correctional institutions such as jails and prisons to probation departments. For example, Benton County, Oregon, solved its eight-year-old jail over-crowding problem by 1986 through shuffling 87 percent of its 480 persons under various court sanctions to the supervision of probation agencies who supervise pretrial releasees and diversions as well as probationers and parolees (Chapman, 1987:24). Within the context of the hydraulic principle noted earlier, this responsibility shift results in greater workloads for proba-tion personnel. And greater workloads usually mean less effective or even ineffective supervision (Lawrence, 1984).

Back door proposals such as more extensive use of parole, administrative early release, or mandatory release because of sentence served or the ac-cumulation of good time credits add similarly to the burden of proba-tion/parole agencies who are often charged with supervising both probationers and parolees. Again, probation/parole officer caseloads are in-creased, and the quality of parole supervision suffers accordingly.

Even prisoners who are subject to mandatory release because they have served their sentences (less the good time credits accumulated) must con-tinue to be supervised by parole officers "on the outside" until the full term of their original sentence has been served (e.g., a prisoner serving a ten-year sentence may be released mandatorily after serving seven years because of good time credits applied against the original sentence length; however, the ex-prisoner continues to be under the supervision of a parole officer for the remaining three years of the original ten-year sentence imposed) (U. S. Parole Commission, 1987:98).

Almost everyone agrees on at least one correctional trend—for whatever reason, *probation departments and their staffs are called upon increasingly to accomplish those supervisory functions which jails and prisons are un-able to accomplish.* Lawrence (1984:14) notes that:

probation is increasingly looked to for help in alleviating the serious problems of overcrowding in jails and prisons. A greater percentage of convicted offenders are being placed on probation—the foremost agency in community corrections—as an al-ternative to incarceration. This increase necessarily results in a greater workload on probation officers: more presentence investigations, larger caseloads, and more paperwork to complete. *The increased pressure on probation often adversely affects the quality of the officers' reports and the supervision provided.* [Emphasis mine]

These increased demands upon probation officers and agencies do little to improve the public image of probation work which suffers from an image of leniency (Fogel, 1981). Some degree of cynicism has insinuated itself into the probation profession. An anonymous sociological lecturer reportedly said that "if probation and parole were done away with today, the crime rate in America would probably go up only about 2 percent. This 2 percent would be probation and parole administrators and line staff who turned to crime only because they could find no other suitable employment for themselves" (Callanan, 1986:16).

Inmate violence, prison riots, and dangerously overcrowded jail and prison conditions in recent years have caused the nation's legislatures, judicial bodies, civil organizations, and the general public to expect much from probation departments and their staffs (Callanan, 1986:16). Changes in sentencing patterns, probation increasingly used as an incentive to elicit guilty pleas from defendants in plea bargaining, and greater use of diversionary strategies to avoid or reduce jail and prison overcrowding have placed extraordinary demands on probation personnel. Callanan (1986:16-17) says that the complex milieu within which probation officers work presents little opportunity for simple solutions, and that probation officers, while realizing that incarcerating everyone convicted of crimes doesn't work, see the ultimate results as overcrowded prisons/jails as well as increased probation officer caseloads.

FELONY PROBATION AND TECHNOLOGY

An intermediate punishment discussed in Chapter 1 was electronic monitoring. In February 1987 the National Institute of Justice conducted a survey of electronic monitoring programs currently used by various jurisdictions and found 53 such programs being conducted in 21 states (Schmidt, 1987:30). Since then, the number of monitoring programs in various jurisdictions has increased substantially.

Corrections officials have been cautious in their consideration of electronic monitoring of offenders. Early experiments have been conducted with extremely low-risk offender groups, misdemeanants, and DUI cases. However, an increasing number of programs are testing electronic monitoring (sometimes coupled with home confinement) on more serious offenders. Simulation experiments are currently being sponsored by the National Institute of Justice where paid program subjects wear electronic wristlets or anklets and computer printouts and feedback are compared with hourly and daily activity logs (Schmidt, 1987:32).

The reliability of these electronic devices has already been demonstrated in Kentucky, Florida, and other jurisdictions (Lilly and Ball, 1987; Palm Beach County, Florida Sheriff's Department, 1987). It is only a matter of time before most jurisdictions adopt monitoring equipment to assist probation officers (and parole officers) in their supervision of low- and high-risk clients. The initial cost of this equipment is high, although offender maintenance fees assessed and collected on a regular basis eventually offset the hardware base costs. At this point, the most promising alternative to large-scale felony probation is intensive supervision and electronic monitoring.

SUMMARY

Prison and jail overcrowding influence every facet of the criminal justice system. Prison/jail overcrowding is defined in various ways including social and spatial density, personal perceptions of privacy, and population density in common areas. Problems of prison and jail overcrowding include increased inmate violence, less effective vocational/educational/counseling programs, legal issues of cruel and unusual punishment and violations of one's right to privacy, increased recidivism rates, and higher rates of psychiatric disorders, suicides, and deaths.

Solutions to prison and jail overcrowding include increasing probation, diversion, earlier parole, increased good time credits, furloughs and work release, restitution and victim compensation, community service, home incarceration and electronic monitoring, split sentencing or shock probation, releasing certain low-risk pretrial detainees on their own recognizance, decriminalizing certain offenses, and lowering or eliminating bail for certain offenses.

Probation agencies are most affected by front door and back door solutions to prison/jail overcrowding. Shifts of responsibility for supervising offenders from jails and prisons to probation departments result in greater caseloads and less effective probation officer/client relations. Technological changes such as the increased use of electronic monitoring systems coupled with intensive supervised probation offer the most promising alternatives to incarceration for the cost-conscious public.

4

Felony Probation, Dangerousness, and Recidivism

.NTRODUCTION

Eventually, 99 percent or more of all offenders, violent and nonviolent, will be released from prisons and jails to walk freely about their communities. A portion of these ex-convicts and releasees will commit new crimes and eventually be reincarcerated. But as has been seen in Chapter 3, prison/jail overcrowding and certain correctional philosophies are directed toward front-end alternatives to incarceration including felony probation. It is reasonable to expect that public concern is heightened as the prospect of nonincarceration for violent and nonviolent criminals becomes more the rule rather than the exception.

This chapter examines in some detail the real or imagined dangerousness actually posed to the public by releasing large numbers of felons to the supervision of various probation programs instead of incarcerating those criminals. Prosecutors, judges, and probation officers pool their information about offenders to evaluate their potential dangerousness if placed on probation. Will the offender recidivate and commit new crimes? Will more harm to society than good result from probation rather than incarceration? In recent years, selective incapacitation has become increasingly popular as a front-end alternative to the prison/jail overcrowding crisis. Some attention will be given to this controversial phenomenon and to the legal, moral, and ethical issues it inspires.

Recidivism is frequently employed as the gauge of a probation program's success or failure. Thus, considerable attention will be given to recidivism, how it is measured, and its usefulness for evaluating the efficacy of felony probation. Finally, a growing trend is *the use of community volunteers and paraprofessionals* to assist probation officers and agencies in monitoring probationers and helping them in various ways. While this volunteerism is

94

certainly helpful to these agencies and officers, it raises certain legal issues which seek resolution. These will be explored as well.

RECIDIVISM DEFINED

The most comprehensive investigation of recidivism by 1988 was conducted by Maltz (1984). Despite the numerous definitions of recidivism Maltz has discovered and described, his own definition of the term reflects an unsettling tentativeness. According to Maltz (1984:1):

recidivism, in a criminal justice context, is the reversion of an individual to criminal behavior after he or she has been convicted of a prior offense, sentenced, and (presumably) corrected. It results from the concatenation of failures: failure of the individual to live up to society's expectations—or failure of society to provide for the individual; a consequent failure of the individual to stay out of trouble; failure of the individual, as an offender, to escape arrest and conviction; failure of the individual as an inmate of a correctional institution to take advantage of correctional programs—or failure of the institution to provide programs that rehabilitate; and additional failures by the individual in continuing a criminal career after release.

Maltz himself uses "recidivism" and "failure" interchangeably (1984:71).

Alternative Definitions of Recidivism

Although Waldo and Chiricos (1977) had identified at least 18 different types of recidivism in an earlier investigation, Maltz (1984:62–64) examined over 90 different studies using the term and derived the following nine categorizations:

1. *Arrest*: this includes an arrest for a new offense (Inciardi, 1971; Fishman, 1977; Cox, 1977); an arrest followed by a court appearance within one year after release from either probation or parole (Coates, Miller, and Ohlin, 1978; Hood, 1966); "criminal arrest" (Hoffman and Stone-Meierhoefer, 1979); recorded police contact (Wolfgang, Figlio, and Sellin, 1972; Murray and Cox, 1979); number of arrests (Waldo and Chiricos, 1977). [Emphasis mine]

2. *Reconviction*: reconviction for any felony (Hopkins, 1976); reconviction or recall for unsatisfactory conduct (Hood, 1966); any new conviction resulting in a sentence of 60 days or more (Gottfredson and Ballard, 1966; Bennett and Ziegler, 1975; Beck and Hoffman, 1976); any new conviction for a felony or "felony-like" offense (Kitchener, Schmidt, and Glaser, 1977); conviction of a "further offense" (Wilkins, 1958). [Emphasis mine]

3. *Incarceration*: jail sentence of more than 3 days and return to prison for either a new offense or a technical violation (Burkhart and Sathmary, 1964);

return to prison (Jacobson and McGee, 1965; Waldo and Chiricos, 1977); return to prison as a parole violator or due to outstanding absconder warrant (Gottfredson and Ballard, 1966); number of commitments to an institution with or without adjudication (Boston University, 1966); return to prison for an administrative violation (Beck and Hoffman, 1976); recommitted to prison with conviction(s) for major offense, same jurisdiction or any other jurisdiction (Mosely and Gerould, 1975); return to prison for at least 30 days within one year of release (from prison, parole, or probation) (LeClair, 1985); return to prison as a parole violator (Kitchener, Schmidt, and Glaser, 1977).

4. *Parole violation*: alcoholic criminality; arrests and fines for drunkenness, disorderly conduct (Hansen and Teilman, 1954); violating rules of parole (Kusuda and Babst, 1964); issuance of a parole violation warrant by District Court or Board of Parole for technical violations or new felony offenses (Lohman, 1967); parole violation (Kantrowitz, 1977); parole violation warrant (Hoffman and Stone-Meierhoefer, 1979).

5. *Parole suspension*: parole suspension with or without new offense (Narloch, Adams, and Jenkins, 1959); suspension (California Adult Authority, 1956); number of parole suspensions (Werner and Palmer, 1976).

6. *Parole revocation*: revocation of parole; parole revocation or bad discharge (Guttman, 1963).

7. *Offense*: new offense or violation of the rules of supervision within two years (Babst and Mannering, 1965); mean number of offenses during a 12-month follow-up period, seriousness of the offense (McEachern and Taylor, 1967; Waldo and Chiricos, 1977).

8. *Absconding*: absconding (Kusuda and Babst, 1964; Inciardi, 1971; Mosely and Gerould, 1975); absconder warrant (Gottfredson and Ballard, 1966; Beck and Hoffman, 1976).

9. *Probation*: observed reconviction rate compared with expected conviction rate (Great Britain Home Office, 1964); drunk arrest rate for municipal court (Ditman and Crawford, 1965); number of months before successful completion of probation (Kawaguchi and Siff, 1967).

Subsequently, Maltz rearranged these definitions into 13 categories and identified the incidence of the use of these recidivism definitions in the 90+ studies he surveyed. These are shown in Table 4.1.

On the basis of the distribution of usage in the studies surveyed, Maltz concluded that "the tabulation . . . should be taken as indicative of the popularity of different measures" (1984:63). Maltz (1984:66) further concluded that "the recidivism definition of choice appears to be . . . arrest recidivism," although the information shown in Table 4.1 shows that "return to prison" (reincarceration), "technical violation" (of probation or parole), and "reconviction" (for new offense, either a misdemeanor or felony un-

Table 4.1   Maltz's Recidivism Definitions Used in Recent Studies (1984)

DEFINITION	FREQUENCY
OFFENSE DATA:	
Recorded police contact......................	2
New offense.................................	16
Severity of offense........................	12
Arrest......................................	20
PAROLE-PROBATION INFRACTIONS:	
Parole suspension..........................	8
Parole revocation..........................	8
Technical violation........................	26
Absconding.................................	10
Probation violation........................	3
COURT APPEARANCE............................	3
RECONVICTION................................	22
SENTENCING..................................	8
RETURN TO PRISON............................	39
GRAND TOTAL.................................	177*

* The large excess of frequencies beyond 90 is attributable
to the fact that some studies used two or more measures of
recidivism simultaneously.

Source: Michael Maltz, Recidivism (1984).

specified) in that order were more frequently cited than "arrest" (the *fourth* most frequently cited measure).

More recent studies have defined recidivism similarly. For instance, recidivism has been used as (1) "return to prison" (Chown and Davis, 1986; Stevens, 1986; LeClair, 1985; Wallerstedt, 1984; Hoffman and Beck, 1985; Oregon Crime Analysis Center, 1984; Clark and Crum, 1985), (2) "program failure" (Stevens, 1986; Eisenberg, 1985b; Andersen and Andersen, 1984), (3) "rearrest" (Gottfredson and Taylor, 1985; Delaware Executive Department, 1984), (4) "probation or parole revoked" (Miller, 1984a; Boudouris, 1983; University of Hawaii-Manoa, 1984; Roundtree, Edwards, and Parker, 1984), (5) "new violations" (Roundtree, Edwards, and Parker, 1984), (6) "repeat a violent offense" (delinquency study by Piper, 1985), (7) "persistent felony offenders" (Wilson, 1985), and even (8) "rehospitalization" of insanity acquittees (Cavanaugh and Wasyliw, 1985).

Some Problems with Past and Present Recidivism Research

There are several problems with much of this recidivism research. First, *a large portion of it focuses upon juvenile delinquents.* Juveniles are atypical of adult probationers or parolees. While it is true that many adult offenders have prior records as juvenile delinquents, recidivism of delinquents is a poor comparative reference when adult probationer recidivism is examined.

A second problem is that British, Scandinavian and other foreign criminal samples are used in some of these recidivism studies. Cross-cultural comparisons complicate rather than simplify recidivism investigations. Other countries have different criminal justice systems with entirely different definitions of specific offenses as crimes. If we are going to examine the implications of felony probation for recidivism and public risk for U. S. offenders, it is perhaps best to adopt a parochial perspective and exclude foreign research. This does not mean that foreign studies of recidivism are unimportant or even less important compared with studies of U. S. offenders, but rather, study comparisons are more legitimate if we restrict our investigations to a single culture and a particular age range within that culture.

It is meaningless, for example, to talk about "probation in Nigeria," since probation as an alternative sanction has only recently been introduced and is applicable only to a small number of offenders. Other more frequent sanctions in Nigeria include capital punishment, imprisonment, and caning or whipping of the buttocks of the offender. Eighty lashes may be ordered for an alcoholic offender, 100 lashes or canings for unlawful sexual relations such as adultery or the use of obscene language against a female, or fewer lashes for offenders under age 45. Female offenders may be lashed or caned no more than twelve times (Cole, Frankowski, and Gertz, 1987:92).

In the Soviet Union, there are no probation officers. Criminals are generally either imprisoned, banished to perform labor in obscure colonies or settlements, or placed in mental institutions (Terrill, 1984:218). Recidivists are subject to increasingly severe penalties and longer periods of confinement as well as the traditional banishment. There aren't many recidivists in the Soviet Union (5 percent among persons on "parole," 9 percent among those sentenced to corrective labor camps, and from 15 to 18 percent among persons conditionally released from labor camps prior to the expiration of their terms (Terrill, 1984:218–219). Therefore, discussing Soviet definitions of recidivism compared with U. S. measures would be an apples-oranges enterprise.

A third general criticism is that much recidivism research deals with parolees rather than probationers. There are several significant distinctions between the two offender aggregates. Without undue elaboration, generally, parolees represent a more serious class of offenders compared with probationers, although increasing numbers of violent offenders are placed on probation according to recent estimates. Petersilia and Turner (1987:160–161) contend that "probationers and prisoners, on the whole, have different characteristics: probationers generally have committed less serious crimes and have fewer prior criminal convictions."

A fourth criticism is that recidivism may or may not mean committing crimes similar or identical to those crimes committed earlier by the offender. Is the person on probation (because of a burglary he/she committed earlier) a recidivist if he/she is subsequently arrested for and convicted of embezzlement, or shoplifting, or vehicular theft, or homicide? Is the person on probation (because of armed robbery committed earlier) a recidivist if he/she is subsequently arrested for forgery, possession of a controlled substance, or selling marijuana? Must one commit identical crimes for which a particular sentence was imposed at an earlier date in order to be classified as a recidivist?

Citizens may apply the logic, once a thief, always a thief. The reasoning is that the offender will commit new crimes similar to those previously committed, if coddled by the courts and released to a probation program. This targets directly community fears about probationers. Are these fears justified?

The Most Meaningful Indicators of Recidivism

There is presently considerable disagreement about which recidivism measure is best at depicting program failures. Although rearrests appear to be popular indicators, rearrests do not necessarily mean the offender has committed new crimes. If a probationer is rearrested, he/she may be released without incident. Probationers are often the first suspects questioned by police if crimes are committed in their vicinity, especially crimes similar to those for which these probationers were originally convicted. An inadequate or unsatisfactory explanation of one's whereabouts when the crime occurred can result in arrest on suspicion. Later, it may turn out the probationer was not involved in the new crime.

Probation revocations are inadequate as well, because these may be based upon rule violations as simple as missing "curfew" by ten minutes or some other minor infraction unrelated to crime. While revocations are usually based on more serious rule violations such as failure to pay timely restitution as ordered or persistent failure to report to the probation officer, technical rule violations are legitimate grounds to argue that the probationer has not abided by the probation agreement. Reincarceration may be the result of a probation or parole revocation, and therefore it, too, is unreliable in measuring one's misdeeds while enjoying either status. Reconvictions for minor offenses may result in revocation of probation also. The public is interested ultimately in whether the offender on probation is going to stay "clean" and refrain from further involvement in criminal activity. Thus, it would seem that *reconviction for a felony within the period of one's probation would emerge as the most direct indicator of program success or failure.* Logically, a felony probationer who commits and is convicted of one or more new felonies has "failed," and this failure is precisely what the probation program is designed to prevent.

One final theoretical question is in order. Within what time period should the recidivism be counted? For example, suppose a 20-year-old probationer (convicted of burglary) fulfills his/her probation term and is freed completely by the court. Suppose this 20-year-old refrains from crime for 30 years. At age 50, the ex-burglar steals a vehicle and is caught and convicted. Is the 50-year-old car thief a recidivist? Was the probation program a "failure" because he/she committed a new crime 30 years later?

It is seemingly more clear-cut in a case where a 20-year-old probationer (convicted of burglary) commits and is convicted of a new serious crime (e.g., armed robbery, burglary, larceny, vehicular theft, or aggravated assault) while on probation or within a few months after being released from a probation program. But what about a lengthy time interval between one crime and another? For most researchers, this time interval has either not been defined or has been arbitrarily defined. In a study of 1,806 federal parolees conducted by Hoffman and Beck (1985), recidivism was arbitrarily defined as the presence of a new sentence of imprisonment exceeding one year for an offense (in all likelihood a felony) committed during a two-year follow-up period (conveniently the duration of Hoffman's and Beck's study). And the Oregon Crime Analysis Center (1984) defined recidivism as "return to prison" during a three-year follow-up. Thus, these definitions seem to rely heavily on the duration of the research project or some other nonrational criteria.

RECIDIVISM AND DANGEROUSNESS: VIOLENT AND PROPERTY OFFENDERS

Monahan (1981a) says predicting dangerousness is one of the most difficult tasks confronting judges and parole boards. For many years, probation has been reserved for and granted more frequently to less violent, presumably harmless property offenders. However, recent trends indicate more serious offenders are being granted probation with increasing frequency. This is one of the front-end safety valves for alleviating the prison overcrowding problem.

Recidivism Among Felony Probationers: An Unclear Picture

Do recidivist/probationers tend to commit crimes similar to those for which they were convicted originally? Will the recidivist/probationer/convicted violent offender be likely to commit one or more new violent crimes?

Likewise, will the recidivist/probationer/convicted property offender commit one or more new property crimes? The information currently available about this general relationship is sketchy at best. We don't know for sure. What we DO know about this relation may be gleaned from several isolated studies, some of which involve parolees rather than probationers. This fact alone presents us with several significant comparison problems. Nevertheless, among 1,670 parolees released from state prisons between 1970 and 1974 and 934 male offenders released between 1975 and 1979, Willstadter (1984) found that (1) recidivism was not particularly high, and (2) recidivists tended to be returned for committing similar offenses to those for which they were originally incarcerated. Similarly, a study of 1,782 offenders released from Oregon state prisons in 1979 showed a 32.2 percent rate of return to prison. In those cases where convictions for new crimes were observed, violent offenders were returned to prison as new violent offenders, while property offenders were returned to prison as new property offenders (Oregon Crime Analysis Center, 1984).

There are apparent inconsistencies regarding which type of offender aggregate is subject to more frequent rearrests. In a study of 3,257 persons released from Delaware prisons in 1980–1982, for example, more than half were rearrested within the first year of their release. The Delaware Executive Department (1984) concluded that "violent offenders tend to get arrested more often than nonviolent offenders." But in their study of 9,549 offenders released from North Carolina state prisons in 1979–1980, Clarke and Crum (1985) found that about 26 percent were reincarcerated because of a conviction for a new offense. However, these researchers concluded "violent felons were less likely to become recidivists than were nonviolent felons and misdemeanants."

Vito (1983:67) alleges "the commonly-held belief that a great number of persons repeat their crimes (recidivate) is not borne out by official statistics." Additionally, Barkdull (1976) blames much of the problem of inconsistencies in recidivism findings on the limited scope of research projects and underfunded investigations. He observes that while there are many good examples of well-designed research projects, the area is so inundated with conflicting results and contradictory findings that it is impossible to draw reliable conclusions (Travis, Schwartz, and Clear, 1983:161).

Conrad (1985) proposes a categorical solution to the problem of distinguishing between property and violent offenders. He observes that intensive probation supervision should be the "disposition of choice for *all* property felons *except rare offenders* who prefer the privacy of a prison cell." Furthermore, he says "*with rare exceptions, all* felons convicted of violent offenses should serve a term in jail or prison, *if only to maintain public confidence that the system is not excessively lenient with offenders guilty of life-threatening crimes.*" [Emphasis mine] Conrad's categorical generalities fail to resolve the problem. In fact, they only serve to compound it. How do we define those "rare exceptions" among property and violent offenders? Conrad fails to make explicit any objective criteria that would permit reliable identifications, however.

SELECTIVE INCAPACITATION: FRAMING THE ISSUES

Selective incapacitation was cited earlier as a means of alleviating prison overcrowding by selectively incarcerating those offenders "most likely" to recidivate (and not incarcerating those with low recidivism potential). Known by other names in past years (e.g., "predictive sentencing," "risk prediction"), selective incapacitation or the statistical prediction of criminality was a product of S. B. Warner and Hornell Hart during the 1920's (von Hirsch, 1987:105). Although their research in predicting criminality dealt primarily with forecasts of parole success or failure, their efforts stimulated others to devise similar predictive tools for probationers and juveniles in later years.

Mislabeled by Forst (1983) as "the latest theory for dealing with crime," selective incapacitation was given considerable prominence as a crime control strategy by the Rand Corporation in California through two 1982 studies of the same large sample of inmates of jails and prisons in California, Michigan, and Texas (Greenwood, 1982; Chaiken and Chaiken, 1982; von Hirsch, 1987:108). David Greenberg (1975) is credited with coining the term, but Greenwood (1982) popularized it through his Rand investigations (von Hirsch, 1987:14).

The RAND Research

Greenwood (1982) and Chaiken and Chaiken (1982) investigated 2,190 male prison and jail inmates, combining survey techniques with personal interviews and self-reports. They recorded inmate characteristics such as age, gender, race, employment history, education, drug use, prior arrests, convictions, and adult and juvenile commitments (Moriarty, 1987:1–2). Greenwood subsequently devised a list of "predictive factors" that might have possible legal relevance for sentencing decisions by the court. Through crosstabulating the level of criminal activity (from inmates' self-reports of crimes they committed during the two years prior to their current commitment) with these previously identified predictive factors, Greenwood devised a seven-point additive scale (Moriarty, 1987:2).

The seven factors in Greenwood's scale were:

1. Prior conviction for the instant offense type;
2. Incarceration for more than half of the preceding two years;
3. Conviction before the age of sixteen;

4. Time served in a state juvenile facility;
5. Drug use during the preceding two years;
6. Drug use as a juvenile;
7. Employment during less than 50 percent of the preceding two years (Greenwood, 1982:50).

Inmates were assigned a "1" for each of these characteristics which were true of them. Offender risk categories were created based on point totals. These categories and point totals were as follows:

RISK CATEGORY	NUMBER OF FACTORS
Low	0–1
Medium	2–3
High	4 or more

Greenwood suggested incarceration for "high-risk" offenders, whereas medium- and low-risk offender groups would be considered for alternative sentencing such as intensive supervised probation or involvement in some other probation program. By selectively incapacitating "high risk" offenders, an effective method of crime control would be established, since "high risk" inmates account for an incredibly high and disproportionate number of crimes compared with their low- and medium-risk offender counterparts.

Greenwood contended that his study demonstrated high predictive utility, although his conclusions were based for the most part on self-reports of previous criminal conduct by inmates studied. The Chaiken and Chaiken (1982) study utilized multiple regression analysis on the same sample of offenders, and, using Greenwood's predictor variables, found for instance that over 60 percent of those classified as "high-rate" robbers had either lower rates or did not commit robberies at all (von Hirsch, 1987:110–111). Thus, they concluded the large number of false positives raised several ethical and moral problems such that the suitability of Greenwood's predictive device should be seriously questioned. The criticisms of the Rand research are well-known (von Hirsch, 1984; von Hirsch, 1987; Blackmore and Welsh, 1983; Blumstein, 1983; Janus, 1985; Gottfredson and Tonry, 1987). In fact, Janus (1985:121) went so far as to say a policy of selective incapacitation was little more than repackaging of the ideas underlying the Salient Factor Score and that such a policy had been operated by the federal system for more than ten years.

The Moral and Ethical Issues of Selective Incapacitation

Tonry (1987:388–400) identifies five major moral and ethical issues and criticisms of selective incapacitation. These are:

1. *Simple Injustice.* If two offenders commit identical crimes in the same jurisdiction but one is incapacitated and the other placed on probation, a basic injustice has occurred. Of course, much rests on the purpose of the punishment which reflects the particular philosophy of the observer. If the philosophy is retribution, differential sentencing is unjustified (Cohen, 1983:39). If the philosophy is "just deserts," the sentence is unjustified as well. Differential sentencing through selective incapacitation appears justified only as a crime control measure or as a means of promoting "justice" for potential victims of those selectively incapacitated (Tonry, 1987:189).

2. *Past and Future Crimes.* Selective incapacitation punishes offenders for crimes they have not committed and may or may not commit if released. Thus, a scheme of punishment for anticipated future criminal conduct but which is based upon ones' past behaviors is morally wrong (von Hirsch, 1987).

3. *False Positives and the "Conviction of Innocents" Analogy.* Predictions of dangerousness and one's risk to the public in the future are seriously flawed. Many persons are labeled as "high risks" although they will not commit future crimes if released. These are known as false positives. Von Hirsch (1987) argues that false positives are unjustifiably penalized. Consider Greenwood's (1982) risk index as an example. This index allocates four points for juvenile or drug-related behaviors or incidents. Conviction before age 16, serving time in a juvenile detention facility, drug use either as a juvenile or during the past year sum to four points. Four or more points places an offender in the "high-risk" category. Reliance on Greenwood's scale in sentencing would bind the court to incapacitate the offender.

Von Hirsch (1987:109) compares Greenwood's scale and its predictive value with seeking to predict the physical condition of women in their ninth month of pregnancy on the basis of self-reports of their symptoms during the ninth month. Von Hirsch says "such predictions may be worthless for forecasting the women's health *after* the ninth month, for reasons I hardly need to explain."

4. *Inappropriate Predictors.* Tonry says that several predictors used in selective incapacitation decisions are status variables such as age, gender, and racial or ethnic identity. These are factors beyond the control of the offender. Thus, it is morally indefensible to base an incarceration decision on such factors. Furthermore, because most states bar public examinations or research inspections of one's juvenile record, investigators are forced to rely upon self-reported delinquent conduct. And any disclosures through self-reports are regarded as unreliable anyway for several apparent reasons. Greenwood's scale could only be applied if offenders chose to disclose their juvenile conduct or drug use through self-reports. To what extent will offenders seal their own fate by admissions of wrongdoing to state or federal officials?

5. *Disparate Racial Impacts.* Selective incapacitation is indirectly influenced by racial and ethnic factors, because these factors are often closely linked with other status variables such as unemployment, educational attainment, vocational skills and experience, residential stability, and income (Tonry, 1987:397–398). To the extent that selective incapacitation decisions are based on factors closely correlated with race, blacks and others will be disproportionately affected by such decisions (Moriarty, 1987; Cohen, 1983:38).

Petersilia and Turner (1987:172–173) have sought to show how the predictive utility of recidivism measures used in selective incapacitation decision-making would be affected if factors highly correlated with race were omitted. Their results were somewhat disappointing. Although predictive accuracy was relatively low to begin with, removal of racially correlated factors did not decrease predictive utility substantially. Therefore, these researchers conclude that "the concern over racially correlated status factors may be exaggerated" (1987:172–173).

However, Minnesota and several other states have implemented sentencing guidelines to overcome sentencing disparities attributable to racial factors. Despite Minnesota's attempt to develop guidelines unaffected by race, the minority population in Minnesota prisons rose significantly after these supposedly objective guidelines went into effect. Petersilia and Turner (1987:173) explain this increase as the result of the continuing influence of race and its association with the "objective" criteria of conviction crime(s) and prior record used by Minnesota in the development of its sentencing grid. In fact, in some jurisdictions white offenders are disadvantaged under a sentencing guideline system because they are more likely than blacks to be alcoholics and drug abusers.

Under the Fourteenth Amendment, all citizens are entitled to equal protection under the law as well as due process. Selective incapacitation has been criticized by researchers as violative of both of these clauses (Tonry, 1987; Morris and Miller, 1985; Morris, 1984). Also, under the Eighth Amendment, the "cruel and unusual punishment" clause has been cited as pertinent to selective incapacitation decisions (Tonry, 1987:381–382). Thus, the Fourteenth and Eighth Amendments of the U. S. Constitution raise three legal issues about prediction devices and their use in sentencing criminals differentially.

First, the "equal protection" clause forbids the use of any classification scheme that deliberately favors one race, religion, political allegiance, ethnic group, or gender over another. Tonry observes that if we use the Constitution for guidance, then in general, whatever is not forbidden is permitted, and little is forbidden (1987:375). Actually, the U. S. Supreme Court is concerned with irrational and directly discriminatory programs and procedures, whereas rational and indirectly discriminatory programs and procedures are left relatively untouched.

Second, under the "due process" clause of the Fourteenth Amendment, the U. S. Supreme Court subjects to scrutiny any scheme that is "fixed and mechanical" or "arbitrary and capricious" (Tonry, 1987:377–378). Essentially, "structured discretion" is permitted and encouraged as lawful. Therefore, as Tonry rightly and persuasively argues, structured discretion under a system of general parole guidelines, for example, would not deny an offender his/her right to due process. The use of prediction devices forecasting an offender's future dangerousness has been approved by the U. S. Supreme Court in the case of *Barefoot v. Estelle* (1983) (upholding the imposition of the death penalty statute in a Texas case involving a psychiatric prediction of future dangerousness) and *Schall v. Martin* (1984) (a juvenile case upholding the constitutionality of New York's juvenile preventive detention statute where the juvenile was predicted as posing a serious risk to society if released (Gottlieb and Rosen, 1984). Tonry suggests that future challenges of dangerousness prediction devices by prospective parolees or probationers as violative of their "due process" rights will no doubt be unsuccessful (1987:380).

Third, the "cruel and unusual punishment" clause of the Eighth Amendment relative to selective incapacitation suggests that imprisoning certain offenders and not others constitutes cruel and unusual punishment for those incarcerated. This is particularly pertinent for persons placed in pretrial detention and who have not been convicted of any criminal offense (Tonry, 1987:381–382). The crucial phraseology is whether the incapacitation is for the *purpose of punishment*. As Tonry (1987:382) says, unless an express intention to punish can be shown (which is highly unlikely in most cases), the state need only show that some legitimate purpose will be served by the special treatment.

In 1987, the U. S. Supreme Court decided in favor of pretrial detention for two alleged organized-crime figures. Although these defendants were challenging their pretrial detention on grounds of "excessive bail" under the Eighth Amendment, the Court upheld the pretrial jailing of two reputed leaders of New York organized-crime families under a 1984 federal law allowing imprisonment of suspects "to protect the safety of any other person in the community" (Gest, 1987:12). Chief Justice William Rehnquist said that pretrial detention in this instance was justified because these Cosa Nostra chieftains posed a "demonstrable danger" (Gest, 1987:12).

Regarding prediction and classification, Tonry (1987:372–373) says that only a handful of generalizations applicable to criminal justice predictions and classifications can be derived from the Supreme Court's interpretation of the U. S. Constitution:

1. Classifications based directly on race, ethnicity, political beliefs, or religion are generally prohibited; reliance on one of these factors must be shown to be justified by a "compelling state interest"—a probative standard that is difficult to meet.

2. Classifications based on sex are often prohibited, and attempts to justify such classifications must be substantially persuasive.

3. Classifications based directly on other factors are nearly always permitted because all that must be shown is that there is a "rational basis" for the classification; the courts defer to legislative and executive classifications, and it is accordingly very difficult to show that a classification lacks a rational basis.

4. Classifications that result in differential impacts on racial or ethnic groups, but indirectly and without the intention to achieve that result, are nearly always permitted (unless a statutory scheme—e.g., an equal-employment opportunity law—is deemed to forbid both intended and unintended differential impacts).

5. Official actions taken before trial involving jail conditions, on the basis of predictions, will generally be sustained even if they infringe on liberty unless they can be shown to be "intended to be punitive."

6. Official actions taken after conviction on the basis of predictions of dangerousness will generally be sustained so long as the sanctions or conditions imposed are within the range authorized by law.

7. Judges (at least, probably all criminal justice system officials) may rely on predictions in making decisions irrespective of the scientific integrity or credibility of the predictive evidence adduced unless they expressly declare that they are relying on evidence that is patently frivolous.

Deservedness and Dangerousness in Sentencing

What an offender "deserves" and what he/she "gets" are two different matters. Many rapists and murderers are placed on probation, while a much higher number of burglars and thieves are given the same punishment. As a collective outsider, the public is inclined to react unfavorably. They probably doubt the wisdom of placing thieves and burglars on probation, and they are even less enthusiastic when it comes to sentencing murderers and rapists to the same status.

As previously seen, a sentencing judge is sensitive to a number of issues. What is the plea bargain agreement before him/her? Does it contain a probation provision? What would be the effect upon prison/jail overcrowding of incarcerating the offender? Every criminal statute prescribes an incarcerative and/or a fine as punishment(s), but for the most part, these punishments are worded "up to" or "no more than." Armed with these sentencing qualifications, judges have considerable latitude in sentencing an offender to probation or denying it.

The question of whether incarceration is deserved or undeserved is irrelevant for many offenders, unless the just deserts philosophy is invoked. The justice model suggests a punishment fitting the crime. Should the offender be punished for past crimes or only for present ones? The crime control model implies greater punishment the more one offends. The rehabilitation model says whatever the offender does, treatment is often relevant in dissuading the offender from future criminal conduct.

How does a judge or parole board decide if an offender is "potentially dangerous"? Should an offender be kept in confinement or not confined on the basis of numerical scores on a "dangerousness" scale? What clear-cut evidence exists supporting such incarcerative or nonincarcerative decisions? There is none, or at least, there is none of a definitive nature that is supported by subsequent empirical tests and research replications (von Hirsch, 1987).

Sometimes, judges and other officials rely on *categorical incapacitation* as a solution to the sentencing and jail/prison overcrowding dilemmas. Categorical incapacitation is more straightforward and involves aggregates of offenders rather than individuals (Blumstein, 1983). Basically, categorical incapacitation removes the "selective" element from the sentencing decision and reduces it to numerical quotients on scales such as Greenwood's (1982). Persons in this or that category receive this or that sentence. Should all murderers be imprisoned? Should all burglars receive probation? Should all robbers be imprisoned? Should all larcenists receive probation? How valid is categorical incapacitation? In view of what Tonry has said concerning certain due process, equal protection, and cruel and unusual punishment issues, it is likely that the U. S. Supreme Court would reject a "fixed and mechanical" sentencing scheme categorical incapacitation proposes (Tonry, 1987:377).

PREDICTIONS OF DANGEROUSNESS AND PUBLIC RISK

Aside from the moral, ethical, and legal issues of selective incapacitation or predictions of dangerousness, how much risk is associated with releasing criminals into the community with or without incarceration? The "cause celebres" such as John Hinckley, Charles Manson, and David Berkowitz represent less than one thousandth of one percent of all criminal cases. Are there significant dangerousness differences between John Hinckley (would-be assassin of President Ronald Reagan), Charles Manson (the "cult" killer of Sharon Tate and others in a "Manson Family" killing), David Berkowitz (the "Son of Sam" killer), Ivan Boesky (felonious New York stock broker facing five years in prison for illegal insider trading), Gary Heidnik (who kept persons in chains in his cellar before killing and butchering them),

Bernhard Goetz (the New York City vigilante who shot and wounded several black youths), and Jake Butcher (Knoxville, Tennessee bank president who is serving 20 years for fraud)?

It is unlikely that Boesky or Butcher will ever be able to obtain a job associated with money exchange such as stock brokerage or banking. By the same token, Manson, Heidnik, and Berkowitz would be unlikely candidates for security work in apartment complexes if paroled. But Goetz and Hinckley are perplexing in that we don't fully understand their original motives, they come from "good families," they don't have prior records, they are not juveniles and have no records as juvenile offenders, they have not been linked with drugs or drug-related offenses, they are not from the lower socioeconomic levels, and they haven't committed previous serious offenses.

How would Greenwood's scale operate in these cases? Boesky, Butcher, Berkowitz, Heidnik, Hinckley and Goetz would be "low-risk" offenders and recommended for probation, while Manson (largely because of his prior record) would be recommended for incarceration, although his score on Greenwood's scale would result in a "moderate" probation recommendation. According to Conrad's (1985) criteria, all of these individuals (with the exception of Goetz and with other "rare exceptions") would be incarcerated for a time and then considered for release. Since Goetz was acquitted anyway, neither Greenwood's nor Conrad's schemes are relevant in his case.

Overpredictions and Underpredictions of Dangerousness

Selective incapacitation and predictions of dangerousness pose the questions of whether a "high-risk" offender ought to be incarcerated and whether a "low-risk" offender ought to receive probation. The major problem with prediction schemes is the tendency for those schemes to *overpredict* or *underpredict*. Error rates in prediction schemes are problematic, primarily because they underpenalize serious or nonserious offenders who recidivate and overpenalize serious or nonserious offenders who don't recidivate.

In the Greenwood (1982) study, Greenwood originally demonstrated an absurdly low false positive rate of 4 percent (i.e., 4 percent of those predicted to be serious recidivists were not). As von Hirsch (1987:110–111) explains, this occurred because Greenwood used as false positives "only those offenders predicted to be 'high-rate' offenders who had, in fact, the lowest reported rates—namely the most extreme category of false positives."

Von Hirsch says that Greenwood failed to treat as false positives those predicted to be high-risk offenders who proved to have medium rates. Von Hirsch demonstrates that the false positive rate was actually *56 percent* in Greenwood's study. Accordingly, Chaiken and Chaiken (1982) analyzed the same data collected by Rand and found that over 60 percent of those classified as high-rate robbers had lower recidivism rates or did not commit robberies at all (von Hirsch, 1987:111). What this means is approximately 60 percent of these inmates would be misclassified as "dangerous" and subject to confinement according to Greenwood's predictions, whereas their actual recidivism and involvement in subsequent serious crimes would be nil.

Monahan (1984) sums it up fairly succinctly by saying "the first generation of research studies on the prediction of violent behavior found such prediction to be *highly inaccurate.*" [Emphasis mine] Monahan recommends that second generation research (whatever that is) should set clear boundaries concerning "its role amidst current policy activity within the criminal justice system." He contends that the future implies greater involvement by psychologists and psychiatrists in dangerousness decisions for parole boards and judicial sentencing. Therefore, these persons (i.e., psychologists, psychiatrists—and we are reasonably certain Monahan would not want to exclude sociologists and experts in criminal justice—and others) "should resist the temptation to make any conclusive judgments that an individual is dangerous."

Monahan recommends the inclusion of salient factors such as the family environment, the work environment, and the peer group environment in which the individual is to function. However, he offers no specific measuring scheme whereby to objectify these variables used in prediction decisions. One may glean from Monahan's recommendations a general responsibility shift from behavioral science professionals to the prosecutors, courts, and parole boards for determining offender life chances. This "cop out" is made explicit by Monahan's recommendation that these professionals "*may be of some help* in assessing the probability of future violence in some cases, but determining whether a person is dangerous 'enough' to justify preventive confinement is *not* the job of mental health professionals." [Emphasis mine] Whose job is it?

Wilkins (1985) says that those who firmly believe they know with certainty what to do about crime and criminals have never studied the subject. Perhaps this is so. Of greater importance, however, is Wilkins' argument that the greatest "myth" to be destroyed today is that decisions about individual offenders will have a significant impact on the incidence and prevalence of crime.

The danger of predictions of offender dangerousness is that whatever measures or criteria are applied, nothing as yet forecasts dangerousness accurately. It is interesting to note that professionals are inordinately concerned with programs with rates of recidivism among probationers and parolees exceeding 30 percent. They scour every explanatory avenue searching for answers which will account satisfactorily for this significant minority of offenders. Travis, Schwartz, and Clear (1983:93) astutely observe that if certain parolees (and probationers) *do not recidivate*, it is quite difficult to pinpoint *that* aspect of their program which led to their conformity to society's laws. [Emphasis mine] Describing and profiling recidivists and serious offenders and using the resulting syntality for this aggregate to predict future offender behaviors and to penalize them accordingly through selective incapacitation are two entirely different operations with drastically dissimilar implications.

If a majority of "high-risk" offenders happen to be black, young, single, unemployed, former juvenile delinquents with drug problems and drug convictions, and possessing prior adult criminal records, should future offenders who happen to have these same characteristics be targeted for harsh sentencing, while those not sharing these characteristics be targeted for leniency? No. Yet, many descriptive studies of recidivists and dangerous offenders promote categorical incapacitation and lead us along such predictive paths. It is a relatively easy lilly-pad leap from a well-articulated list of offender characteristics to a decision-making situation where those same characteristics are used as predictors of future behavior. Granted, we need descriptive information, but at this stage, no one is sure of how such information ought to be applied in predictions of future dangerousness for probationers and parolees (Wright, Clear, and Dickson, 1984).

The Reality of Greater Risk Through Felony Probation versus the Parole Alternative

Several significant steps have been taken by states as well as the federal government either to abolish or seriously curtail the decision-making power of parole boards and judges. Determinate sentencing undermines parole board discretion about inmate early-release decisions, and mandatory sentencing further binds both judges and parole boards regarding whether to incarcerate an offender and for how long. In short, both probation and parole are subjects of considerable controversy at present (Gottfredson and Gottfredson, 1988:176).

Some research has shown that if offenders recidivate, they tend to commit acts similar to those for which they were originally convicted (Heuser, 1985; Oregon Crime Analysis Center, 1984). This is not conclusive, however. Other equally inconclusive research has shown that some property offenders progress to more serious crimes and recidivate more frequently (Eisenberg, 1985b), violent offenders tend to commit less serious offenses and recidivate less (Boudouris, 1983), and violent offenders tend to recidivate more (Chown and Davis, 1986).

Closely related to predicting the relative dangerousness of parolees and probationers and whether they will recidivate is the decision of pretrial release for defendants with felonious charges against them. Gottfredson and Gottfredson (1988:93) say that "the ability to make such judgments accurately and the consequences of errors are topics that have attracted much social scientific attention in recent years. The results of these studies *cast serious doubt on current abilities to predict with great accuracy the statistically rare events of failure to appear at trial and pretrial crime*." [Emphasis mine]

Presumably, the trend is away from leniency and toward a "get tough" policy for criminals as well as a potential deterrent for would-be offenders. At the same time, intermediate punishments have been or are being devised as conciliatory inputs to the controversy over incarceration or nonincarceration as a rehabilitative tool, a "justice" aim, or a "just deserts-retributionist" view.

It does not necessarily follow that because some offenders are incarcerated, they are "naturally" more serious compared with those not incarcerated. *Some* murderers (not many, but "some") are placed on probation, as well as *some* robbers, *many* burglars, *many* thieves, and numerous arsonists and muggers. Obviously, the more serious the conviction, the greater the likelihood of a sentence of incarceration rather than probation. From this we might infer categorically greater seriousness for those incarcerated compared with those sentenced to probation of some type. Judicial bias enters the picture as well, as evidence suggests judges place the "best risks" on probation while confining the poorest risks to prison in the first place. Gottfredson and Gottfredson (1988:194) compare the probationer-parolee difference to the apples-oranges analogy. In fact, these investigators say that "if we ask who is placed on probation, some observed differences with selected imprisoned offenders may be cited (they tend to be younger, to be convicted of less serious offenses, and to have shorter prior records) . . . but a detailed profile of such differences generalizable to probationers and prisoners in general, cannot be given . . . [because] . . . the necessary research has not been done" (1988:198).

Morris and Miller (1985) offer the view that using predictions of dangerousness, however sophisticated, for the purpose of making incarceration or probation decisions requires a "political judgment balancing the risk and harm to society with the intrusion on the liberty of each member of a preventatively detained group. Not all types of prediction are equally satisfactory." Simple predictive tools often work as well as or better than more complex ones (Gottfredson and Gottfredson, 1985). But Morris and Miller (1985) warn that:

in the context of sentencing, the controlling principle for the use of predictions of dangerousness is that the base expectancy rate of violence [computed from a predictive tool] for the criminal predicted as dangerous must be shown by reliable evidence to be substantially higher than the base expectancy rate of another criminal with a closely similar record, convicted of a closely similar crime, but not predicted to be unusually dangerous, *before the greater dangerousness of the former may be relied upon to intensify or extend his punishment.* [Emphasis mine]

Farrington and Tarling (1985) add that because prediction and prediction methods will never be 100 percent accurate, and since these predictions no doubt have crucial implications for offenders during sentencing or parole consideration, in the interests of justice they should be as accurate as possible. More theoretically based criteria are needed, as well as more empirical research on the validity and reliability of dangerousness measures.

But one fact must be acknowledged for both parolees and probationers considered as the general criminal class: *most of these persons will eventually be released into the community, despite community sentiment to the contrary.* Many current experimental and/or operational community-based probation programs maximize community participation through the use of volunteers and paraprofessionals who assist probation officers in their supervisory tasks (Latessa, Travis, and Allen, 1983). The same phenomenon is occurring in the operation of halfway houses and other facilities designed to accommodate parolees (McCarthy and McCarthy, 1984:369–388). The use of volunteers is frequently attributable to staff shortages due to agency funding limitations and restrictions.

Thus, regardless of the philosophy of corrections one espouses, a consistent and compelling objective of virtually all programs for both probationers and parolees is *crime control* (Eaglin and Lombard, 1984). Those offenders who are more intensively supervised seem to do better in their vocational/educational programs as well as exhibit lower rates of recidivism (Pearson, 1985; Pearson and Bibel, 1986; Latessa, 1987; Clear, Flynn, and Shapiro, 1987). However, some research shows little or no relation between a probationer's or parolee's program successfulness and the level of contacts with his/her probation/parole officer, where risk level is held constant (Eisenberg, 1986a).

Gottfredson and Gottfredson (1988:182) say that thus far, (1) no optimal caseload has been demonstrated, and (2) no clear evidence of reduced recidivism, simply by reduced caseload size, has been found. And as these researchers argue, although pronouncements about reduced officer caseloads as effective are without empirical support, they often serve political ends rather than humanitarian ones—such as assisting managers of agencies secure larger budgets and resources despite their impotent contribution to reducing offender recidivism. Interestingly, these experts indicate intensive supervision may backfire because with more intensive monitoring, probationers and parolees may be cited for more technical violations associated with their release agreements (1988:199).

Petersilia (1986b) expresses best the sentiments of many corrections professionals as new intensive probation supervision programs are subjected to close community scrutiny. She says that probation's long-term survival may depend on the success of these middle-range (intermediate punishment) programs, and that if probation can adapt its methods of supervision and service to deal with higher-risk offenders in the community, then probation will find itself back in the public's favor and in the center of corrections policy.

SUMMARY

Much attention has been devoted in recent years to studies of recidivism among probationers and parolees. Recidivism is often equated with a program's failure or success. Studies of recidivism show mixed and frequently contradictory results, although these are explained largely by how recidivism is defined as well as the target groups investigated.

More popular recidivism measures include rearrests, reconvictions, and reincarcerations, although parole or probation revocations, the filing of new charges, the failure to complete vocational/educational training programs, and absconding are other alternatives used. The most meaningful indicators of recidivism seem to be rearrests and reconvictions for new and serious offenses, although experts disagree over a uniform conceptualization of the term.

Much of the recidivism research conducted thus far has focused upon juvenile offenders or parolees, groups quite different from probationers. Some of this research has occurred in other countries where different laws are applicable and varying standards apply. Public concern with recidivism is with the dangerousness to the citizenry posed by the early release of offenders through parole or through bypassing incarceration entirely through granting probation. Increased use of felony probation in recent years has raised issues of dangerousness and societal risk.

While most jurisdictions have risk/needs assessment devices to predict one's potential dangerousness, no measures have yet been devised to gauge this phenomenon accurately. One option has been to suggest that certain offenders be selectively incapacitated on the basis of predictable risk levels. There are several moral, ethical, and legal issues involved in selective incapacitation such as punishing offenders in the present for crimes they may or may not commit in the future. The Rand Corporation has extensively researched several offender groups, and selective incapacitation has been recommended. These recommendations have been challenged on several methodological and theoretical grounds, however. There is a tendency for many prediction devices to "overpredict" and "underpredict," thus penalizing certain false positives more harshly and being too lenient with false negatives.

There is a general trend toward greater reliance upon community-based corrections programs for managing increasing numbers of probationers, many of whom are dangerous. Community involvement in such programs, through the use of volunteers and paraprofessionals, works to the advantage of program officials where the program is made more acceptable to the general community. However, legal issues and liabilities arise as less experienced volunteer workers become involved in offender monitoring and supervision.

5

The Future of Felony Probation

THE CONTROVERSY IN RETROSPECT

Whether felons should be granted probation is a moot question because currently, a majority of felons in most jurisdictions are being sentenced to probationary programs. Keenly interested in this controversial practice is the Rand Corporation and two of its leading social researchers, Joan Petersilia and Peter Greenwood. The conclusion they reach is that *felony probation poses a serious threat to public safety* (Petersilia, Turner, Kahan, and Peterson, 1985:381; Greenwood, 1982). Although their work has been subjected to intense criticism from various researchers in part because of the unrepresentative samples of felons selected for investigation and the unusually high recidivism rates reported among these persons, their investigations have been provocative (Travis, Latessa, and Vito, 1987; Latessa, 1987; Fichter, Hirschburg, and McGaha, 1987).

Some Standards from Rand

Furthermore, a set of policy recommendations has been devised by these investigators suggesting radical restructuring of several important components of the criminal justice system. These policy recommendations include:

1. *The mission of probation and the responsibilities of probation agencies should be redefined, limited, and explicitly stated, by statute if necessary.*
2. *In response to changes in the probation population, the system should redefine the role and powers of probation officers.*
3. *The risk/needs assessment scales promoted by the National Institute of Corrections and adopted by many probation departments nationwide should be strongly endorsed.*

4. *State criminal justice systems should develop punitive community-based alternatives to prison for convicted felons, even where problems of severe prison overcrowding have not yet occurred* (1985:388–389).

Although there is a certain ambiguity about these recommendations and we can take issue with *how* such diffuse objectives can be achieved logistically among so many different and competing agencies and organizations, they do reflect a general pattern occurring in the research literature. In short, their ideas are consistent with other advocates of probation reform in recent years. It is not expected that sweeping changes as recommended will occur overnight. In fact, many programs reported or referred to in this book are only in experimental stages in selected jurisdictions in some states. Large-scale, national, or even statewide adoptions of new programs have not occurred with great frequency, in spite of the call for such reforms from so many correctional experts and agencies during the last two decades.

It is unclear, for instance, about who should redefine the mission of probation and how probation officers can be given more power in their supervisory roles. Risk/needs assessment scales have been around for some time, although their predictive utility is questionable. Even now it may be premature to encourage large-scale adoption of existing scales for offender classification and management (Gottfredson and Gottfredson, 1988). The problem of false positives raises certain moral and ethical issues, and selective incapacitation fosters such numbers of false positives that the general concern for fairness and equity in punishment is heightened.

And the Rand encouragement of the inclusion of "punitive" elements in existing community-based probation programs is an outgrowth of the "get tough" or "just deserts" or "retributionist" philosophies stimulated in part by the impotence of rehabilitation associated with these programs. This is not an attack on *all* probation programs. Rather, programs that are currently serving only custodial functions and offering only token supervision for offender-clients are targeted for the development of more punitive policies.

The Rand recommendations include an examination of how much and in what ways prison (and jail) overcrowding affects the criminal justice system's treatment of offenders, who uses presentence investigation reports, could their design be improved as well as their purposes, the clarification of the mission of chief probation officers, and how rates of probationer recidivism compare with incarcerated offenders (1985:390–391; Greenwood, 1982; Chaiken and Chaiken, 1982).

Policy Recommendations as Guideposts

These Rand conclusions and recommendations have been selected to preface this closing chapter for several reasons. First, *their studies of felony probation have been extremely provocative throughout the corrections com-*

munity. Great interest in establishing workable probation programs has been inspired by their research showing a 65 percent failure rate of a large sample of felony probationers in the late 1970's. Second, while the Rand Corporation and Peter Greenwood didn't invent selective incapacitation, *they have certainly generated ample controversy over the use of selective incapacitation in conjunction with sentencing practices and reforms.* The Rand endorsement and promotion of risk/needs assessment indices devised by the National Institute of Corrections confirms this specific policy aim. Third, *the policy recommendations are, for the most part, legitimate and well-intentioned.* More than a few corrections experts are skeptical about the sophistication of existing risk/needs devices that purportedly forecast one's dangerousness, and they believe the use of such instruments is premature and possibly violative of offender rights to "due process" and "equal protection" under the U. S. Constitution.

The fourth and probably most important reason is that in view of *when* these policy recommendations were prepared (1983–1984), *they function now as a standard against which recent developments in probation programs can be compared.* Thus, we can see whether one or more of their original aims have been realized in subsequent research and whether significant changes have occurred in former criminal justice policies and practices. Have the mission of probation and the diverse responsibilities of probation agencies changed? Have the roles and powers of probation officers been redefined in recent years? Have risk/needs assessment scales been adopted by many probation departments? Have punitive community-based alternatives to prison for convicted felons been established?

Although Gottfredson and Gottfredson (1988) say much more needs to be done in these and other related areas, generally the response to all questions above is conditionally affirmative. "Conditionally affirmative" means that, yes, the mission, roles, powers, and functions of probation officers as well as their affiliated agencies and departments have been transformed in recent years. Many community-based program alternatives have been or are being established and are in various stages of implementation and/or experimentation. Risk/needs instruments have been or are being devised and used increasingly for sentencing, screening, classification, and other purposes. However, critics of these cumulative efforts are reluctant to pass judgment and issue definitive progress reports. It is clear we have "come a long way," but no one is sure where we are at present.

The research suggestions of the Rand investigators are as interesting as their policy recommendations. These suggestions also function as standards against which present research efforts may be contrasted. Currently, we know a great deal about prison and jail overcrowding, how it occurs, and how it can be alleviated. The litigation explosion and the staggering numbers of civil and criminal actions filed annually by prisoners against their administrative authorities and guards and the response of the U. S. Supreme

Court to selected suits have effected substantial improvements in offender treatment in many jails and prisons through court-ordered compliance with both old and new regulations and standards. Increasing numbers of probation/parole officers and agencies are also falling prey to civil and criminal litigation from their target clientele. And recidivism rates of various offender groups are increasingly reviewed and described by investigators.

Significant Events of the 1980's Influencing Felony Probation

Much of what has transpired in the 1980's in corrections generally has been prompted by debates, concerns, studies, and recommendations among and from researchers, corrections officials, and legislators in the 1970's. Several significant events have occurred which are causing serious changes in offender processing at virtually every point in the criminal justice system. It is imperative that we understand the important events which have spawned such changes in order to appreciate more fully the context in which felony probation is couched.

It is also important that the *interrelatedness* of each of these events is acknowledged and should function as a "given" in subsequent discussion. At least thirteen more or less specific changes, innovations, and/or shifts have occurred, particularly during the 1980's, which have affected and will continue to affect the future of felony probation in various ways. These events have been arranged below in a reasonably logical fashion, although their respective chronologies differ.

1. *The philosophical shift in correctional thinking from rehabilitation to "just deserts" and crime control.* The U. S. Sentencing Commission has drastically overhauled the federal sentencing process, with the general aim of crime control (U. S. Sentencing Commission, 1987:1.3). Many state jurisdictions have moved from the rehabilitation mode toward punishments consistent with "just deserts," deterrence, and crime control. Every state has examined or is examining its sentencing and punishment schemes and reevaluating them in view of this general philosophical shift. Various offender programs are likewise being reevaluated.

2. *The Bail Reform Act of 1984.* The year 1984 was significant in several respects as will be seen. It signaled the passage of several important Acts which have subsequently altered the future of many defendants and convicted offenders. Especially important are the pretrial detention provisions of the Act which permit judges the discretion of denying bail and authorizing the detention of any defendant *who may flee or pose a danger to any other person in the community* (18 U.S.C., Sec. 3142(d)(2), 1988). This provision was challenged in 1987 and the U. S. Supreme Court ruled in favor of the government. The increased use of pretrial detention has aggravated jail overcrowding. This Act has also contributed to the formulation of

measures of public risk or dangerousness designed to forecast which offenders "pose a danger" to the public, although these measures have generated much controversy among corrections experts and others (Gottlieb and Rosen, 1984).

3. *The Comprehensive Crime Control Act of 1984.* By authority granted by the Comprehensive Crime Control Act of 1984 (Public Law 98-473), the U. S. Sentencing Commission was created to establish sentencing policies and practices for the federal criminal justice system (U. S. Sentencing Commission, 1987:1.1). Under this same authority, the U. S. Sentencing Commission is given broad authority to review and rationalize the federal sentencing process (1987:1.1). The Act requires the offender to serve virtually all of any prison sentence imposed, because it abolishes parole in 1992 and substantially restructures good behavior adjustments (1987:1.1).

4. *The Sentencing Reform Act of 1984.* This is actually Chapter II of the Comprehensive Crime Control Act of 1984 which was subsequently amended under Public Law 99-363 and labeled "The Sentencing Guideline Adjustment Act of 1986." Under this Act, a presumptive sentencing guidelines scheme was established which went into effect November 1, 1987. Thereafter, federal district judges must select a sentence within the guidelines, and the reasons for any departures from these guidelines must be specified.

5. *The shift from indeterminate to determinate, presumptive, and/or mandatory sentencing.* Beginning with Maine, several states have changed their sentencing schemes from indeterminate to determinate and/or presumptive schemes. These changes have resulted in less judicial discretion (theoretically) in sentencing offenders. In reality, the significance of this shift as eroding judicial sentencing power is questionable. Basically, the shift signifies (again theoretically) greater certainty of incarceration for criminal convictions. It also signifies less discretionary authority of parole boards (or their abolishment) in granting prisoners early release. The elimination of sentencing disparities is cited as a major reason for this general sentencing shift.

6. *The abolition of parole boards or limitations of parole board authority.* One result of determinate, presumptive, and mandatory sentencing is that parole board discretion is either severely curtailed or totally eliminated as has been done in some jurisdictions. Currently about two-thirds of the states as well as the federal government utilize parole boards for making early release decisions for inmates. Many of these jurisdictions combine several sentencing schemes together with parole board decision-making.

7. *Increased use of split-sentencing and shock probation.* The U. S. Sentencing Commission (1987) has established provisions for split sentences or short terms of incarceration for offenders in certain offense ranges. The Commission's view is that "the definite prospect of prison, though the term is short, will act as a significant deterrent to many of these crimes, particularly when compared with the status quo where probation, not prison, is

the norm" (1987:1.9). Both state and federal jurisdictions retain fairly broad discretion in sentencing offenders to short terms, usually in jails or minimum-security facilities. This adds also to jail overcrowding, if only for a relatively brief period.

8. *Greater jail and prison overcrowding.* Given the sentencing schemes noted above, we will never resolve satisfactorily the jail and prison overcrowding situation. Newly enacted sentencing schemes and those proposed add to prison populations rather than lessen them. The result in some states is contracting with locally-operated jails to handle prison overflows. This aggravates the jail overcrowding problem in affected jurisdictions. The overcrowding issue is also a consideration in plea bargaining terms as well as sentencing decisions (Champion, 1988a).

9. *Greater civil and criminal litigation filed by jail and prison inmates.* Record numbers of civil and criminal suits are filed by inmates of jails and prisons annually against jail and prison officials. The 1980's have been labeled the era of the "litigation explosion," and it is unlikely that the explosion will abate in the near future. These suits take valuable court time and cause judges and others to seek solutions to speed up criminal case processing. One result is greater pressure on prosecutors and judges to consider probation alternatives as inducements to elicit guilty pleas from offenders.

10. *Recidivism and selective incapacitation.* No direct and consistent evidence of rising recidivism rates among probationers or parolees has been presented in the criminal justice literature. However, recidivism is often equated with program failure, and selective incapacitation is increasingly considered as one very controversial solution. Targeting high-risk offenders for incarceration and low-risk offenders for probation, especially through various dangerousness measures which have not yet proved fully reliable or valid, raises moral, ethical, and legal issues relating to due process, equal protection, and general fairness under the law. Large numbers of false positives and false negatives cast doubt on our ability to forecast dangerousness and recidivism accurately.

11. *Technological developments.* Relatively recent technological innovations in corrections affecting probationers to an increasing degree are electronic monitoring systems. Offenders in some jurisdictions must wear tamper-resistant anklets or wristlets which emit electronic signals and can be monitored by telephone equipment or through radio signal emissions from great distances. As our technological sophistication increases in this most promising and innovative area, more officials will be inclined to favor placing formerly high-risk offenders in electronic monitoring programs as a means of increasing the level of crime control.

This list is certainly not exhaustive, but it represents several significant events or changes that have altered drastically the lives of offenders, especially probationers. Each event is both partially independent of and dependent upon the other events listed. No concerted effort has been made by any agency or governmental bureau to coordinate these events. They have occurred at roughly the same point in time and have inadvertently conspired to weave an interesting contextual framework within which corrections officials, judges, and others must operate when processing criminals. Where we have been and where we are going regarding felony probation is easier to understand if we contemplate at least these antecedents.

It is clear also from an examination of the correctional literature that much emphasis has been placed in recent years on improving the administration, operation, and overall quality of intensive probation supervision programs. Also highlighted have been efforts by the American Correctional Association and other groups to foster improvements in probation officer education and training. Therefore, expanded and continuing efforts will be observed in the following areas affecting the quantity and quality of felony probation.

More community-based programs as intermediate punishments and intensive supervised probation. Increasing numbers of probationers have created the need for better services and offender monitoring. Programs in New Jersey, Georgia, and Oregon have demonstrated reasonably low rates of recidivism for handling low- and medium-risk offenders. Although these programs are sometimes faulted for their biased selections of program participants (i.e., those least likely to recidivate or "fail"), they are growing in popularity and use in many jurisdictions. In turn, these community-based facilities offer prosecutors and judges a wider variety of options in sentencing offenders. Home incarceration or confinement or assignment to a community center, together with curfews and other restrictions, restitution, and victim compensation programs render probation an increasingly desirable (and punitive) alternative to satisfy both public and professionals alike.

Better training of probation/parole officers and administrative/supervisory personnel. The American Correctional Association, National Institute of Justice, and other agencies have made significant efforts to improve the quality of personnel in all correctional sectors. Minimum education requirements and specialized training programs lead to the recruitment of more qualified specialists to deal with low-risk or high-risk offender groups on either probation or parole. These training improvements are important, inasmuch as probation and parole work are becoming increasingly hazardous (Renzema, 1987).

THE REHABILITATION MODEL AND ITS COMPETITION

Most certainly the treatment or rehabilitation model is not dead. Among federal officials, for instance, the Comprehensive Crime Control Act of 1984 was designed to further "the basic purposes of criminal punishment, i.e., deterring crime, incapacitating the offender, providing just punishment, and *rehabilitating the offender"* (U. S. Sentencing Commission, 1987:1.1). [Emphasis mine] In a single sentence, the Commission blended several punishment philosophies and aims: deterrence, incapacitation, justice (and "just deserts"), and rehabilitation.

But the treatment orientation and its emphasis on offender rehabilitation has undergone severe criticisms from both within and without the correctional field. Reports of recidivism among probationers as high as 65 or 70 percent associated with *any* program cause observers to question the utility of the program as a rehabilitative device. Probation agencies and their officers or agents are at a disadvantage initially because of citizen expectations envisioning these organizations and personnel as the primary forces of crime control for probationers. In reality, these persons and agencies must manage or monitor whatever clients the courts decide to send them. Therefore, when probationers recidivate, the programs and personnel are most frequently the first to be blamed for not controlling effectively their offender populations. Of course, the courts originally sentence offenders to probation, not probation departments. But as we have seen, prosecutors and the judiciary are most intractable and intransigent when it comes to implementing and/or abiding by sentencing reforms.

The public lacks a basic understanding of the complexity of the legal system and the hydraulic nature of it. Incarcerating more offenders means overcrowding existing penal facilities or constructing new ones. Building new prisons and jails is expensive, and the taxpayer bears the financial burden for new construction. Besides, overcrowding increases the likelihood of court-ordered prison and jail population reductions which also add to the ranks of offenders roaming freely about the community (Cavender, 1984). Yet, the general shift from indeterminate to determinate and presumptive sentencing occurring in many jurisdictions is increasing rather than decreasing prisoner populations (Lombardi and Lombardi, 1986; Goodstein and Hepburn, 1985). In 1984, 2,400 top state and local corrections officials were surveyed and they disclosed through interviews that the most important issue facing the criminal justice system today is prison and jail overcrowding (Gettinger, 1984). However, diverting greater numbers of offenders to probation programs expands the limited resources of probation departments and raises officer caseloads to excessive levels. If prosecutors and judges increasingly restrict the use of probation as a bargaining tool for guilty pleas in only the most minor cases, court dockets will quickly become glutted and extremely sluggish in case processing.

It is unfortunate that citizens equate probationer freedom in the community with leniency, whereas incarceration is interpreted as the only "just" punishment. However, growing community participation in selected community-based intensive probation supervision programs is doing much to dispel many of the myths and misconceptions citizens may hold about these programs and the clientele they serve.

The "get tough on crime" movement is currently strong and enjoys a broad constituency. However, some critics warn of the hazards of becoming too punitive through the philosophy that "nothing works but punishment" (Nagel, 1984). A critic of Washington State's presumptive sentencing system, enacted through the Sentencing Reform Act of 1981, has examined the role of community-based corrections as an alternative to confinement. Lovell (1985) interviewed 43 Washington administrators of various criminal justice agencies and personally examined sites of different community programs. He concluded that intensive community supervision should serve as a distinct alternative to total confinement. And he also indicated probation and community corrections officers can best fulfill roles closely associated with services brokerage and practical counseling. However, the therapeutic value of such treatment programs has only limited utility for most offenders. Lovell recommends coercive post-release supervision for periods of limited duration, rather than confining short-term felons habitually to county jails and other local facilities.

In a 1985 survey of 120 chief probation officers, Petersilia (1986c) found that many probation agencies have been expected to implement certain control-oriented programs for probationers. Among the tasks to be performed by these officers are intensive probationer supervision, supervised community service, electronic monitoring, urine testing, and house arrest monitoring. In short, these officers perceive themselves as expected to ensure offender control rather than to perform any type of rehabilitative function.

Recent developments in community-based intensive supervision programs as well as a better-trained and educated force of probation officers and ancillary workers operate to enhance overall program effectiveness in several broad respects. Thus, multiple objectives may be served simultaneously, even though they may appear to be in conflict. The prospects for offender rehabilitation have been greatly improved in recent years through restitution programs, victim compensation provisions, community service, and home confinement with curfew. Probation services are becoming crime control services as well, without seriously diminishing their treatment value or philosophy.

SYSTEM CONSTRAINTS AND "JUST DESERTS": MORAL AND ETHICAL CONSIDERATIONS OF FELONY PROBATION

Ethically, morally, and even legally, there is little, if anything, wrong with felony probation. Many professionals agree it is not necessary that all felons should or need to be incarcerated. The most pressing ethical, moral, or legal issue is *how felony probation is administered*. Who gets felony probation and who doesn't get it? Decision-making by judges is far from perfunctory at either the state or federal level (Champion, 1987a, 1987b, 1988a; Cramer, 1981; Frazier and Bock, 1982). Some evidence shows that in U. S. district courts, being age 60 or over compared with being under 60 is likely to double the chances of convicted felons of being sentenced to probation, regardless of their prior records or current offense severity (Champion, 1988a). Obviously, judges use several other criteria as well as the rationale for sentences they impose.

Besides their personal judgment, statutory penalties, and/or sentencing guidelines (depending on the jurisdiction), judges also rely on prosecutorial recommendations in sentencing felons. In over 90 percent of the cases, the prosecutor "cuts a deal" with the defendant or his/her attorney through plea bargaining which both parties believe to be mutually advantageous. The "deal" may contain a recommendation for probation, split-sentencing, or even an agreement *not to recommend anything at all*. The judge also considers the information contained in presentence investigations, if such reports have been ordered by the court. Often such information, including a recommendation from the probation officer preparing the report, is persuasive.

Among the policy recommendations made by the Rand researchers, risk/needs assessment scales recommended by the National Institute of Corrections (NIC) were strongly endorsed (Petersilia, Turner, Kahan, and Peterson, 1985:388–389). A probation risk-assessment instrument developed by the State of Wisconsin and recognized by the NIC has received much attention and widespread use throughout the United States in recent years (Wright, Clear, and Dickson, 1984). However, the lack of validation of this instrument has led to problems such as inappropriate application in jurisdictions dissimilar to Wisconsin. Wright, Clear, and Dickson (1984) say on the basis of the research they have conducted, that there are serious questions about the state-of-the-art of risk-prediction devices in general, and that sentencing and type of punishment decisions about offenders based on the results of such instruments are premature and should be approached with caution.

Brown and Cochran (1984) have studied the impact of a risk/needs assessment device developed and used by probation officers in the Commonwealth of Massachusetts. On the basis of their examination of 1,963 adults and juveniles who were placed under risk/need supervision in 1982, these researchers demonstrated the need for greater probation officer contacts with high-risk probationers than persons with characteristics placing them in low-risk groups. Offenders with high-risk scores based on an initial assessment and classification were found to be more likely to commit new offenses compared with low-risk offenders.

Some support exists for the use of risk-assessment devices for short-term behavioral forecasts only rather than long-range ones (Morris and Miller, 1985). A recurring problem is overpenalizing persons predicted to be dangerous and who turn out not to be, and underpenalizing those predicted not be dangerous and who commit further harmful offenses. This is the familiar "false positive/false negative" issue, and it causes more than a little concern about the ethics of dangerousness predictors and their utilization by judges, prosecutors, parole boards, and even probation officers. But Morris and Miller (1985) also say that within the range of "deserved" punishment or control, relative predictions of dangerousness may properly influence dispositional decisions by judges and others.

Little evidence exists supporting the view that sentencing offenders more harshly acts as a deterrent to their potential for future criminal conduct. Examining deterrence-oriented articles over the period 1950–1979, DiChiara and Galliher (1984) have discovered mixed and inconclusive results about the relationship between deterrence and punishment. Their research shows a clear and convincing shift from anti-punishment toward justice-related ideologies during the 30-year period, however. Also, they report increased statistical sophistication in deterrence research which has often taken precedence over ethical considerations.

The justice emphasis is revealed in the shift from indeterminate to determinate sentencing in many jurisdictions. But Hamm (1987) and others argue that the justice model as a sentencing guide is a myth that limits our understanding of policies endorsed and practiced by state and federal officials (Smith, 1987). Mandatory minimum and determinate sentencing statutes in jurisdictions such as Illinois have been justified by legislatures on the basis of their predicted deterrent and incapacitative effects. But the results in Illinois thus far have been disappointing. Originally viewed by Illinois authorities as a significant crime control strategy, determinate sentencing has not controlled crime. Rather, it has lessened defendant incentives to plead guilty, thereby increasing the probability of case dismissals or acquittals due to heavy court caseloads. It has also resulted in lower conviction and imprisonment rates (Witayapanyanon, 1987).

Recognition of certain system constraints is an important factor influencing sentencing decisions as well. It is currently logistically impossible to imprison everyone convicted of crimes. Besides, it is simply not practical. However, decisions must be made about offenders, especially serious ones. The fact that considerable uncertainty is associated with predictive devices should not mean that persons involved in the sentencing process should reject them outright. They can be helpful, particularly if they are transformed into probabilities and added to other information used by judges, prosecutors, and probation officers (Wilkins, 1985).

It is highly unlikely that decisions about individual offenders will seriously curtail the incidence and prevalence of crime. Wilkins (1985) suggests that sentencing decisions as well as other crucial choices affecting probationers and parolees involve a *shared responsibility* as the moral alternative. But where prediction instruments are used in criminal justice decision-making, they should be as accurate as possible in the interests of justice (Farrington and Tarling, 1985).

PUBLIC OPINION VERSUS SYSTEM LIMITATIONS

There may be a propensity among corrections officials and legislators to overestimate citizen concern about probation and other correctional programs (Conrad, 1984b). In fact, an examination of a series of polls commencing with the Louis Harris survey for the Joint Commission on Correctional Manpower and Training through the 1982 ABC News Poll of Public Opinion on Crime indicates that some experts are inclined to oversimplify public attitudes about crime and corrections programs (Flanagan and Caulfield, 1984). To claim that the public has become increasingly "punitive" and to base correctional policy on this assumption is simply unwarranted. The public mood is a complex composite of attitudes suggesting social defense as a priority rather than greater offender punishment. Obviously, many gaps presently exist in our knowledge of public opinion about correctional policy, largely because the available data are episodic, highly topical and uneven in quality and breadth as well as overly general (Flanagan and Caulfield, 1984).

Programs demonstrating some tax relief through offender employment in order to compensate victims, defray partially the cost of their rehabilitative assistance, and support their families are more likely to be accepted by the public generally than those services which appear to be primarily custodial (Cullen and Travis, 1984). A middle ground is sought by corrections authorities such that former abuses and misuses of coercion and indeterminacy can be minimized if not entirely eliminated (Nagel, 1984). Intermediate punishments offer this possibility (McCarthy, 1987).

Intermediate punishments including home confinement or house arrest with or without electronic monitoring, community-based probation programs, and intensive supervised probation are among the intermediate alternatives offering punishment as well as a chance for offender rehabilitation. These programs promote offender restitution, victim compensation, and community service as punitive, yet functional, goals. At the same time, a large offender aggregate is diverted from incarceration and overcrowding is alleviated to a degree. But intermediate punishments are not a general panacea for overcrowding. The solution to overcrowding is a task to be shared by several criminal justice agencies.

TECHNOLOGICAL CHANGE AND FELONY PROBATION

This book has explored several increasingly popular options as alternatives to incarceration for felony offenders. The consensus seems to be that *crime control* is the primary consideration in offender sentencing, followed by more punitive and retributionist objectives consistent with "just deserts."

Alternative punishments that happen to be rehabilitative as well appear to be desirable but unnecessary conditions, according to those most critical and apathetic toward probation generally.

Annually, growing numbers of serious felons are placed in probationary programs with control emphases. These are intensive supervised programs such as those currently used by Georgia, New Jersey, and Oregon officials. Largely because of this influx of more dangerous offenders, probation work has become increasingly dangerous (Renzema, 1987). But at the same time, an increasingly educated and more sophisticated probation officer work force is emerging with the capability of meeting the challenges of supervising more dangerous clientele.

One intermediate punishment offering much promise for the future as a major crime control strategy is electronic monitoring (Ball and Lilly, 1985, 1987). Stephens (1987) observes that "twenty-first century corrections can be humane, effective, and efficient. The technology to contain, control, and correct offenders is evolving rapidly, as are ideas to use it successfully and economically. The biggest 'if' in the path of implementation of this new wave of corrections seems to be the one of 'will'—the will of correctional officials to advocate the changes necessary to deliver this utopia." Certainly a significant role will be played in the control of offenders through the establishment and use of effective electronic monitoring systems.

But the matter is more complex than Stephens suggests. It involves more than just the "will" of corrections officials to take effective advantage of corrections technology as it applies to felony probationers. Such systems must be court-approved and validated in much the same way as prediction devices must be tested and validated before using them in sentencing decisions. As has been seen, electronic monitoring experiments are underway in several jurisdictions including Kentucky, California, Oregon, and Florida. Thus far, study results show considerable promise for effective offender surveillance and monitoring.

But legal and ethical hurdles must be overcome before electronic surveillance will be accepted nationally. The privacy issue is a dominant theme among critics of electronic monitoring. The "Big Brother" analogy is revived as a general criticism, and experts are quick to point out the extremely high direct costs incurred initially when commencing an electronic monitoring program. But the greater feasibility and economy of electronic monitoring compared with incarceration in either jails or prisons, particularly coupled with a program involving house arrest, has already been demonstrated in several jurisdictions (Lilly and Ball, 1987; Lilly, Ball, and Wright, 1987; Palm Beach County, Florida Sheriff's Department, 1987). But even persons heavily involved in electronic monitoring research are cautious. In a personal conversation with Bob Lilly in late 1987, he advised that while there is unlimited potential for electronic monitoring in corrections, much more needs to be done to solve various technical problems.

Closely related to the increased use of technology in corrections is the involvement of the private sector in probation, parole, and prison services. Several private agencies currently operate to monitor probationers and juveniles, often with electronic monitoring equipment. But the privatization of corrections, though growing in popularity, is extremely controversial. Is "prison for profit" a viable alternative to save taxpayer dollars? Should private enterprises take over correctional institutions or be permitted to monitor probationers on a national scale?

Corrections officials frequently consider the privatization movement ill-advised and professionally unprepared to take over tasks presently performed by persons trained to deal with serious prisoners, probationers, and/or parolees. Legal questions are raised as well concerning the accountability issue. What policies should govern the accountability of private prison or community-based probation program management? But Janus (1987) says that government authorities and policymakers are turning more and more toward the private sector for solutions to their prison and jail overcrowding problems.

STATE AND FEDERAL TRENDS: A SUMMARY

The trend is toward greater use of probation as an alternative to incarceration at the state and federal levels. Conrad (1984b) says that although probation should not be expected to control crime, community-based corrections can maximize their efficiency by improving their surveillance and investigative functions as well as their general services. Crime itself is seen largely as an economic problem confronting society as a whole rather than one to be solved by corrections agencies. Some persons believe, however, that probation can function to reduce crime by providing effective services and intervention for its clientele (Harris, 1984).

It is anticipated that one result of the new U. S. Sentencing Commission guidelines which went into effect in November 1987 will be a systematic rise in the number of incarcerated offenders. However, it is not expected that federal prisons will bear the brunt of this population increase. Within certain sentencing ranges, the new guidelines provide for either probation or split-sentencing, with short-term commitments to minimum-security institutions or correctional centers.

At the state level, a similar trend should be observed. Contrary to the bleak predictions of corrections pessimists that prisons and jails will be flooded as one result of major sentencing reforms and determinate or presumptive sentencing, the hydraulic nature of the criminal justice system has operated in recent years to adjust for these predicted increases through several options. Some of these options include greater "good time" credits for prison inmates, shock probation, and greater use of diversion in less serious felony cases. Greater use of intermediate punishments also explains why drastic prison population increases have not occurred beyond those normally expected based on projections from previous years.

The future for probation officers suggests that they will be called upon more frequently to "double" as special masters who are expected to implement court-ordered jail and prison improvements (Nielsen, 1984). Probation officers, however, will help to minimize the costly operational expenses associated with prison and jail improvements by being given more important supervisory responsibilities over more offenders. Their roles in community-based intensive supervisory programs will increase in importance during the next few years, and they will be assisted greatly by paraprofessionals and interested community volunteers to perform their tasks more efficiently and productively. They will become more than just "service brokers" for the clientele they manage.

Among other states, Connecticut corrections officials agree that the most fruitful approach to managing larger numbers of convicted felons is not through incarceration, but rather through intensive supervision probation programs. For several years, these officials relied upon imprisonment as the only punitive recourse. Such reliance caused massive prison overcrowding rather rapidly (Citizens Crime Commission of Connecticut, Inc., 1984).

For many jurisdictions, felony probation has become an economic and legal necessity in view of court-ordered prison population reductions and various feasible probation alternatives. The technological and logistical capabilities exist among corrections professionals to ensure that the growth of felony probation can be "controlled" as an effective means of crime control. But the responsibility for crime control is shared by all members of the criminal justice community, not just probation agencies. Communities are also involved, especially as growing numbers of community-based programs are established in many jurisdictions.

Myren (1988:33–34) underscores the fact that considerable interdependence exists among the various criminal justice components, and that the emphasis is indeed shifting away from the narrow concern with incarceration toward a more general "deprivation of liberty" conceptualization. He observes that "policy makers and practitioners are realizing that the specific justice system in which they operate is, in reality, part of a complex system of systems, and that these systems are so interrelated that no one of them can be understood, much less implemented, without consideration of the integral relationships involved" (1988:34). Again, intermediate punishments are consistent with this different concept of deprivation of liberty.

Felony probation will succeed on a national scale if proper control can be effected over an increasingly dangerous probationer population. Necessities for successful programs include feedback mechanisms to spot existing program weaknesses and regular evaluations of the quality of services provided (Travis, 1984). Perhaps the most compelling argument favoring the continuance and eventual increased use of felony probation is implementing a strong system of offender accountability, both to themselves as well as to the persons they have victimized. Victim rights as well as a general concern for equity, fairness, and respect for probationers as human beings must be the primary priorities of any probation program (Harlow, 1984; Fogel, 1984).

Bibliography

Abadinsky, Howard
  1987 PROBATION AND PAROLE: THEORY AND PRACTICE. Englewood Cliffs, NJ: Prentice-Hall.

Aikman, Alex B.
  1986 "Volunteer Lawyer-Judges Bolster Court Resources." NIJ REPORTS, 195:1–6.

Allen, G. Frederick
  1985 "The Probationers Speak: Analysis of the Probationers' Experiences and Attitudes." FEDERAL PROBATION, 49:67–75.

Allen, Harry E., Chris W. Eskridge, Edward J. Latessa, and Gennaro F. Vito
  1985 PROBATION AND PAROLE IN AMERICA. New York, NY: Macmillan.

Allen, Harry E., Edward J. Latessa, and Gennaro F. Vito
  1987 "Corrections in the Year 2000." CORRECTIONS TODAY, 49:92–96.

Allen, Harry E. and Richard P. Seiter
  1976 "The Effectiveness of Halfway Houses: A Reappraisal of a Reappraisal." CHITTY'S LAW JOURNAL, 24:196–200.

Allen, N. E., E. W. Carlson, and E. C. Parks
  1979 CRITICAL ISSUES IN ADULT PROBATION. Washington, DC: Law Enforcement Assistance Administration.

Allied Engineering
  1985 MAINE STATEWIDE CORRECTIONAL MASTER PLAN: FINAL REPORT, VOLUME I: EXECUTIVE SUMMARY OF RECOMMENDATIONS. Gorham, ME: Ehrenkrantz Group.

Allinson, Richard
  1982 "Crisis in the Jails." CORRECTIONS MAGAZINE, 8:18–23.

Alschuler, Albert W.
  1976 "The Trial Judge's Role in Plea Bargaining." COLUMBIA LAW REVIEW, 76:1059–1154.

  1979a "Plea Bargaining and Its History." LAW AND SOCIETY REVIEW, 13:211–245.

  1979b "The Trial Judge's Role in Plea Bargaining." COLUMBIA LAW REVIEW, 76:1059–1154.

American Correctional Association
  1986 "Federal Bureau of Prisons Budget." CORRECTIONS TODAY, 48:42.

Andersen, Brian David, and Kevon Andersen
    1984   PRISONERS OF THE DEEP. San Francisco, CA: Harper & Row.

Anson, Richard H.
    1986   AN EXAMINATION OF AN INTENSIVE PROBATION PROGRAM
           FOR ALCOHOL OFFENDERS. Albany, GA: Department of Criminal Jus-
           tice, Albany State College.

Austin, James
    1986   "Using Early Release to Relieve Prison Crowding: A Dilemma for Public
           Policy." CRIME AND DELINQUENCY, 32:404–502.

Austin, James, and B. Krisberg
    1982   "The Unmet Promise of Alternatives to Incarceration." CRIME AND
           DELINQUENCY, 28:374–409.

Austin, James, Barry Krisberg, and Shirley Melnicoe
    1985   MARIN COUNTY JAIL ALTERNATIVES STUDY: FINAL REPORT.
           San Francisco, CA: National Council on Crime and Delinquency.

Babst, Dean, and John W. Mannering
    1965   "Probation versus Imprisonment for Similar Types of Offenders: A Com-
           parison by Subsequent Violations." JOURNAL OF RESEARCH IN
           CRIME AND DELINQUENCY, 2:60–71.

Ball, Richard A., and J. Robert Lilly
    1985   "Home Incarceration: An International Alternative to Institutional Incar-
           ceration." INTERNATIONAL JOURNAL OF COMPARATIVE AND AP-
           PLIED CRIMINAL JUSTICE, 9:85–97.

    1987   "The Phenomenology of Privacy and the Power of the State: Home Incar-
           ceration with Electronic Monitoring." In CRITICAL ISSUES IN
           CRIMINOLOGY AND CRIMINAL JUSTICE, J. E. Scott and T. Hirschi,
           eds. Beverly Hills, CA: Sage.

Barkdull, Walter L.
    1976   "Probation: Call It Control—and Mean It." FEDERAL PROBATION,
           40:3–8.

Beck, James, and Peter Hoffman
    1976   "Time Served and Release Performance: A Research Note." JOURNAL OF
           RESEARCH IN CRIME AND DELINQUENCY, 13:127–132.

Bell, D.
    1984   "Plea Bargaining: Contradiction or Justice?" In LEGAL ISSUES IN
           CRIMINAL JUSTICE, S. Letman, E. Edwards, and D. Bell, eds. Cincin-
           nati, OH: Pilgrimage Press.

Bennett, Lawrence A.
    1987   "A Reassessment of Intensive Service Probation." In INTERMEDIATE
           PUNISHMENTS: INTENSIVE SUPERVISION, HOME CONFINE-
           MENT, AND ELECTRONIC SURVEILLANCE, B. McCarthy, ed. Mon-
           sey, NY: Criminal Justice Press.

Bennett, Lawrence A., and Max Ziegler
    1975   "Early Discharge: A Suggested Approach to Increased Efficiency in
           Parole." FEDERAL PROBATION, 39:27–30.

Bensinger, Gad J., and Magnus Seng
1986   "Probation in Illinois: Some New Directions." FEDERAL PROBATION, 50:66–73.

Black, Henry Campbell
1979   BLACK'S LAW DICTIONARY. St. Paul, MN: West Publishing Company.

Blackmore, John, and Jane Welsh
1983   "Selective Incapacitation: Sentencing According to Risk." CRIME AND DELINQUENCY, 29:504–528.

Block, Michael K., and William M. Rhodes
1987   "The Impact of the Federal Sentencing Guidelines." NATIONAL INSTITUTE OF JUSTICE NIJ REPORTS, No. 205 (September/October):2–9.

Blumberg, Abraham
1967   CRIMINAL JUSTICE. Chicago, IL: Quadrangle Books.
1979   CRIMINAL JUSTICE: ISSUES AND IRONIES (2d ed.) New York, NY: New Viewpoints.

Blumstein, Alfred
1968   "Free Enterprise Corrections: Using Industry to Make Offenders Economically Viable." PRISON JOURNAL, 48:26–28.
1983   "Selective Incapacitation as a Means of Crime Control." AMERICAN BEHAVIORAL SCIENTIST, 27:87–108.
1984a   "Sentencing Reforms: Impacts and Implications." JUDICATURE, 68:129–135.
1984b   "Sentencing Reforms: Impacts and Implications." JUDICATURE, 68:129–139.

Blumstein, Alfred, and Joseph B. Kadane
1983   "An Approach to the Allocation of Scarce Imprisonment Resources." CRIME AND DELINQUENCY, 29:546–560.

Boland, Barbara, and Brian Forst
1985   "Prosecutors Don't Always Aim to Pleas." FEDERAL PROBATION, 49:10–15.

Boston University
1966   "Educational Counselors: Training for a New Definition of After-Care of Juvenile Parolees." In THE EFFECTIVENESS OF CORRECTIONAL TREATMENTS, D. Lipton et al., eds. New York, NY: Praeger.

Bottomley, A. Keith
1984   "Dilemmas of Parole in a Penal Crisis." THE HOWARD JOURNAL OF CRIMINAL JUSTICE, 23:24–40.

Boudouris, James
1983   THE RECIDIVISM OF RELEASEES FROM THE IOWA STATE PENITENTIARY AT FORT MADISON. Des Moines, IA: Iowa Division of Adult Corrections.
1985   THE REVOCATION PROCESS IN IOWA. Des Moines, IA: Iowa Department of Corrections, Bureau of Data, Research, and Planning.

Brantingham, Patricia L.
  1985 "Sentencing Disparity: An Analysis of Judicial Consistency." JOURNAL
        OF QUANTITATIVE CRIMINOLOGY, 1:281–305.

Brennan, Tim
  1985 OFFENDER CLASSIFICATION AND JAIL CROWDING: EXAMINING
        THE CONNECTION BETWEEN POOR CLASSIFICATION AND THE
        PROBLEM OF JAIL CROWDING. Boulder, CO: HSI, Inc.

Brereton, D., and J. D. Casper
  1981 "Does It Pay to Plead Guilty? Differential Sentencing and the Function of
        Criminal Courts." LAW AND SOCIETY REVIEW, 16:45–70.

Brown, Marjorie E., and Donald Cochran
  1984 EXECUTIVE SUMMARY OF RESEARCH FINDINGS FROM THE
        MASSACHUSETTS   RISK/NEED   CLASSIFICATION   SYSTEM,
        REPORT #5. Boston, MA: Office of the Commissioner of Probation.

Bucknew, D., et al.
  1983 EVALUATION OF THE STRUCTURED PLEA NEGOTIATIONS
        PROJECT: FINDINGS OF AN EXPERIMENT IN THREE CITIES.
        Washington, DC: Inslaw, Inc.

Bureau of Justice Statistics
  1986   CRIME AND JUSTICE FACTS, 1985. Washington, DC: U. S. Government
         Printing Office.

  1987a PROBATION AND PAROLE, 1985. Washington, DC: U. S. Department
         of Justice.

  1987b BJS DATA REPORT, 1986. Washington, DC: U. S. Department of Jus-
         tice, Bureau of Justice Statistics.

  1987c CRIMINAL VICTIMIZATION IN THE UNITED STATES, 1986.
         Washington, DC: U. S. Department of Justice, Bureau of Justice Statistics.

Burkhart, Walter R., and Arthur Sathmary
  1964 "An Evaluation of a Treatment Control Program for Narcotics Offenders,
        Phases 1 and 2." JOURNAL OF RESEARCH IN CRIME AND DELIN-
        QUENCY, 1:47–52.

Burks, David N., and N. Dean DeHeer
  1986 "Jail Suicide Prevention." CORRECTIONS TODAY, 48:52–88.

Byrne, James M.
  1986 "The Control Controversy: A Preliminary Examination of Intensive Proba-
        tion Supervision Programs in the United States." FEDERAL PROBA-
        TION, 50:4–16.

Cahalan, Margaret Werner, and Lee Anne Parsons
  1986 HISTORICAL CORRECTIONS IN THE UNITED STATES, 1850–1984.
        Washington, DC: Bureau of Justice Statistics.

California Adult Authority
  1956 "Special Intensive Parole Unit: Phase I: Fifteen Man Caseload Study." In
        THE EFFECTIVENESS OF CORRECTIONAL TREATMENTS, Lipton et
        al., eds. New York, NY: Praeger.

California Joint Committee for Revision of the Penal Code
  1984   PRISON OVERCROWDING: EMERGENCY MEASURES AND ALTER-
         NATIVE FORMS OF PUNISHMENT. Sacramento, CA: California Joint
         Committee for Revision of the Penal Code.

Call, Jack E.
  1987   "Lower Court Responses to Supreme Court Decisions on Prison and Jail
         Overcrowding." Unpublished paper presented at American Society of
         Criminology, Montreal, Canada (November).

Callanan, Thomas J.
  1986   "Pointers for Probation and Parole Leadership." CORRECTIONS TODAY,
         48:76–81.

Camp, George, and Camille Camp
  1985   CORRECTIONS YEARBOOK. South Salem, NY: Criminal Justice In-
         stitute.

Carlson, Eric, and Evalyn Parks
  1979   CRITICAL ISSUES IN ADULT PROBATION: ISSUES IN PROBATION
         MANAGEMENT. Washington, DC: U. S. Department of Justice.

Casper, Jonathan D., David Brereton, and David Neal
  1981   THE IMPLEMENTATION OF THE CALIFORNIA INDETERMINATE
         SENTENCING LAW. Palto Alto, CA: Stanford University.

Cavanaugh, James L., and Orest E. Wasyliw
  1985   "Treating the Not Guilty by Reason of Insanity Outpatient: A Two-Year
         Study." BULLETIN OF THE AMERICAN ACADEMY OF
         PSYCHIATRY AND THE LAW, 13:407–416.

Cavender, Gray
  1984   "A Critique of Sentencing Reform." JUSTICE QUARTERLY, 1:1–16.

Cecil, Joe S.
  1985   ADMINISTRATION OF JUSTICE IN A LARGE APPELLATE COURT.
         THE NINTH CIRCUIT INNOVATIONS PROJECT. Washington, DC:
         Federal Judicial Center.

Chaiken, Jan M., and Marcia R. Chaiken
  1982   VARIETIES OF CRIMINAL BEHAVIOR. Santa Monica, CA: The Rand
         Corporation.

Champion, Dean J.
  1987a "Probation Trends in Felony Cases: A Look at Prosecutorial Decision-
         Making in Plea Bargaining Agreements." JOURNAL OF CONTEM-
         PORARY CRIMINAL JUSTICE, 3:25–37.

  1987b "Felony Offenders, Plea Bargaining, and Probation: A Case of Extra-
         Legal Exigencies in Sentencing Practices." JUSTICE PROFESSIONAL,
         2:1–18.

  1987c "District Attorneys and Plea Bargaining: An Analysis of the Prosecutorial
         Priorities Influencing Negotiated Guilty Pleas." THE PROSECUTOR,
         20:25–32.

  1988a "The Severity of Sentencing: Do Federal Judges Really Go Easier on
         Elderly Felons?" In OLDER OFFENDERS: PERSPECTIVES IN

CRIMINOLOGY AND CRIMINAL JUSTICE, B. McCarthy, ed. New York, NY: Praeger.

1988b "Private Counsels and Public Defenders: A Look At Weak Cases, Prior Records, and Leniency in Plea Bargaining." JOURNAL OF CRIMINAL JUSTICE, (forthcoming).

1988c "Felony Plea Bargaining and Probation: A Growing Judicial and Prosecutorial Dilemma." JOURNAL OF CRIMINAL JUSTICE, (forthcoming).

Chandler, Henry P.
1987 "Latter-Day Procedures in the Sentencing and Treatment of Offenders in the Federal Courts." FEDERAL PROBATION, 51:10–19.

Chapman, Jack
1987 "Benton County, Oregon: Managing Its Inmate Population." CORRECTIONS TODAY, 49:20–24.

Chown, Bill, and Steven Davis
1986 RECIDIVISM AMONG OFFENDERS INCARCERATED BY THE OKLAHOMA DEPARTMENT OF CORRECTIONS: A SURVIVAL DATA ANALYSIS. Oklahoma City, OK: Oklahoma Department of Corrections.

Church, T. W.
1976 "Plea Bargaining, Concessions, and the Courts: Analysis of a Quasi Experiment." LAW AND SOCIETY REVIEW, 10:377–401.

1979 "In Defense of 'Bargain Justice.' " LAW AND SOCIETY REVIEW, 13:509–525.

Citizens Crime Commission of Connecticut, Inc.
1984 CONNECTICUT INTENSIVE SUPERVISION PROBATION. Hartford, CT: Citizens Crime Commission of Connecticut, Inc.

Clarke, Stevens H.
1987 "Probationer Recidivism and Alternative Classification Strategies." Unpublished paper presented at American Society of Criminology Meetings, Montreal, Canada (November).

Clarke, Stevens H., and Larry Crum
1985 RETURNS TO PRISON IN NORTH CAROLINA. Chapel Hill, NC: Institute of Government, University of North Carolina at Chapel Hill.

Clarke, Stevens H., et al.
1983 NORTH CAROLINA'S DETERMINATE SENTENCING LEGISLATION: AN EVALUATION OF THE FIRST YEAR'S EXPERIENCE. Chapel Hill, NC: Governor's Crime Commission and the NIJ.

Clear, Todd R., Suzanne Flynn, and Carol Shapiro
1987 "Intensive Supervision in Probation: A Comparison of Three Projects." In INTERMEDIATE PUNISHMENTS, Belinda R. McCarthy, ed. Monsey, NY: Criminal Justice Press.

Clear, Todd R., and Vincent O'Leary
1983 CONTROLLING THE OFFENDER IN THE COMMUNITY. Lexington, MA: Lexington Books.

Clements, William
    1987 "Recidivism and Alternative Correctional Treatment." Unpublished paper presented at American Society of Criminology Meetings, Montreal, Canada (November).

Coates, Robert B., Alden D. Miller, and Lloyd E. Ohlin
    1978 DIVERSITY IN A YOUTH CORRECTIONAL SYSTEM: HANDLING DELINQUENTS IN MASSACHUSETTS. Cambridge, MA: Ballinger.

Coffey, Betsy B.
    1986 "Community Corrections: An Equal Partner." CORRECTIONS TODAY, 48:44–46.

Cohen, Fred
    1986 "Corrections Law Developments: The Mentally Disordered Prisoner." CRIMINAL LAW BULLETIN, 22:372–376.

Cohen, Jacqueline
    1983 "Incapacitation as a Strategy for Crime Control: Possibilities and Pitfalls." In CRIME AND JUSTICE: AN ANNUAL REVIEW OF RESEARCH, M. Tonry and N. Morris, eds. Chicago, IL: University of Chicago Press.

Cole, George F., Stanislaw J. Frankowski, and Marc G. Gertz (eds.)
    1987 MAJOR CRIMINAL JUSTICE SYSTEMS: A COMPARATIVE SURVEY (2d ed.). Beverly Hills, CA: Sage.

Connecticut Prison and Jail Overcrowding Commission
    1985 PRISON AND JAIL OVERCROWDING: A REPORT TO THE GOVERNOR AND LEGISLATURE. Hartford, CT: Office of Policy and Management.

Conrad, John P.
    1981 "Where There's Hope, There's Life." in Fogel and Hudson, JUSTICE AS FAIRNESS: PERSPECTIVES ON THE JUSTICE MODEL, Cincinnati, OH: Anderson Publishing Company.

    1984a "Corrections and Its Constituencies." PRISON JOURNAL, 64:47–55.

    1984b "The Redefinition of Probation: Drastic Proposals to Solve an Urgent Problem." In PROBATION AND JUSTICE, P. McAnany, D. Thomson, and D. Fogel, eds. Cambridge, MA: Oelgeschlager, Gunn, and Hain.

    1985 THE DANGEROUS AND THE ENDANGERED. Lexington, MA: Lexington Books.

Contact Center, Inc.
    1986 "1986 Jail Survey Finds Crowding, Litigation." CORRECTIONS COMPENDIUM, 11:12–14.

Conti, Samuel D., et al.
    1985 HUDSON COUNTY (NJ) CIP EVALUATION. North Andover, MA: National Center for State Courts, New England Office.

Corbett, Ronald P., and Ellsworth A. L. Fersch
    1985 "Home as Prison: The Use of House Arrest." FEDERAL PROBATION, 49:13–17.

Corliss, Robert K.
    1983   JAIL POPULATION REDUCTION PROJECT: A STUDY OF THE GE-
           NESSEE COUNTY JAIL POPULATION AND RECOMMENDATIONS
           FOR REDUCING THE POPULATION. Albany, NY: State Commission on
           Corrections.

Cox, George H.
    1977   THE RELATIVE IMPACT OF GEORGIA'S INSTITUTIONAL TRAIN-
           ING PROGRAMS ON THE POST-RELEASE BEHAVIOR OF ADULT
           MALE OFFENDERS. Atlanta, GA: Department of Offender Rehabilita-
           tion.

Cox, Verne C., Garvin McCain, and Paul B. Paulus
    1985   "Prison Crowding and Stress." CORRECTIONS TODAY, 47:12–14.

Craddock, Amy
    1987   "Classification and Correctional Policies: An Empirical Assessment." Un-
           published paper presented at the American Society of Criminology Meet-
           ings, Montreal, Canada (November).

Cramer, James A.
    1981   COURTS AND JUDGES. Beverly Hills, CA: Sage.

Cullen, Francis T., and K. E. Gilbert
    1982   REAFFIRMING REHABILITATION. Cincinnati, OH: Anderson Publish-
           ing Company.

Cullen, Francis T., Gregory A. Clark, and John F. Wozniak
    1985   "Explaining the Get Tough Movement: Can the Public Be Blamed?"
           FEDERAL PROBATION, 49:16–24.

Cullen, Francis T., and Lawrence F. Travis III
    1984   "Work as an Avenue of Prison Reform." NEW ENGLAND JOURNAL ON
           CRIMINAL AND CIVIL CONFINEMENT, 10:45–64.

Cunniff, Mark A.
    1987   SENTENCING OUTCOMES IN 28 FELONY COURTS. Washington, DC:
           National Association of Criminal Justice Planners.

Davis, Steven
    1985   MENTALLY   HANDICAPPED   INMATES   IN   THE   OKLAHOMA
           DEPARTMENT OF CORRECTIONS. Oklahoma City, OK: Oklahoma
           Department of Corrections.

del Carmen, Rolando V.
    1986   POTENTIAL LIABILITIES OF PROBATION AND PAROLE OFFI-
           CERS. Cincinnati, OH: Anderson.

del Carmen, Rolando V., and Harlee Field
    1985   MODEL GUIDELINES FOR PROBATION REVOCATION: A MAN-
           UAL. Washington, DC: National Institute of Corrections.

del Carmen, Rolando V., and F. Trook-White
    1986   LIABILITY ISSUES IN COMMUNITY SERVICE SANCTIONS. Wash-
           ington, DC: U. S. National Institute of Corrections.

del Carmen, Rolando V., and Joseph B. Vaughn
1986 "Legal Issues in the Use of Electronic Surveillance in Probation." FEDERAL PROBATION, 50:60–69.

Delaware Executive Department
1984 RECIDIVISM IN DELAWARE: A STUDY OF REARREST AFTER RELEASE FROM INCARCERATION. Dover, DE: Delaware Executive Department Statistical Analysis Center.

DiChiara, Albert, and John F. Galliher
1984 "Thirty Years of Deterrence Research: Characteristics, Causes, and Consequences." CONTEMPORARY CRISES, 8:243–263.

Ditman, Keith S., and George Crawford
1965 "The Use of Court Probation in the Management of the Alcohol Addict." Los Angeles, CA: Alcoholism Research Clinic, UCLA Health Services Center.

Duffie, Henry C.
1987 "Probation—the Best-Kept Secret Around." CORRECTIONS TODAY, 49:122–127.

Dukakis, Michael S.
1985 A BALANCED PLAN TO END PRISON OVERCROWDING. Boston, MA: Office of the Governor.

Eaglin, James B., and Patricia A. Lombard
1984 "Statistical Risk Prediction as an Aid to Probation Caseload Classification." FEDERAL PROBATION, 48:25–30.

Eisenberg, Michael
1985a RELEASE OUTCOME SERIES: HALFWAY HOUSE RESEARCH. Austin, TX: Texas Board of Pardons and Paroles.

1985b FACTORS ASSOCIATED WITH RECIDIVISM. Austin, TX: Texas Board of Pardons and Paroles.

1985c SELECTIVE EARLY RELEASE: RESEARCH-BASED CRITERIA. Austin, TX: Texas Board of Pardons and Paroles.

1986a "INTENSIVE CASELOAD PILOT PROJECT: RESEARCH REPORT. Austin, TX: Texas Board of Pardons and Paroles.

1986b PAROLE SUPERVISION: ADMINISTRATIVE TIME STUDY. Austin, TX: Texas Board of Pardons and Paroles.

1986c CASE CLASSIFICATION: TWO YEAR OUTCOME STUDY. Austin, TX: Texas Board of Pardons and Paroles.

Ekland-Olson, Sheldon, Dennis M. Barrick, and Lawrence E. Cohen
1983 "Prison Overcrowding and Disciplinary Problems: An Analysis of the Texas Prison System." JOURNAL OF APPLIED BEHAVIORAL SCIENCE, 19:163–176.

Erlinder, C. Peter, and David C. Thomas
  1985   "Prohibiting Prosecutorial Vindictiveness While Protecting Prosecutorial Discretion: Toward a Principled Resolution of a Due Process Dilemma." JOURNAL OF CRIMINAL LAW AND CRIMINOLOGY, 76: 321–328.

Erwin, Billie S.
  1986   "Turning Up the Heat on Probationers in Georgia." FEDERAL PROBATION, 50:17–24.

Eskridge, Chris W.
  1986   "Sentencing Guidelines: To Be or Not To Be?" FEDERAL PROBATION, 50:70–76.

Faine, J. R., and E. W. Bohlander
  1976   SHOCK PROBATION: THE KENTUCKY EXPERIENCE. Bowling Green, KY: 8Western Kentucky University.

Farbstein, Jay, and Richard Goldman
  1983   HOUSING PRETRIAL INMATES: THE COSTS AND BENEFITS OF SINGLE CELLS, MULTIPLE CELLS, AND DORMITORIES. Sacramento, CA: Sacramento County Board of Corrections.

Farr, K. A.
  1984   "Administration and Justice: Maintaining Balance Through an Institutionalized Plea Negotiation Process." CRIMINOLOGY, 22:257–272.

Farrington, David P., and Roger Tarling
  1985   PREDICTION IN CRIMINOLOGY. Albany, NY: State University of New York Press.

Feeley, Malcolm M.
  1983   COURT REFORM ON TRIAL: WHY SIMPLE SOLUTIONS FAIL. New York, NY: Basic Books.

Fichter, Michael, Peter Hirschburg, and Johnny McGaha
  1987   "Increased Felony Probation: Is It the Answer to Overcrowded Prisons?" Unpublished paper presented at the ACJS meetings, St. Louis, Missouri (March).

Finckenauer, J. O.
  1982   SCARED STRAIGHT! AND THE PANACEA PHENOMENON. Englewood Cliffs, NJ: Prentice-Hall.

Finn, Peter
  1984a   "Prison Crowding: The Response of Probation and Parole." CRIME AND DELINQUENCY, 30:141–153.

  1984b   "Judicial Responses to Prison Crowding." JUDICATURE, 67:318–326.

  1985   "Decriminalization of Public Drunkenness: Response of the Health Care System." JOURNAL OF STUDIES ON ALCOHOL, 46:7–23.

Fishman, Robert
  1977   CRIMINAL RECIDIVISM IN NEW YORK CITY: AN EVALUATION OF THE IMPACT OF REHABILITATION AND DIVERSION SERVICES. New York, NY: Praeger.

Flanagan, Timothy, and Susan Caulfield
1984 "Public Opinion and Prison Policy: A Review." PRISON JOURNAL, 64:31–46.

Flango, Victor E., Robert T. Roper, and Mary E. Elsner
1983 THE BUSINESS OF STATE TRIAL COURTS. Williamsburg, VA: National Center for State Courts.

Florida Law Review
1970 "Accepting the Indigent Defendant's Waiver of Counsel and Plea of Guilty." FLORIDA LAW REVIEW, 13:453–459.

Flynn, Leonard E.
1986 "House Arrest: Florida's Alternative Eases Crowding and Tight Budgets." CORRECTIONS TODAY, 48:64–68.

Fogel, David
1975 WE ARE THE LIVING PROOF. Cincinnati, OH: Anderson.

1979 ". . .WE ARE THE LIVING PROOF. . ." Cincinnati, OH: Anderson Publishing Company.

1981 JUSTICE AS FAIRNESS: PERSPECTIVES ON THE JUSTICE MODEL. Cincinnati, OH: Anderson Publishing Company.

1984 "The Emergence of Probation as a Profession in the Service of Public Safety: The Next Ten Years." In PROBATION AND JUSTICE, P. D. McAnany, D. Thomson, D. Fogel, eds. Cambridge, MA: Oelgeschlager, Gunn, and Hain.

Fogel, David, Patrick McAnany, and Doug Thomson
1980 "Probation as the Pursuit of Justice." Paper presented at the American Probation and Parole Association, Niagara Falls, NY, October 29, 1980.

Fogg, Vern
1988 "An Effective Alternative: Colorado's Intensive Supervision." CORRECTIONS TODAY, 50:50–53.

Forst, Brian
1983 "Selective Incapacitation: An Idea Whose Time Has Come?" FEDERAL PROBATION, 46:19–22.

Fox, Vernon
1977 COMMUNITY-BASED CORRECTIONS. Englewood Cliffs, NJ: Prentice-Hall.

Frazier, C. E., and E. W. Bock
1982 "Effects of Court Officials on Sentence Severity: Do Judges Make A Difference?" CRIMINOLOGY, 20:257–272.

French, Laurence
1986 "Treatment Considerations for the Mentally Retarded Inmates." CORRECTIVE AND SOCIAL PSYCHIATRY AND JOURNAL OF BEHAVIOR TECHNOLOGY AND THERAPY, 32:124–129.

Friday, P. C., D. M. Petersen, and H. E. Allen
1973 "Shock Probation: A New Approach to Crime Control." GEORGIA JOURNAL OF CORRECTIONS, 1:1–13.

Gable, Ralph K.
    1986   "Application of Personal Telemonitoring to Current Problems in Correc-
           tions." JOURNAL OF CRIMINAL JUSTICE, 4:167–176.

Gaes, Gerald G.
    1985   "The Effects of Overcrowding in Prison." In CRIME AND JUSTICE: AN
           ANNUAL REVIEW OF RESEARCH, M. Tonry and N. Morris, eds.
           Chicago, IL: University of Chicago Press.

Garry, Eileen
    1984   OPTIONS TO PRISON CROWDING. Washington, DC: National Criminal
           Justice Reference Service, U. S. National Institute of Justice.

Geerken, Michael, and Walter Gove
    1975   "Deterrence: Some Theoretical Considerations." LAW AND SOCIETY
           REVIEW, 9: 497–514.

Gertz, Marc G., and Albert C. Price
    1985   "Variables Influencing Sentencing Severity: Intercourt Differences in Con-
           necticut." JOURNAL OF CRIMINAL JUSTICE, 13:131–139.

Gest, Ted
    1987   "No Bail for the Baddest." U. S. NEWS AND WORLD REPORT, June 8,
           1987.

Gettinger, Stephen
    1984   ASSESSING CRIMINAL JUSTICE NEEDS. Washington, DC: U. S. Na-
           tional Institute of Justice.

Gilsinan, James F.
    1986   "Creating a Reform Environment: A Case Study in Community Corrections
           and Coalition Building." CRIMINAL JUSTICE POLICY REVIEW, 1:328–
           343.

Glaser, Daniel
    1987   "Classification for Risk." In PREDICTION AND CLASSIFICATION, Don
           M. Gottfredson and M. Tonry, eds. Chicago, IL: University of Chicago
           Press.

    1984   "Six Principles and One Precaution for Efficient Sentencing and Correc-
           tion." FEDERAL PROBATION, 48:22–28.

Golbin, James J.
    1983   INTENSIVE SPECIAL SUPERVISION: THE DEVELOPMENT OF A
           PROMISING PROBATION STRATEGY FOR SERIOUS OFFENDERS.
           Suffolk County, NY: Suffolk County Department of Probation.

Goodstein, Lynne, and John Hepburn
    1985   DETERMINATE AND IMPRISONMENT: A FAILURE OF REFORM.
           Cincinnati, OH: Anderson Publishing Company.

Gottfredson, Don M., and K. B. Ballard
    1966   "Differences in Parole Decisions Associated with Decision Makers."
           JOURNAL OF RESEARCH IN CRIME AND DELINQUENCY, 3:112–119.

Gottfredson, Don M., and Michael Tonry
    1987   PREDICTION AND CLASSIFICATION: CRIMINAL JUSTICE DE-
           CISION MAKING. Chicago, IL: University of Chicago Press.

Gottfredson, Michael R., and Don M. Gottfredson
1988   DECISION MAKING IN CRIMINAL JUSTICE: TOWARD THE RA-
TIONAL EXERCISE OF DISCRETION. (2d ed.) New York, NY: Plenum
Press.

Gottfredson, Stephen D.
1984   "Institutional Responses to Prison Overcrowding." NEW YORK UNIVER-
SITY REVIEW OF LAW AND SOCIAL CHANGE, 12:259–273.

Gottfredson, Stephen D., and Don M. Gottfredson
1985   "Screening for Risk among Parolees: Policy, Practice, and Method." In
PREDICTION IN CRIMINOLOGY, D. P. Farrington and R. Tarling, eds.
Albany, NY: SUNY Press.

Gottfredson, Stephen D., and Ralph B. Taylor
1985   PREDICTION   OF   RECIDIVISM: NEIGHBORHOOD   EFFECTS.
Washington, DC: U. S. National Institute of Justice.

1983   THE CORRECTIONAL CRISIS: PRISON POPULATION AND PUBLIC
POLICY. Washington, DC: U. S. Department of Justice, National Institute
of Justice.

Gottlieb, Barbara, and Phillip Rosen
1984   PUBLIC DANGER AS A FACTOR IN PRETRIAL RELEASE: SUM-
MARIES OF STATE DANGER LAWS. Washington, DC: Toborg Associates.

Gray, Richard
1986   "Probation: An Exploration in Meaning." FEDERAL PROBATION,
50:26–31.

Great Britain Home Office
1964   THE SENTENCE OF THE COURT: A HANDBOOK FOR COURTS ON
THE TREATMENT OF OFFENDERS. London, UK: Her Majesty's
Stationery Office.

Greenberg, David F.
1975   "The Incapacitative Effect of Imprisonment: Some Estimates." LAW AND
SOCIETY, 2:541–580.

Greenfeld, Lawrence A.
1985   EXAMINING RECIDIVISM. Washington, DC: Bureau of Justice Statistics.

1986a   PRISONERS IN 1985. Washington, DC: U. S. Department of Justice,
Bureau of Justice Statistics.

1986b   PROBATION AND PAROLE, 1984. Washington, DC: U. S. Department
of Justice, Bureau of Justice Statistics.

1987   PROBATION AND PAROLE, 1985. Washington, DC: U. S. Department
of Justice, Bureau of Justice Statistics.

Greenwood, Peter W.
1982   SELECTIVE INCAPACITATION. Santa Monica, CA: The Rand Corporation.

Guttman, Evelyn S.
  1961 "MMPI Measured Changes in Treated and Untreated Youth Authority
        Wards Judged in Need of Psychiatric Treatment." Sacramento, CA:
        California Youth Authority.
  1963 "Effects of Short-Term Psychiatric Treatment on Boys in Two California
        Youth Authority Institutions." Research Report No. 36. Sacramento, CA:
        California Youth Authority.

Hackett, Judith C., et al.
  1987 CONTRACTING FOR THE OPERATION OF PRISONS AND JAILS.
        Washington, DC: National Institute of Justice.

Hagan, J., and K. Bumiller
  1983 "Making Sense of Sentencing: A Review and Critique of Sentencing
        Research." In RESEARCH IN SENTENCING, A. Blumstein, ed.
        Washington, DC: National Academy of Science.

Hall, Andy
  1987 SYSTEMWIDE STRATEGIES TO ALLEVIATE JAIL OVERCROWD-
        ING. Washington, DC: National Institute of Justice.

Hall, Jane N.
  1985 "Identifying and Serving Mentally Retarded Inmates." JOURNAL OF
        PRISON AND JAIL HEALTH, 5:29–38.

Hamm, Mark S.
  1987 "Determinate Sentencing in Indiana: An Analysis of the Impact of the Jus-
        tice Model." Unpublished paper presented at American Society of
        Criminology Meetings, Montreal, Canada (November).

Hammrock, Edward R., and Anne Marie Santangelo
  1985 "Sentencing Disaster? Will Determinate Sentencing Do The Job?" COR-
        RECTIONS TODAY, 47:91–93.

Hansen, Hans A., and Karl Teilmann
  1954 "A Treatment of Criminal Alcoholics in Denmark." QUARTERLY JOUR-
        NAL OF STUDIES ON ALCOHOL, 25:246–287.

Harlow, Nora
  1984 "Implementing the Justice Model in Probation." In PROBATION AND
        JUSTICE, P. D. McAnany, D. Thomson, and D. Fogel, eds. Cambridge,
        MA: Oelgeschlager, Gunn, and Hain.

Harris, M. Kay
  1984 "Rethinking Probation in the Context of the Justice Model." In PROBA-
        TION AND JUSTICE, P. McAnany, D. Thomson, and D. Fogel (eds).
        Cambridge, MA: Oelgeschlager, Gunn, and Hain.

Hartke, Kenneth L.
  1984 "Work Units in Theory and Practice." CORRECTIONS TODAY,
        46:66–68.

Hawkes, Mary Ann
  1985 "Rhode Island: A Case Study in Compliance." CORRECTIONS TODAY,
        47:167–183.

Herrington, Lois Haight
  1986 "Dollars and Sense: The Value of Victim Restitution." CORRECTIONS
         TODAY, 48:156–160.

Hester, Thomas
  1987 PROBATION AND PAROLE, 1986. Washington, DC: U. S. Department
         of Justice, Bureau of Justice Statistics.

Heuser, James Paul
  1985 TRAFFIC AND NON-TRAFFIC OFFENDERS INCARCERATED IN
         AND RELEASED FROM AN OREGON STATE CORRECTIONAL IN-
         STITUTION IN 1980–1981. Salem, OR: Oregon Crime Analysis Center.

Hoffman, Peter B.
  1983 "Screening for Risk: A Revised Salient Factor Score, (SFS 81)." JOURNAL
         OF CRIMINAL JUSTICE, 11:539–547.

Hoffman, Peter B., and Sheldon Adelberg
  1980 "The Salient Factor Score: A Nontechnical Overview." FEDERAL
         PROBATION, 44:44–52.

Hoffman, Peter B., and James L. Beck
  1985 "Recidivism among Released Federal Prisoners: Salient Factor Score and
         Five-Year Follow-Up." CRIMINAL JUSTICE AND BEHAVIOR, 12:501–
         507.

Hoffman, Peter B., and Barbara Stone-Meierhoefer
  1979 "Post-Release Arrest Experiences of Federal Prisoners: A Six-Year Fol-
         lowup." JOURNAL OF CRIMINAL JUSTICE, 7:193–216.

  1980 "Reporting Recidivism Rates: The Criterion and Follow-up Issues." JOUR-
         NAL OF CRIMINAL JUSTICE, 8:53–60.

Hood, Roger
  1966 HOMELESS BORSTAL BOYS: A STUDY OF THEIR AFTER-CARE
         AND AFTER-CONDUCT. London, UK: Bell and Sons.

Hopkins, Andrew
  1976 "Imprisonment and Recidivism: A Quasi-Experimental Study." JOURNAL
         OF RESEARCH IN CRIME AND DELINQUENCY, 13:13–32.

Houk, Julie M.
  1984 "Electronic Monitoring of Probationers: A Step Toward Big Brother?"
         GOLDEN GATE UNIVERSITY LAW REVIEW, 14:431–446.

Huggins, M. Wayne
  1986 "Urban Jails: Facing the Future." CORRECTIONS TODAY, 48:114–120.
         Illinois Governor's Task Force on Prison Crowding.

  1983 RECOMMENDATIONS. Springfield, IL: Governor's Task Force on
         Prison Crowding.

Immarigeon, Russ
  1987 "Privatizing Adult Imprisonment in the U. S.: A Bibliography."
         CRIMINAL JUSTICE ABSTRACTS (March):123–139.

Inciardi, James
    1971   "Use of Parole Prediction with Institutionalized Narcotics Addicts." JOUR-
           NAL OF RESEARCH IN CRIME AND DELINQUENCY, 8:65–73.

Innes, Christopher A.
    1986   POPULATION DENSITY IN STATE PRISONS. Washington, DC: Bureau
           of Justice Statistics.

Jacobson, Frank, and Eugene McGee
    1965   "Englewood Project: Re-Education: A Radical Correction of Incarcerated
           Delinquents." Englewood, CO: Federal Correctional Institution.

Jamieson, Katherine M., and Timothy J. Flanagan (eds.)
    1987   SOURCEBOOK OF CRIMINAL JUSTICE STATISTICS—1986. Wash-
           ington, DC: U. S. Department of Justice, Bureau of Justice Statistics.

Janus, Michael G.
    1985   "Selective Incapacitation: Have We Tried It? Does It Work?" JOURNAL
           OF CRIMINAL JUSTICE, 13:117–129.

    1987   "Privatization of Corrections: Symbolic and Public Policy Issues." Un-
           published paper presented at the American Society of Criminology Meet-
           ings, Montreal, Canada (November).

Jaros, D., and R. I. Mendelsohn
    1967   "The Judicial Role and Sentencing Behavior." MIDWEST JOURNAL OF
           POLITICAL SCIENCE, 11:471–488.

Johnson, Fred R.
    1928   PROBATION FOR JUVENILES AND ADULTS. New York, NY: Cen-
           tury.

Johnson, Judith, Keith McKeown, and Roberta James
    1984   REMOVING THE CHRONICALLY MENTALLY ILL FROM JAIL:
           CASE STUDIES OF COLLABORATION BETWEEN LOCAL
           CRIMINAL JUSTICE AND MENTAL HEALTH SYSTEMS. Washington,
           DC: National Coalition for Jail Reform.

Judicature
    1984   "Comment." JUDICATURE, 68:161–171, 181–189.

Kantrowitz, Nathan
    1977   "How to Shorten the Follow-up Period in Parole Studies." JOURNAL OF
           RESEARCH IN CRIME AND DELINQUENCY, 14:222–236.

Kapsch, Stefan J., and Diane M. Luther
    1985   PUNISHMENT AND RISK MANAGEMENT AS AN OREGON SANC-
           TIONING MODEL. Portland, OR: Oregon Prison Overerowding Project.

Kastenmeier, Robert W.
    1986   "Corrections and Crowding: A Legislator's Perspective." CORRECTIONS
           TODAY, 48:38–42.

Kawaguchi, Ray M., and Leon M. Siff
    1967   "An Analysis of Intensive Probation Services—Phase II." Los Angeles,
           CA: Research Report No. 29, Los Angeles County Probation Department.

Kennedy, Daniel B.
1984   "A Theory of Suicide While in Police Custody." JOURNAL OF POLICE SCIENCE AND ADMINISTRATION, 12:191–200.

Kerle, Kenneth E., and Francis R. Force
1982   THE STATE OF OUR NATION'S JAILS, 1982. Washington, DC: National Sheriff's Association.

Kipnis, K.
1976   "Criminal Justice and the Negotiated Plea." ETHICS, 86:93–106.

Kirp, David L., Mark G. Yudof, and Marlene S. Franks
1986   GENDER JUSTICE. Chicago, IL: University of Chicago Press.

Kitchener, Howard, Annesley K. Schmidt, and Daniel Glaser
1977   "The Deterrent Effect of Capital Punishment: An Assessment of the Estimates." In DETERRENCE AND INCAPACITATION, A. Blumstein, J. Cohen, and D. Nagin, eds. Washington, DC: National Academy of Sciences.

Kizziah, Carol A.
1984   THE STATE OF THE JAILS IN CALIFORNIA, REPORT #1, OVERCROWDING IN THE JAILS. Sacramento, CA: California Board of Corrections.

Kleck, G.
1981   "Racial Discrimination in Criminal Sentencing: A Critique and Evaluation of Evidence with Additional Evidence on the Death Penalty." AMERICAN SOCIOLOGICAL REVIEW, 46:783–805.

Kline, Susan
1987   JAIL INMATES, 1986. Washington, DC: Bureau of Justice Statistics.

Knoxville News-Sentinel
1987   "Woman, 70, Gets Six Years in Sevierville, Tennessee." September 23, 1987, A20.

Kusuda, Paul H., and Dean V. Babst
1964   "Wisconsin Base Expectancies for Adult Male Parolees: Preliminary Findings on the Relationship of Training, Work and Institutional Adjustment." Milwaukee, WI: Department of Public Welfare.

Lane, Michael P.
1986   "A Case for Early Release." CRIME AND DELINQUENCY, 32:399–403.

Langbein, J. H.
1979   "Understanding the Short History of Plea Bargaining." LAW AND SOCIETY REVIEW, 13:261-272.

Latessa, Edward J.
1983   THE FIFTH EVALUATION OF THE LUCAS COUNTY ADULT PROBATION DEPARTMENT'S INCARCERATION DIVERSION UNIT. Cincinnati, OH: University of Cincinnati Criminal Justice Program.

1986   "The Cost Effectiveness of Intensive Supervision." FEDERAL PROBATION, 50:70–74.

1987 "Intensive Supervision: An Eight Year Follow-Up Evaluation." Paper presented at the Academy of Criminal Justice Sciences Meetings, St. Louis, MO.

Latessa, Edward, and Harry Allen
1982a "Halfway Houses and Parole: A National Assessment." JOURNAL OF CRIMINAL JUSTICE, 10:153–163.

Latessa, Edward J., and Harry E. Allen
1982b MANAGEMENT ISSUES IN PAROLE. San Jose, CA: San Jose State University Foundation.

Latessa, Edward J., Lawrence F. Travis, and Harry E. Allen
1983 "Volunteers and Paraprofessionals in Parole: Current Practices." JOURNAL OF OFFENDER COUNSELING SERVICES AND REHABILITATION, 8:91–106.

Lauen, Roger J.
1984 "Community Corrections? Not in My Neighborhood!— Developing Legitimacy." CORRECTIONS TODAY, 46:117–130.

Lawrence, Richard A.
1984 "Professionals or Judicial Civil Servants? An Examination of the Probation Officer's Role." FEDERAL PROBATION, 48:14–21.

1985 "Community-Based Corrections: Are They Effective?" CORRECTIONS TODAY, 47:108–112.

LeClair, Daniel P.
1985 THE EFFECT OF COMMUNITY REINTEGRATION ON RATES OF RECIDIVISM: A STATISTICAL OVERVIEW OF DATA FOR THE YEARS 1971–1982. Boston, MA: Massachusetts Department of Corrections.

Lemert, Edwin M.
1951 SOCIAL PATHOLOGY. New York, NY: McGraw-Hill.

1967 HUMAN DEVIANCE, SOCIAL PROBLEMS, AND SOCIAL CONTROL. Englewood Cliffs, NJ: Prentice-Hall.

1974 "Beyond Mead: The Societal Reaction to Deviance." SOCIAL PROBLEMS, 21:458–468.

Library Information Specialists, Inc.
1983a ALTERNATIVE FINANCING OF JAIL CONSTRUCTION. Boulder, CO: Information Center, U.S. National Institute of Corrections.

1983b SUICIDE IN JAILS. Boulder, CO: Information Center, U. S. National Institute of Corrections.

Lilly, J. Robert, and Richard A. Ball
1987 "A Brief History of House Arrest and Electronic Monitoring." NORTHERN KENTUCKY LAW REVIEW, 3:343–374.

Lilly, J. Robert, Richard A. Ball, and Jennifer Wright
1987 "Home Incarceration with Electronic Monitoring in Kenton County, Kentucky: An Evaluation." In INTERMEDIATE PUNISHMENTS, B. McCarthy, ed. Monsey, NY: Criminal Justice Press.

Lindner, Charles, and Margaret R. Savarese
1984 "The Evolution of Probation: University Settlement and the Beginning of Statutory Probation in New York City." FEDERAL PROBATION, 48:3–12.

Lindquist, Charles A.
1984 "The Private Sector in Corrections: Contracting Probation Services from Community Organizations." FEDERAL PROBATION, 48:58–64.

Logan, Dianne
1986 "Harris County Juvenile Probation Department: Growing Services, Shrinking Budget." CORRECTIONS TODAY, 48:22–26.

Lohman, Joseph D.
1967 "The Intensive Supervision Caseloads: A Preliminary Evaluation." Berkeley, CA: School of Criminology, University of California at Berkeley.

Lohman, Joseph D., et al.
1967 THE INTENSIVE SUPERVISION CASELOAD: A PRELIMINARY EVALUATION: THE SAN FRANCISCO PROJECT SERIES REPORT #11. Berkeley, CA: University of California at Berkeley.

Lombardi, John H., and Donna M. Lombardi
1986 "Objective Criteria: More Harm Than Good?" CORRECTIONS TODAY, 48:86–87.

Lombardo, Lucien X.
1981 GUARDS IMPRISONED. New York, NY: Elsevier.

Lovell, David G.
1985 SENTENCING REFORM AND THE TREATMENT OF OFFENDERS. Olympia, WA: Washington Council on Crime and Delinquency.

Lurigio, Arthur J.
1987 "The Perceptions and Attitudes of Judges and Attorneys Toward Intensive Supervised Probation." FEDERAL PROBATION, 51:16–24.

Mahoney, Barry, Larry L. Sipes, and Jeanne A. Ito
1985 IMPLEMENTING DELAY REDUCTION AND DELAY PREVENTION PROGRAMS IN URBAN TRIAL COURTS: PRELIMINARY FINDINGS FROM CURRENT RESEARCH. Williamsburg, VA: National Center for State Courts.

Maltz, Michael D.
1984 RECIDIVISM. Orlando, FL: Academic Press.

Martin, Steven J., and Sheldon Ekland-Olson
1987 TEXAS PRISONS: THE WALLS CAME TUMBLING DOWN. Austin, TX: Texas Monthly Press, Inc.

Martinez, Pablo, and Antonio Fabelo
1985 TEXAS CORRECTIONAL SYSTEM: GROWTH AND POLICY ALTERNATIVES. Austin, TX: Texas Criminal Justice Policy Council.

Martinson, Robert
1974 "What Works? Questions and Answers about Prison Reform." THE PUBLIC INTEREST, 35:22–54.

Martinson, Robert, and J. Wilks
   1977   "Save Parole Supervision." FEDERAL PROBATION, 41:23–27. Maryland
          Criminal Justice Coordinating Council.

   1984   REPORT. Towson, MD: Criminal Justice Coordinating Council, Commit-
          tee on Prison Overcrowding.

Mather, L. M.
   1979   PLEA BARGAINING OR TRIAL? THE PROCESS OF CRIMINAL CASE
          DISPOSITION. Lexington, MA: Lexington Press.

Maynard, Douglas W.
   1984   INSIDE PLEA BARGAINING: THE LANGUAGE OF NEGOTIATION.
          New York, NY: Plenum.

McAnany, Patrick D.
   1984   "Mission and Justice: Clarifying Probation's Legal Context." In PROBA-
          TION AND JUSTICE, P. McAnany, D. Thomson, D. Fogel, eds.
          Cambridge, MA: Oelgeschlager, Gunn, and Hain.

McAnany, Patrick D., Doug Thomson, and David Fogel (eds.)
   1984   PROBATION AND JUSTICE: RECONSIDERATION OF A MISSION.
          Cambridge, MA: Oelgeschlager, Gunn, and Hain.

McCarthy, Belinda R.
   1985   "An Analysis of Detention." JUVENILE AND FAMILY COURT JOUR-
          NAL, 36:49–50.

McCarthy, Belinda R. (ed.)
   1987   INTERMEDIATE   PUNISHMENTS: INTENSIVE   SUPERVISION,
          HOME CONFINEMENT, AND ELECTRONIC SURVEILLANCE. Mon-
          sey, NY: Willow Tree Press.

   1988   OLDER OFFENDERS: PERSPECTIVES IN CRIMINOLOGY AND
          CRIMINAL JUSTICE. New York, NY: Praeger.

McCarthy, Belinda R., and Charles A. Lindquist
   1985a "Ambiguity and Conflict in Sentencing Research: Partial Resolution
          Through Crime-Specific Analysis." JOURNAL OF CRIMINAL JUSTICE,
          13:155–169.

   1985b "Certainty of Punishment and Sentence Mitigation in Plea Behavior."
          JUSTICE QUARTERLY, 2:363–383.

McCarthy, Belinda R., and Bernard J. McCarthy
   1984   COMMUNITY-BASED CORRECTIONS. Monterey, CA: Brooks/Cole
          Publishing Company.

McDonald, William F.
   1985   PLEA BARGAINING: CRITICAL ISSUES AND COMMON PRAC-
          TICES. Washington, DC: U. S. Department of Justice, National Institute of
          Justice.

McEachern, Alexander W., and Edward M. Taylor
   1967   THE EFFECTS OF PROBATION. Los Angeles, CA: Youth Studies
          Center, University of Southern California.

McGillis, Daniel
1987 THE FEDERAL CIVIL JUSTICE SYSTEM. Washington, DC: U. S. Department of Justice, Bureau of Justice Statistics.

McShane, Marilyn
1985 THE EFFECT OF DETAINER ON PRISON OVERCROWDING. Huntsville, TX: Criminal Justice Center, Sam Houston State University.

Meador, Daniel J.
1983 "Straightening Out Federal Review of State Criminal Cases." OHIO STATE LAW JOURNAL, 44:273–285.

Meeker, James W.
1984 "Criminal Appeals Over the Last 100 Years: Are the Odds of Winning Increasing?" JOURNAL OF CRIMINAL JUSTICE, 22:551–571.

Meierhoefer, Barbara S., and Eric V. Armen
1985 THE CASELOAD EXPERIENCES OF THE DISTRICT COURTS FROM 1972 TO 1983: A PRELIMINARY ANALYSIS. Washington, D C : U.S. Federal Judicial Center.

Miller, Dallas H.
1984a A SURVEY OF RECIDIVISM RESEARCH IN THE UNITED STATES AND CANADA. Boston, MA: Massachusetts Department of Correction.

1984b A DESCRIPTION OF WORK RELEASE JOB PLACEMENTS FROM MASSACHUSETTS STATE CORRECTIONAL FACILITIES DURING 1982. Boston, MA: Massachusetts Department of Corrections.

Miller, Eugene, and Charles W. Cansfield
1987 "Rebuilding the Past: Renovation is a Viable Option." CORRECTIONS TODAY, 49:22–24.

Miller, H. S., James A. Cramer, and W. F. McDonald
1978 PLEA BARGAINING IN THE UNITED STATES: PHASE I REPORT. Washington, DC: U. S. Government Printing Office.

Minnesota Sentencing Guidelines Commission
1984 THE IMPACT OF THE MINNESOTA SENTENCING GUIDELINES: THREE YEAR EVALUATION. St. Paul, MN: Minnesota Sentencing Guidelines Commission.

Monahan, John
1981a PREDICTING VIOLENT BEHAVIOR. Beverly Hills, CA: Sage.

1981b THE CLINICAL PREDICTION OF VIOLENT BEHAVIOR. Rockville, MD: U. S. Department of Health and Human Services.

1984 "The Prediction of Violent Behavior: Toward a Second Generation of Theory and Policy." AMERICAN JOURNAL OF PSYCHIATRY, 141:10–15.

Moore, Charles A.
1987 "Can Sentencing Reform Work? A Four-Year Evaluation of Determinate Sentencing in Minnesota." Unpublished paper presented at the ASC Meetings, Montreal, Canada (November).

Moran, T. Kenneth, and Charles Lindner
  1985 "Probation and the Hi-Technology Revolution: Is A Re- Conceptualization of the Traditional Officer Role Inevitable?" CRIMINAL JUSTICE REVIEW, 10:25–32.

Morelli, Richard S.
  1986 "The Effects of Five-year Mandatory Sentencing in Pennsylvania." JUSTICE ANALYST, 1:1–8.

Moriarty, Laura J.
  1987 "Ethical Issues of Selective Incapacitation." CRIMINAL JUSTICE RESEARCH BULLETIN, 3:1–5.

Morris, Norval
  1974 THE FUTURE OF IMPRISONMENT. Chicago, IL: University of Chicago Press.

  1984 "On Dangerousness in the Judicial Process." THE RECORD OF THE ASSOCIATION OF THE BAR OF THE CITY OF NEW YORK, 39:102–128.

Morris, Norval, and Marc Miller
  1985 "Predictions of Dangerousness." In CRIME AND JUSTICE: AN ANNUAL REVIEW OF RESEARCH, M. Tonry and N. Morris, eds. Chicago, IL: University of Chicago Press.

  1987 PREDICTIONS OF DANGEROUSNESS IN THE CRIMINAL LAW. Washington, DC: National Institute of Justice.

Moseley, William, and Margaret Gerould
  1975 "Sex and Parole: A Comparison of Male and Female Parolees." JOURNAL OF CRIMINAL JUSTICE, 3:47–58.

Mullen, Joan
  1985 CORRECTIONS AND THE PRIVATE SECTOR. Washington, DC: National Institute of Justice.

Murphy, Joseph P.
  1987 "Some Axioms for Probation Officers." FEDERAL PROBATION, 51:20–23.

Murray, Charles A., and Louis A. Cox, Jr.
  1979 JUVENILE CORRECTIONS AND THE CHRONIC DELINQUENT. Washington, DC: American Institutes for Research.

Myren, Richard A.
  1988 LAW AND JUSTICE: AN INTRODUCTION. Monterey, CA: Brooks/Cole.

Nagel, S. S.
  1982 "Discretion in the Criminal Justice System: Analyzing, Channeling, Reducing, and Controlling It." EMORY LAW REVIEW, 31:603–633.

Nagel, William G.
  1984 "Corrections and Punishment." CORRECTIONS TODAY, 46:32–62.

Nardulli, Peter F., Roy B. Fleming, and James Eisenstein
  1985 "Criminal Courts and Bureaucratic Justice: Concessions and Consensus in
        the Guilty Plea Process." JOURNAL OF CRIMINAL LAW AND
        CRIMINOLOGY, 76:1103–1131.

Narloch, R. P., S. Adams, and K. J. Jenkins
  1959 "Characteristics and Parole Performance of California Youth Authority
        Early Releases." Sacramento, CA: California Youth Authority, Research
        Report No. 7.

National Council on Crime and Delinquency
  1973 "The Nondangerous Offender Should Not Be Imprisoned: A Policy State-
        ment." CRIME AND DELINQUENCY, 19:449–460.

National Institute of Justice
  1973 COMMUNITY CORRECTIONAL CENTERS. Washington, DC: U. S.
        Government Printing Office.

  1986 THE FEDERAL CIVIL JUSTICE SYSTEM. Washington, DC: U. S.
        Government Printing Office.

  1987 BJS DATA REPORT, 1986. Washington, DC: Bureau of Justice Statistics.

Nelson, Paul L.
  1985 "Marketable Skills." CORRECTIONS TODAY, 47:70.

New Jersey Governor's Management Improvement Plan
  1983 DEPARTMENT OF CORRECTIONS: THE CORRECTIONAL SYSTEM,
        STRATEGIC ISSUES AND ALTERNATIVES. Trenton, NJ: Governor's
        Management Improvement Plan.

Newman, Graeme
  1983 JUST AND PAINFUL. New York, NY: Macmillan.

Nielsen, Dennis W.
  1984 "U. S. Probation Officers as Jail Monitors: A New Responsibility on the
        Horizon?" FEDERAL PROBATION, 48:29–33.

Oklahoma State Board of Corrections
  1984 RECOMMENDATIONS FOR CONTROLLING PRISON POPULATION
        GROWTH: A RESPONSE TO HB 1483. Oklahoma City, OK: Oklahoma
        Department of Corrections.

O'Leary, Vincent, and Todd Clear
  1984 DIRECTIONS FOR COMMUNITY CORRECTIONS IN THE 1990'S.
        Washington, DC: U. S. Department of Justice, National Institute of Correc-
        tions.

Oregon Crime Analysis Center
  1984 RECIDIVISM OF RELEASEES FROM OREGON CORRECTIONS IN-
        STITUTIONS. Salem, OR: Oregon Crime Analysis Center.

Orsagh, Thomas, and Mary Ellen Marsden
  1985 "What Works When: Rational-Choice Theory and Offender Rehabilita-
        tion." JOURNAL OF CRIMINAL JUSTICE, 13:269–277.

Orsagh, Thomas, and Mary Ellen Marsden
    1987   "Inmates + Appropriate Programs = Effective Rehabilitation." CORREC-
           TIONS TODAY, 49:174–180.

Padgett, John F.
    1985   "The Emergent Organization of Plea Bargaining." AMERICAN JOURNAL
           OF SOCIOLOGY, 90:753–800.

Palm Beach County, Florida Sheriff's Department
    1987   "Palm Beach County's In-House Arrest Work Release Program." In IN-
           TERMEDIATE PUNISHMENTS, Belinda McCarthy, ed. Monsey, NY:
           Willow Tree Press.

Parisi, N.
    1980   "Combining Incarceration and Probation." FEDERAL PROBATION,
           44:3–12.

Paulus, Paul, Garvin McCain, and Verne Cox
    1985   "The Effects of Crowding in Prisons and Jails." In REACTIONS TO
           CRIME: THE PUBLIC, THE POLICE, COURTS, AND PRISONS, D. Far-
           rington and J. Gunn, eds. New York, NY: Wiley.

Pearson, Frank S.
    1985   "New Jersey's Intensive Supervision Program: A Progress Report."
           CRIME AND DELINQUENCY, 31:393–410.

Pearson, Frank S., and Daniel B. Bibel
    1986   "New Jersey's Intensive Supervision Program: What is it Like? How is it
           Working?" FEDERAL PROBATION, 50:25–31.

Pennsylvania Commission on Crime and Delinquency
    1985   A STRATEGY TO ALLEVIATE OVERCROWDING IN PENNSYL-
           VANIA'S PRISONS AND JAILS. Harrisburg, PA: Commission on Crime
           and Delinquency, Prison and Jail Overcrowding Task Force.

Petersilia, Joan M.
    1983   RACIAL DISPARITIES IN THE CRIMINAL JUSTICE SYSTEM.
           Washington, DC: U. S. Department of Justice, National Institute of Correc-
           tions.

    1985a "Rand's Research: Felony Probation." CORRECTIONS TODAY, 47:36–
           38.

    1985b "Rand's Research: A Closer Look." CORRECTIONS TODAY, 47:37–40.

    1985c "Community Supervision: Trends and Critical Issues." CRIME AND
           DELINQUENCY, 31: 86–95.

    1985d PROBATION AND FELONY OFFENDERS. Washington, DC: Bureau of
           Justice Statistics.

    1986a EXPLORING THE OPTION OF HOUSE ARREST. Santa Monica, CA:
           The Rand Corporation.

    1986b TAKING STOCK OF PROBATION REFORM. Santa Monica, CA: The
           Rand Corporation.

    1986c "Exploring the Option of House Arrest." FEDERAL PROBATION,
           50:50–55.

1987   EXPANDING OPTIONS FOR CRIMINAL SENTENCING. Santa Monica, CA: The Rand Corporation.

Petersilia, Joan M., and Susan Turner
1987   "Guideline-based Justice: Prediction and Racial Minorities." In PREDIC-TION AND CLASSIFICATION, D. M. Gottfredson and M. Tonry, eds. Chicago, IL: University of Chicago Press.

Petersilia, Joan M., Susan Turner, James Kahan, and Joyce Peterson
1985   GRANTING FELONS PROBATION: PUBLIC RISKS AND ALTERNA-TIVES. Santa Monica, CA: The Rand Corporation.

Petersilia, Joan M., Susan Turner, and Joyce Peterson
1986   PRISON VERSUS PROBATION IN CALIFORNIA: IMPLICATIONS FOR CRIME AND OFFENDER RECIDIVISM. Santa Monica, CA: The Rand Corporation.

Phillips, Barry
1983   OVERCROWDING IN MASSACHUSETTS PRISONS: SOURCES AND SOLUTIONS. Boston, MA: Massachusetts Joint Legislative Committee on Human Services and Elderly Affairs.

Piper, Elisabeth S.
1985   "Violent Recidivism and Chronicity in the 1958 Philadelphia Cohort." JOURNAL OF QUANTITATIVE CRIMINOLOGY, 1:319–344.

Pope, Peter B.
1986   "How Unreliable Factfinding Can Undermine Sentencing." YALE LAW REVIEW, 95: 1258–1282.

Price, Albert C., et al.
1983   "Judicial Discretion and Jail Overcrowding." JUSTICE SYSTEM JOUR-NAL, 8:222–238.

Probation Association
1939   JOHN AUGUSTUS: FIRST PROBATION OFFICER. New York, NY: Probation Association.

Pugh, Michael, and Mark Kunkel
1986   "The Mentally Retarded Offenders Program of the Texas Department of Corrections." PRISON JOURNAL, 66:39–51.

Quinlan, J. Michael
1987   "The New Man at the Top." CORRECTIONS TODAY,49:16–20.

Renzema, Marc
1987   "An Analysis of the Dangerousness of Probation and Parole Work." Un-published paper presented at the American Society of Criminology Meet-ings, Montreal, Canada (November).

Rhode Island Governor's Commission
1984   RHODE ISLAND'S OVERCROWDED PRISONS. Providence, RI: Rhode Island Governor's Commission.

Robbins, Ira P.
1986   "Privatization of Corrections: Defining the Issues." FEDERAL PROBA-TION, 50:24–30.

Rockowitz, Ruth J.
  1986a   "Developmentally Disabled Offenders: Issues in Developing and Maintaining Services." PRISON JOURNAL, 66:19–23.

Rockowitz, Ruth J. (ed.)
  1986b   "The Developmentally Disabled Offender." PRISON JOURNAL, 66:1–92.

Romero, Joseph, and Linda M. Williams
  1983   "Group Psychotherapy and Intensive Probation Supervision: A Comparative Study." FEDERAL PROBATION, 47:36–42.

Rothman, David J.
  1980a   CONSCIENCE AND CONVENIENCE: THE ASYLUM AND ITS ALTERNATIVES IN PROGRESSIVE AMERICA. Boston, MA: Little, Brown.

  1980b   THE DISCOVERY OF THE ASYLUM. Boston, MA: Little, Brown.

  1983   "Sentencing Reforms in Historical Perspective." CRIME AND DELINQUENCY, 29:631–647.

Roundtree, George A., Dan W. Edwards, and Jack B. Parker
  1984   "A Study of the Personal Characteristics of Probationers as Related to Recidivism." JOURNAL OF OFFENDER COUNSELING, 8:53–61.

Ruback, R., and Timothy S. Carr
  1984   "Crowding in a Women's Prison: Attitudinal and Behavioral Effects." JOURNAL OF APPLIED SOCIAL PSYCHOLOGY, 14:57–68.

Rubenstein, M., and T. White
  1979   "Alaska's Ban on Plea Bargaining." LAW AND SOCIETY REVIEW, 13:367–383.

San Francisco Jail Overcrowding Committee
  1985   REPORT TO THE MAYOR FROM THE JAIL OVERCROWDING COMMITTEE. San Francisco, CA: Mayor's Criminal Justice Council.

Santamour, Miles
  1986   "The Offender with Mental Retardation." PRISON JOURNAL, 66:3–18.

Sapp, Allen D.
  1984   ADMINISTRATION RESPONSES TO PRISON OVERCROWDING: A SURVEY OF PRISON ADMINISTRATORS. Warrenburg, MO: Central Missouri State University.

Schmidt, Annesley K.
  1986   "Electronic Monitors." FEDERAL PROBATION, 50:56–59.

Schmidt, Annesley K., and Christine E. Curtis
  1987   "Electronic Monitors." In INTERMEDIATE PUNISHMENTS, Belinda R. McCarthy, ed. Monsey, NY: Criminal Justice Press.

Serrill, Michael S.
  1970   "Determinate Sentencing: History, Theory, Debate." CORRECTIONS MAGAZINE, 3:3–12.

Shane-DuBow, Sandra, Alice P. Brown, and Eric Olsen
  1985   SENTENCING REFORM IN THE UNITED STATES: HISTORY, CON-
          TENT, AND EFFECT. Washington, DC: U. S. Department of Justice.

Sims, Brian, and Jack O'Connell
  1985   EARLY RELEASE: PRISON OVERCROWDING AND PUBLIC POLICY
          IMPLICATIONS. Olympia, WA: Washington Office of Financial Manage-
          ment.

Singer, Richard G.
  1979   JUST DESERTS: SENTENCING BASED ON EQUALITY AND
          DESERT. Cambridge, MA: Ballinger.

  1980   "The WOLFISH Case: Has the BELL Tolled for Prisoner Litigation in the
          Federal Courts?" In LEGAL RIGHTS OF PRISONERS, Geoffrey Alpert,
          ed. Beverly Hills, CA: Sage.

  1984   "Desert Sentencing and Prison Overcrowding: Some Doubts and Tentative
          Answers." NEW YORK UNIVERSITY REVIEW OF LAW AND SOCIAL
          CHANGE, 12:85–110.

Smith, Alexander B., and Alexander Bassin
  1984   "Research in a Probation Department: Twenty-two Years Later." FED-
          ERAL PROBATION, 48:25–28.

Smith, Alexander B., Harriet Pollack, and E. Warren Benton
  1987   "Sentencing Problems: A Pragmatic View." FEDERAL PROBATION,
          51:67–74.

Smith, Freddie V.
  1984   "Alabama SIR Program." CORRECTIONS TODAY, 46:129–132.

Smith, J. Steven
  1987   "After a Decade of Determinate Sentencing: Probation Officers' At-
          titudes." Unpublished paper presented at the American Society of
          Criminology Meetings, Montreal, Canada (November).

Spohn, Cassia, John Gruhl, and Susan Welch
  1986   "The Ethics of Plea Bargaining." Unpublished paper presented at the an-
          nual meeting of the Academy of Criminal Justice Sciences, Orlando,
          Florida (March).

Spohn, Cassia, Susan Welch, and John Gruhl
  1985   "Women Defendants in Court: The Interaction Between Sex and Race in
          Convicting and Sentencing." SOCIAL SCIENCE QUARTERLY, 66:178–
          185.

Steinberg, Allen
  1984   "From Private Prosecution to Plea Bargaining: Criminal Prosecution, the
          District Attorney, and American Legal History." CRIME AND DELIN-
          QUENCY, 30:568–592.

Stephens, Gene
  1987   "Corrections in the 21st Century." Unpublished paper presented at the
          American Society of Criminology Meetings, Montreal, Canada (Novem-
          ber).

Steppe, Cecil H.
  1986   "Public Support: Probation's Backbone." CORRECTIONS TODAY, 48:12–16.

Stevens, Reid D.
  1986   "The Effect on Recidivism of Attaining the General Educational Development Diploma." JOURNAL OF OFFENDER COUNSELING, 7:3–9.

Stewart, James K.
  1986   "Felony Probation: An Ever-Increasing Risk?" CORRECTIONS TODAY, 48:94–102.

Stienstra, D.
  1985   JOINT TRIAL CALENDARS IN THE WESTERN DISTRICT OF MISSOURI. Washington, DC: Federal Judicial Center.

Stitt, B. G., and S. Siegel
  1986   "The Ethics of Plea Bargaining." Unpublished paper presented at the annual meeting of the Academy of Criminal Justice Sciences, Orlando, Florida (March).

Struckhoff, David R.
  1987   "Selective Incapacitation." CORRECTIONS TODAY, 49:30–34.

Suall, Irwin
  1987   "Extremist Groups Seek Recruits in Prisons." USA TODAY, 116:23–29.

Sumner, George W.
  1985   "Nevada: Adapting to Rapid Growth." CORRECTIONS TODAY, 47:86–88.

Sutton, L. P.
  1978   VARIATIONS IN FEDERAL CRIMINAL SENTENCES: A STATISTICAL ANALYSIS AT THE NATIONAL LEVEL. Albany, NY: Criminal Justice Research Center.

Taylor, William J.
  1985   "Training: ACA Priority." CORRECTIONS TODAY, 47:24–29.

Terrill, Richard J.
  1984   WORLD CRIMINAL JUSTICE SYSTEMS: A SURVEY. Cincinnati, OH: Anderson Publishing Company.

Thomas, Charles W.
  1986   "Corrections in America: Its Ambiguous Role and Future Prospects." In THE DILEMMAS OF PUNISHMENT: READINGS IN CONTEMPORARY CORRECTIONS, K.C.Haas and G.P. Alpert, eds. Prospct Heights,IL: Waveland Press.

Tonry, Michael
  1987   "Prediction and Classification: Legal and Ethical Issues." In PREDICTION AND CLASSIFICATION, D. M. Gottfredson and M. Tonry, eds. Chicago, IL: University of Chicago Press.

Tonry, Michael, and Norval Morris (eds.)
  1985   CRIME AND JUSTICE: AN ANNUAL REVIEW OF RESEARCH. Chicago, IL: University of Chicago Press.

Travis, Kevin M., and Francis J. Sheridan
1983 "Community Involvement in Prison Siting." CORRECTIONS TODAY, 45:14–15.

Travis, Lawrence F. III
1984 "Intensive Supervision in Probation and Parole." CORRECTIONS TODAY, 46:34–40.
1985 PROBATION, PAROLE, AND COMMUNITY CORRECTIONS. Prospect Heights, IL: Waveland Press.

Travis, Lawrence F. III, Edward J. Latessa, and Gennaro F. Vito
1987 "Felony Probation: An Examination of the Research." Unpublished paper presented at the Midwestern Criminal Justice Association, Chicago, Illinois (October).

Travis, Lawrence F. III, Martin D. Schwartz, and Todd R. Clear
1983 CORRECTIONS: AN ISSUES APPROACH (2d ed.) Cincinnati, OH: Anderson Publishing Company.

U. S. Department of Justice
1985 PRISON GANGS, THEIR EXTENT, NATURE AND IMPACT ON PRISONS. Washington, DC: Bureau of Justice Statistics.
1987 UNIFORM CRIME REPORTS: CRIME IN THE UNITED STATES. Washington, DC: U. S. Government Printing Office.

U. S. General Accounting Office
1985 ORGANIZED CRIME FIGURES AND MAJOR DRUG TRAFFICKERS: PAROLE DECISIONS AND SENTENCES SERVED. Washington, DC: U. S. Government Printing Office.

U. S. Parole Commission
1984 UNITED STATES PAROLE COMMISSION: RULES AND PROCEDURES. Washington, DC: U. S. Department of Justice.
1987 RULES AND PROCEDURES MANUAL. Washington, DC: U. S. Parole Commission.

Uhlman, T., and D. Walker
1979 "A Plea is No Bargain." SOCIAL SCIENCE QUARTERLY, 60:218–234.

United States Code
1988 U. S. CODE ANNOTATED. St. Paul, MN: West.

United States Sentencing Commission
1987 UNITED STATES SENTENCING COMMISSION GUIDELINES MANUAL. Washington, DC: U. S. Sentencing Commission, October, 1987.

University of Hawaii-Manoa
1984 RECIDIVISM OF 1979 ADULT PROBATION, THIRD CIRCUIT COURT. Honolulu, HI: Youth Development and Research Center.

Unnever, J. D., C. E. Frazier, and J. C. Henretta
1980 "Race Differences in Criminal Sentencing." SOCIOLOGICAL QUARTERLY, 21:197–206.

Vernon's Annotated Code of Criminal Procedure
   1979   Vernon's Annotated Code of Criminal Procedure of the State of Texas. St.
          Paul, MN: West.

Vito, Gennaro F.
   1978   "Shock Probation in Ohio: A Re-Examination of the Factors Influencing
          the Use of an Early Release Program." OFFENDER REHABILITATION,
          3:123–132.

   1983   "Reducing the Use of Imprisonment." In CORRECTIONS: AN ISSUES
          APPROACH (2d ed.), L. Travis, M. Schwartz, and T. Clear, eds. Cincin-
          nati, OH: Anderson.

   1984   "Developments in Shock Probation: A Review of Research Findings and
          Policy Implications." FEDERAL PROBATION, 48:22–27.

   1986   "Felony Probation and Recidivism: Replication and Response." FEDERAL
          PROBATION, 50:17–25.

von Hirsch, Andrew
   1976   DOING JUSTICE. New York, NY: Hill and Wang.

   1983   "Recent Trends in American Criminal Sentencing Theory." MARYLAND
          LAW REVIEW, 42:6–36.

   1984   "The Ethics of Selective Incapacitation: Observations on the Contemporary
          Debate." CRIME AND DELINQUENCY, 30:175–194.

   1985   PAST OR FUTURE CRIMES: DESERVEDNESS AND DANGEROUS-
          NESS IN THE SENTENCING OF CRIMINALS. New Brunswick, NJ: Rut-
          gers University Press.

   1987   PAST OR FUTURE CRIMES: DESERVEDNESS AND DANGEROUS-
          NESS IN THE SENTENCING OF CRIMINALS. New Brunswick, NJ: Rut-
          gers University Press.

von Hirsch, Andrew, and K. Hanrahan
   1978   ABOLISH PAROLE? Washington, DC: U. S. Government Printing Office.

Wainwright, Louie L.
   1985   "Correctional Officer: Agent of Change." CORRECTIONS TODAY,
          47:50–54.

Wald, Michael S.
   1986   "Judging the Judges: What Standards Should Voters Use?" CRIME AND
          SOCIAL JUSTICE, 25:70–77.

Waldo, Gordon P., and Theodore G. Chiricos
   1977   "Work Release and Recidivism: An Empirical Evaluation of a Social
          Policy." EVALUATION QUARTERLY, 1:87–108.

Waldron, J. A., and H. R. Angelino
   1977   "Shock Probation: A Natural Experiment on the Effect of a Short Period of
          Incarceration." PRISON JOURNAL, 57:45–52.

Walker, Samuel
   1985   SENSE AND NONSENSE ABOUT CRIME: A POLICY GUIDE.
          Monterey, CA: Brooks/Cole Publishing Company.

Wallerstedt, John F.
1984   RETURNING TO PRISON. Washington, DC: Bureau of Justice Statistics.

Washington Governor's Emergency Commission on Prison Overcrowding
1983   REPORT OF THE GOVERNOR'S EMERGENCY COMMISSION ON PRISON OVERCROWDING. Olympia, WA: Office of the Governor.

Washington State Sentencing Guidelines Commission
1985   SENTENCING PRACTICES UNDER THE SENTENCING REFORM ACT: A PRELIMINARY REPORT. Olympia, WA: Sentencing Guidelines Commission.

Webb, Gary L.
1984   THE PRISON ORDEAL. Fayetteville, GA: Coker.

Weisheit, Ralph, and Sue Mahan
1988   WOMEN, CRIME, AND CRIMINAL JUSTICE. Cincinnati, OH: Anderson Publishing Company.

Werner, Eric, and Ted Palmer
1976   "Psychological Characteristics of Successful and Unsuccessful Parolees: Implications of Heteroscedastic and Non-linear Relationships." JOURNAL OF CRIME AND DELINQUENCY, 13:165–178.

Westerfield, Louis
1984   "A Study of the Louisiana Sentencing System and Its Relationship to Prison Overcrowding: Some Realistic Solutions." LOYOLA LAW REVIEW, 30:5–86.

Wilkins, Leslie T.
1958   "A Small Comparative Study of the Results of Probation." BRITISH JOURNAL OF CRIMINOLOGY, 8:201-209.

1985   "The Politics of Prediction." In PREDICTION IN CRIMINOLOGY, D. P. Farrington and R. Tarling, eds. Albany, NY: State University of New York Press.

Willstadter, R.
1984   TIME SERVED: DOES IT RELATE TO CRIMINAL RECIDIVISM? FINAL REPORT NO. 1, DECEMBER 1984. Seattle, WA: Spectrum Analysis.

Wilson, Deborah G.
1985   PERSISTENT FELONY OFFENDERS IN KENTUCKY: A PROFILE OF THE INSTITUTIONAL POPULATION. Louisville, KY: Kentucky Criminal Justice Statistical Analysis Center.

Wilson, M. J.
1983   RESTITUTION AS AN ALTERNATIVE TO INCARCERATION: AN INTERRUPTED TIME SERIES ASSESSMENT OF FIVE FEDERALLY FUNDED RESTITUTION PROGRAMS. Eugene, OR: Institute of Political Analysis.

Witayapanyanon, Tamasak
  1987 "Illinois' Mandatory Minimum and Determinate Sentencing Law." Un-
        published paper presented at American Society of Criminology Meetings,
        Montreal, Canada (November).

Wolfgang, Marvin E., Robert M. Figlio, and Thorsten Sellin
  1972 DELINQUENCY IN A BIRTH COHORT. Chicago, IL: University of
        Chicago Press.

Wood, Dorothy, Jean Verber, and Mary Reddin
  1985 A STUDY OF THE INMATE POPULATION OF THE MILWAUKEE
        COUNTY JAIL. Milwaukee, WI: Wisconsin Correctional Service and
        Benedict Center for Criminal Justice.

Wright, Kevin N.
  1986 IMPROVING CORRECTIONAL CLASSIFICATION THROUGH A
        STUDY OF THE PLACEMENT OF INMATES IN ENVIRONMENTAL
        SETTINGS. Binghamton, NY: Center for Social Analysis, SUNY.

Wright, Kevin N., Todd R. Clear, and Paul Dickson
  1984 "Universal Applicability of Probation Risk-Assessment Instruments: A
        Critique." CRIMINOLOGY, 22:113–134.

CASES CITED

Barefoot v. Estelle (1983) 103 S. Ct. 3383
Bell v. Wolfish (1979) 441 U. S. 520
Bordenkircher v. Hayes (1978) 434 U.S. 357
Boykin v. Alabama (1969) 395 U.S. 238
Brady v. United States (1970) 397 U.S. 742
Jones v. United States (1983) 103 S. Ct. 3043
Kelleher v. Henderson (1976) 531 F. 2d 78
McCarthy v. United States (1969) 394 U.S. 459
Rhodes v. Chapman (1981) 452 U.S. 337
Ruiz v. Estelle (1982) 679 F. 2d 1115
Schall v. Martin (1984) 104 S. Ct. 2403
Shepherd v. United States (1979) 618 F. 2d 702
Sundeberg v. Alaska (1982) 652 P. 2d 113
United States v. French (1983) 466 U.S. 960
United States v. Garcia (1980) 617 F. 2d 1176
United States v. Lynch (1983) 699 F. 2d 839

Name Index

Adams, S., 96
Addams, Jane, 3
Aikman, Alex B., 38
Allen, G. Frederick, 14-15
Allen, Harry E., 2-3, 9, 30, 69, 113
Allen, N. E., 21
Allied Engineering, 84
Allinson, Richard, 76
Alschuler, Albert W., 35, 38
American Correctional Association, 88, 122
Andersen, Brian David, 97
Andersen, Kevon, 97
Angelino, H. R., 31
Anson, Richard H., 80
Augustus, John, 1-3, 7
Austin, James, 25, 81, 83

Babst, Dean V., 96
Ball, Richard A., 9, 27-30, 85, 93, 128
Ballard, K. B., 95-96
Barkdull, Walter L., 21, 101
Barrick, Dennis M., 80
Bassin, Alexander, 10
Beck, James L., 95-97, 100
Bell, D., 39-40
Bennett, Lawrence A., 95
Bensinger, Gad J., 22-24, 31
Benton, E. Warren, 47-48, 53, 55, 61-62
Berkowitz, David, 108-109
Bibel, Daniel B., 24, 113
Black, Henry Campbell, 1
Blackmore, John, 6, 103
Block, Michael K., 54, 56, 65-66
Blumberg, Abraham, 37
Blumstein, Alfred, 7, 84, 87, 103
Bock, E. W., 35, 40, 125
Boesky, Ivan, 108-109
Bohlander, E. W., 31

Boland, Barbara, 39
Boston University, 96
Bottomley, A. Keith, 2
Boudouris, James, 97, 111
Brantingham, Patricia L., 60
Brennan, Tim, 76, 85
Brereton, D., 35, 40, 59
Brown, Alice P., 12, 35, 49-50, 60
Brown, Marjorie E., 125
Bucknew, D., 40
Bumiller, K., 41
Bureau of Justice Statistics, 33, 36-37, 48
Burkhart, Walter R., 95
Burks, David N., 80
Butcher, Jake, 109
Byrne, James M., 13, 18-19

Cahalan, Margaret Werner, 4
California Adult Authority, 96
California Joint Committee for Revision of the Penal Code, 83-85, 90
Call, Jack E., 77, 79
Callanan, Thomas J., 92
Camp, Camille, 76
Camp, George, 76
Cansfield, Charles W., 84
Carlson, Eric W., 21
Carr, Timothy S., 80
Casper, J. D., 35, 40, 59
Caulfield, Susan, 127
Cavanaugh, James J., 97
Cavender, Gray, 18, 123
Cecil, Joe S., 37
Chaiken, Jan M., 102-103, 109, 117
Chaiken, Marcia R., 102-103, 109, 117
Champion, Dean J., 31, 38, 40-44, 63-65, 121, 125
Chandler, Henry P., 61

Subject Index

About the Author

DEAN J. CHAMPION is Professor of Sociology at the University of Tennessee–Knoxville. He received his Ph.D. in 1965 from Purdue University. Dr. Champion is the author of *Basic Statistics for Social Research, Sociology of Organizations, Methods and Issues in Social Research, Corrections in the United States, Introduction to Criminal Justice*, and *Probation and Parole in the United States*. His contributions have appeared in *Journal of Criminal Justice, Criminal Justice Review, Federal Probation,* the *American Journal of Sociology*, and numerous others. Dr. Champion's current research focuses on plea bargaining.